Glenn & Sue Hawks
950 Fairview Road
Ojai, California 93023

D1602612

Glenn & Sue Hawks
119 Don Felipe Way
Ojai, Calif 93023

HEBREW
ROOTS

OF

MORMONISM

DAVID THOMAS

CFI
AN IMPRINT OF CEDAR FORT, INC.
SPRINGVILLE, UTAH

HEBREW ROOTS

OF
MORMONISM

DAVID THOMAS

CFI
AN IMPRINT OF CEDAR FORT, INC.
SPRINGVILLE, UTAH

ISBN 13: 978-1-4621-1136-7

Published by CFI, an imprint of Cedar Fort, Inc., 2373 W. 700 S., Springville, UT 84663
Distributed by Cedar Fort, Inc., www.cedarfort.com

LIBRARY OF CONGRESS CATALOGING-IN-PUBLICATION DATA

Thomas, David, 1962 January 14- author.
  Hebrew roots of Mormonism / David Thomas.
      pages cm
  Includes bibliographical references and index.
  Summary: An examination of the historical battle for orthodoxy in the early Christian Church between Hebrew Christians, Hellenized Christians, and Gnostic Christians.
  ISBN 978-1-4621-1136-7 (alk. paper)
  1. Church history--Primitive and early church, ca. 30-600. 2. Christianity and other religions--Judaism--History. 3. Mormon Church--Doctrines. 4. Great Apostasy (Mormon doctrine) I. Title.

  BX8643.G74T49 2012
  270.1--dc23

                    2012042453

Cover design by Angela D. Olsen
Cover design © 2013 Lyle Mortimer
Edited and typeset by Emily S. Chambers

Printed in the United States of America

10 9 8 7 6 5 4 3 2 1

FOR MY SWEETHEART, LYNN

Contents

PREFACE

This is my disclaimer. I do not profess to be an academic or scholar on early Christian history. I do not hold a history or theological degree from a major university. I am not a professor or anyone of any significance in the realm of religious studies. Early Christianity, however, is my passion and this scholarly work is the result.

I have to admit that I do have a bias. I am a member of The Church of Jesus Christ of Latter-day Saints (the Mormon Church). I have a testimony of the restored gospel of Jesus Christ and that does color my analysis and conclusions. My desire in this work is to attempt to make sense out of historical Christianity and the place where The Church of Jesus Christ of Latter-day Saints fits within that history.

The conclusions that I draw in this work are my own and do not reflect the opinions or positions of any church or other religious organization. I have spent the past decade reading and studying early Christianity, developing a thoughtful respect for the second- and third-century converts to the Christian movement. I am drawn to the sacrifices and challenges they faced. Persecution was a constant; death was a common occurrence.

There are many who suggest that the man Jesus is not an historical figure at all. They question the lack of archeological evidence. Josephus includes Jesus of Nazareth as a mere footnote within his historical treatise of the Jewish people.[1] If this Jesus of Nazareth was the founder of such a great movement, why is he merely a footnote to historians of the time?

I believe the answer is rather simplistic—to ancient historians, Jesus was a mortal man, just another Jewish heretic, and his followers were small in number. The Romans used crucifixion with regularity. Hence, Jesus's crucifixion was of no great consequence. To the victor go the spoils. To historians of the time, Jesus's death ended whatever had been the theological battle between himself and the Jewish leadership. Why would they bother to write about it?

Jesus's resurrection was not widely published throughout Judea or the Galilee. While to Jesus's followers, His appearance after the crucifixion was a manifestation of divine power, to the rest of society, it was a myth propagated by Jesus's followers, who had stolen His body from the tomb.

It was not until the Apostolic ministries that the teachings of Jesus moved out of a regional setting. These ministries are well documented in the annals of history, and there is ample archeological evidences of their lives and teachings.

However, there is a greater reason for the absence of direct evidence of Jesus—the first principle of His gospel is faith. Faith in Him and His existence as our Lord and Redeemer. Consequently, our conversion to the teachings of Christ requires a measure of trust. That is why no one can ever prove by physical means that Jesus was real or that He is God, the Savior of the world. He intentionally made it so.

As a practicing member of the Mormon faith, Jesus Christ, His life and ministry, is essential to what I believe. However, at times I have been troubled by other Christian denominations who do not view the Mormons as followers of Christ. Why would they say such a thing? This book is my attempt to answer that very question.

NOTES

1. Flavius Josephus, 4 vols., *Antiquities of the Jews* (Grand Rapids, MI: Baker Book House, 1998), 4: 244–65.

INTRODUCTION

TWO ROADS DIVERGED IN A WOOD, AND I—
I TOOK THE ONE LESS TRAVELED BY,
AND THAT HAS MADE ALL THE DIFFERENCE.

—ROBERT FROST, "THE ROAD NOT TAKEN"

ARE MORMONS CHRISTIAN?

The Christian world is a broad mosaic of many different faiths, all professing a belief and devotion to Jesus Christ as Savior and Redeemer of mankind. Notwithstanding such, The Church of Jesus Christ of Latter-day Saints, sometimes referred to as the Mormon Church, is generally characterized by other Christian faiths—principally protestant churches, but also the Roman Catholic Church—in a less than favorable light. Why? What is the cause of such hostility? What are its origins?

The purpose of this book is to test a theological hypothesis as to why, historically, other Christian denominations do not consider the Mormons Christians; for Mormonism is a lot older than it appears, and that is the rub. There came a time in Christianity where there was a divergence in the road—one road led to traditional Christianity and the other led to Mormon Christianity, and as the poet suggests, "that has made all the difference."

Of course, at the meridian of time when Jesus of Nazareth lived and preached, there were not any Mormons—or were there? Jesus's disciples were sent abroad to all the world to gather in those who would accept Christianity. However, the church that Christ built was not in Rome but rather in Jerusalem among the Jews. The Hebrews were the original adherents to what historians term the *Jesus Movement*. These Hebrew Christians were the dominant sect in Christianity for three hundred years following the death of the Savior. Yet while the Christian Church grew, the Hebrew contingent of Christianity remained static. Soon the Hebrews were in the minority among Christians, replaced by the Greeks, Romans, and Jews of the Diaspora. What was once a church of Judea and Israel had become the Church of Rome with side tours to Alexandria and Antioch. As the Church grew, many of its doctrines began to change. Those in Rome adapted, those in Jerusalem did not. The Hebrews remained ensconced in the Apostolic Church, the church according to Peter, James, and John, and not the one preached by the students of Paul. Tension grew between these contingents. The Roman Church designated its major congregations as Constantinople, Alexandria, and Antioch. Jerusalem was thrown in as an afterthought, not because it was an important city in the Church, but rather out of respect for the city of origin of the faith. Jerusalem and the Hebrew Christians had become the step sister. It was only a matter of time before a confrontation on the future of the Church would come. And come it did, in AD 325 at the Council of Nicaea, when the Roman Church claimed that its doctrines were orthodoxy and those of the Hebrews in Jerusalem were heretical. Soon everything Hebrew would be eliminated by the Church, a mere footnote to history. Or maybe not even a footnote; for the Roman Church never wanted the Hebrew Christian heretical doctrines to ever see the light of day again. The Hebrews were crushed, they either gave up their beliefs, or like Arius, they were exiled and excommunicated.

As renown Christian scholar Bruce Shelley writes,

> There were two main cultures, however—the Jewish and the Hellenistic (or Greek). The original disciples were Jews. But many of their early converts, as we have seen, were gentile proselytes of the Jewish synagogues. Thus, two sharply contrasting cultural backgrounds were obvious almost from the start. The two forces, Jewish and Hellenistic, represented two contrasting influences in the thought of the church. To the Jewish Christian, God was one. He had been the God of the Jew for a long time. When they clearly recognized that he was also the

true God of all men, they still accepted him as the personal God they had always known. He was recognized by his personal name, Jehovah or Yahweh. His unity was a personal unity. To the Greek believers, on the other hand, the unity of God was an abstraction. They reached their ideas about God by philosophical refinement, by the processes of almost mathematical thought. No doubt the Hellenists accepted the personal attributes of God in their surrender to Christianity, but the more abstract, philosophical idea was in their blood. Thus, we can see how history and culture made a difference in the way the two peoples thought and spoke.[1]

This view of the battle between Hellenized Christians (Greeks) and Hebrew Christians (Jews) is not unique. German scholar F. C. Baur (1792–1860) maintained that earliest Christianity, before the books of the New Testament had been completed, was characterized by a conflict between Jewish Christians, who wanted to maintain distinctive ties to Judaism and so keep Christianity as a particularist religion (it was Jewish), and Gentile Christians, who wanted to sever those ties in order to make it a universalistic religion (it was for everyone).[2]

Baur asserted that Peter led the Jewish Christians and Paul led the Gentile Christians. He further hypothesized that the books in the New Testament show this battle—Revelation is a Jewish Christian type and Paul's letters are a Gentile Christian type and hence are anti-Jewish in content—the law of Moses is no longer necessary.[3]

Unlike the other heretical variant in the Roman Church, that of Gnosticism, which kept springing up from surprisingly new sources every few hundred years, the Hebrew version of Christianity was eradicated and did not reappear. That is, until the spring of 1820 in upstate New York.

By this time, the Roman Church had divided since the Reformation took place three hundred years before. Protestant churches like the Presbyterians, Methodists, Unitarians, Baptists, Calvinists, and other evangelical branches of the Church had splintered off from the Roman Catholic Church. Although these branches of the Catholic Church fought between themselves for followers, they all came from the same tree trunk and hence had the same view of the heretical Hebrew Christians. It had been fifteen hundred years since they were wiped off the face of the earth to rise no more.

The reason the Roman Catholic Church and the reformist would have been wary of the old Hebrew doctrines was because of how widespread those doctrines had been in the first three centuries of the Church. It had taken over three hundred years for the Catholic Church to win primacy over the Hebrews. It had been the only serious challenge to the Greeks who would become the Catholics. Yes, Martin Luther and John Calvin had injured the orthodox superiority of the Catholic Church, but these reformers were not in league with the old Hebrew Christians. With the Hebrews, it had been a fight for the future of the faith, and the Roman Church had almost lost. For if the Hebrews had won, Christianity as we know it today would be much different. There would be reformers—there always are—but many of the grounding doctrines of all Christianity would have been altered.

It wasn't that the Hebrews were better organizers or more intelligent than the Roman Church. Rather it was the appeal of the Hebrew Christian doctrines, most of which came directly from Jesus Christ through the Apostles Peter, James, and John. These doctrines were popular and spoke of a special relationship of God to mankind. The very nature of God had been at the center of the disagreement between the Greek and Hebrew Christians. The Greek belief in God was framed by the philosophies of the dominant Hellenistic culture of the dark ages, while the Hebrew belief was intertwined with that of the Jews and sons of Israel.

What a surprise for the Christian world when a young boy of fourteen first told of his vision of God the Father and Jesus Christ. Even more surprising and concerning was what Jesus Christ had told the boy; namely, that the Christian churches were off course and that the boy was to lead not a reformation of the Church, but instead a restoration of the original faith. That faith happened to be Hebrew Christianity and the boy was Joseph Smith.

Joseph Smith tells of the enormous persecution that he came under almost immediately. He couldn't understand why. Not even Martin Luther was hunted as he was, and Luther's *95 Theses* had been a declaration of war against the Catholic Church. What made Smith's discovery so much more threatening? As previously stated, the answer is simple: of all the variants of Christianity that the Roman Catholic Church and its reformist offspring feared, it was not the new-age cultists or the Gnostic branches; rather, it was the one belief system that nearly defeated Hellenistic Christianity in the fourth century—the Hebrew Christians were back. The doctrines of the Hebrews came to young Joseph through a religious record of Jews and other descendants of Israel who fled Jerusalem at the time of the Babylonian conquest, had wandered in the desert, voyaged to the new world guided by God, and lived the doctrines of Hebrew Christianity. After Christ's Resurrection, the Apostle John tells us of a conversation wherein Jesus referred to other sheep He had that were not of this fold (meaning those followers in Jerusalem) and that He needed to visit them as well. Those were the descendants of those who came to the new world six hundred years before. Christ visited the Americas. The mythology of the American Indians, Aztecs, Mayans, and others, told of a white god who had visited their ancestors and had promised to return one day. It is for this reason that the Native Americans welcomed Columbus and Cortez to their shores. They thought that these white men were the returning Savior promised in their traditional stories. This religious record of the doctrines of Hebrew Christianity and the culture and wars of this civilization are contained in the Book of Mormon. This book is a history book of sorts, similar to the Holy Bible. Wherein, as we will see, the Bible has been altered over time and thus the doctrines of the Hebrews therein have been modified or deleted in their entirety, the Book of Mormon is a pure version of Hebrew cosmology. Its history is of two great nation states, the Nephites and the Lamanites. The history runs approximately one thousand years, from 600 BC to approximately AD 400, ending with the complete destruction of the Nephite nation. It was the Nephites who kept the records of their fathers before them. On the eve of the destruction of their nation, the records of one thousand years of history and religious doctrines were abridged by the Prophet General Mormon and then entrusted to his son, Captain Moroni. Moroni wandered for some twenty years, hiding from the Lamanites who continued to hunt down stragglers of the old Nephite nation. He finally buried the abridged records (which were on golden plates engraved in reformed Egyptian, the language of their fathers) in a hill called Cumorah, which is located today by Palmyra, New York. There the pure Hebrew Christian doctrines stayed safe until the Lord was ready. Until the long winter night of the Apostasy, foretold by the

Apostle Paul, was over. Fitting that young Joseph went to a grove to pray in the spring, the ending of winter and the beginning of new life.

This is what the other Christian denominations feared. This is why Joseph was forced to hide the plates and was forced to flee time and time again for his life. He and this ancient secret were not safe. It could destroy Hellenistic Christianity. There was no way that the ancient Hebrew religion would ever be allowed to survive. It had to be crushed. The Mormons were driven from New York to Ohio and then to Missouri, where Governor Boggs placed an extermination order on Mormons if any were found in the state. The Mormons were hunted like animals, and they were forced to leave all of their possessions and to flee north to Illinois. There they established the largest city in the state, Nauvoo, on the banks of the Mississippi River. Nevertheless, it was merely a matter of time before their enemies attacked them again. The Prophet Joseph Smith was murdered in June of 1844 and the Mormons, led by Brigham Young, fled west out of the United States, the only religious organization that ever fled the jurisdictional boundaries of the United States due to religious bigotry and persecution. The First Amendment held no sway to those of other Christian denominations. Extinguishing the Mormons would once and for all destroy the Hebrew Christian doctrines that would be Hellenism's undoing.

This is the reason that although the Mormons are devout and devoted disciples of the Savior, Jesus Christ, they are not accepted in the Christian world. It is said that they believe in Christ, but it's a different Christ from the orthodoxy of Christendom. They are correct, for the Christ preached by the Mormons is the Hebrew Christian Christ, the Christ who came to this mortal sphere, preached how we can return to the Father of our spirits, died on Calvary, and was resurrected. The nature of Christ and God the Father was much different to the Hebrews than it was to the Hellenized Church, the Church of Rome, the Church of the Greeks. It is different from the protestant churches of today as well. It is the return of the true orthodox Christians and the teachings of the Apostles during the meridian of time.

This book's goal is to lay out this history and discuss the battle for Christianity's soul in the early Church and how Mormonism is the restored Church of Jesus Christ, of which the Hebrew Christians were members.

NOTES

1. Bruce L. Shelley, *Church History in Plain Language*, 2nd ed. (Thomas Nelson, Nashville, TN: 1995), 48–49.
2. Bart D. Ehrman, *Lost Christianities* (Oxford University Press, New York: 2003), 171–172.
3. Ibid.

CHAPTER 1

THE ORIGINS OF CHRISTIANITY

When did Christianity begin? Was it with the birth of Jesus of Nazareth? The Apostle Matthew spends most of his Gospel citing to prophesies from the Old Testament that speak and prophesy of a coming Messiah, whom Matthew asserts is this same Jesus. Consequently, we are left with a legitimate religious question: When exactly did Christianity begin? If the ancient prophets knew of Jesus, didn't they teach His doctrine?

In the early days following Jesus's ascension and before the days of Pentecost, the "Jesus Movement," as it was termed, was thought of as simply a branch of Judaism. In fact, all early converts were Jews. Until Cornelius, most, if not all, of the Apostles, believed that one had to be a Jew or a convert to Judaism before one could be baptized into the Church of Jesus Christ. This ended with Peter's vision of unclean animals, which signified that Christ's gospel was for all peoples, not just the Jews.[1]

So if the gospel that Christ taught was not simply for the Jews but for all people, couldn't the same be said of the doctrines taught by the ancient prophets of the Old Testament? They were prophesying of Jesus and His gospel to more than just ancient Israel.

Hence, one may draw the conclusion that Christianity, the gospel of Jesus Christ, is of ancient origin. Certainly that is what Christ's Apostles and the early Apostolic Fathers believed. For example, Paul preached that the gospel was given to Abraham around 2000 BC,[2] and to Moses,[3] as well as to Old Testament Israel at approximately 1350 BC.[4] The famous theologian of the second century AD, Ignatius, bishop of Antioch, preached that the prophets of the Old Testament preached of Christ.[5] The Christian scholar Tatian, as well as Church Father Theophilus, and the famous Christian historian bishop Eusebius all noted that the gospel is older than the Greeks or written languages, and was practiced by Abraham, whom they called a Christian.[6] According to bishop Athanasius of Alexandria in the fourth century AD, the gospel of Christ was even taught to Adam.[7]

In fact, the Apostle Paul preached that the law of Moses was a lesser law to the gospel, meant to prepare the Jews for the restoration of the gospel during the meridian of time.[8] What's more, in the Epistle of Barnabas, chapter fourteen, it provides that Moses received the gospel on Mount Sinai when he came down the first time, but broke those tablets when he saw the Hebrews worshiping a golden calf. He returned to the Hebrews after receiving a new tablet, the lesser law, known as the law of Moses.

Early Christianity understood the various dispensations and recognized that the gospel itself was not new. The Apostolic Father Ignatius, bishop of Antioch, testified in approximately AD 108:

> For the divine prophets [referring to the ancient Patriarchs and prophets of old] lived according to Jesus Christ. Therefore they were also persecuted, being inspired by his grace, to convince the disobedient that there is one God, who manifested himself through Jesus Christ his son. . . .
>
> Should any one, beginning from Abraham, and going back to the first man, pronounce those who have had the testimony of righteousness, Christians in fact, though not in name, he would not be far from the truth. . . . They obviously knew the Christ of God, as he appeared to Abraham, communed with Isaac, spoke to Jacob; and that he communed with Moses and the prophets after him. . . . Whence it is evident that the religion delivered to us in the doctrine of Christ is not a new nor a strange doctrine; but if the truth must be spoken, it is the first and only true religion.[9]

Consequently, it is my belief that Christianity is the original religion of Adam. Some have referred to this theory as "Dispensationalism." A dispensation is defined as a period of time wherein God has an authorized representative upon the earth. The New Testament equates dispensation with a household stewardship; "that is, God establishes His household on the earth and gives the stewardship for running that household to particular individuals—His prophets."[10]

Between dispensations occurs an apostasy, or a falling away from the pure gospel. The next dispensation begins at the conclusion of this apostasy with direct contact between God and man, generally through the calling of a prophet who restores the ancient religion; namely, the gospel of Jesus Christ.

ADAM'S RELIGION; THE BEGINNINGS OF REVEALED RELIGION

What was Adam's religion?[11] What did he know and believe about his relationship to God, his creator? And what did God expect from Adam? In addressing Adam, I will attempt to stay as close as possible to the written record and avoid conjecture and even informed speculation.

As Moses records in Genesis:

And God said, Let us make man in our image, after our likeness: and let him have dominion over the fish of the sea, and over the fowl of the air, and over the cattle, and over all the earth, and over every creeping thing that creepeth upon the earth.

So God created man in his own image, in the image of God created he him; male and female created he them.

And God blessed them, and God said unto them, Be fruitful, and multiply, and replenish the earth, and subdue it: and have dominion over the fish of the sea, and over the fowl of the air, and over every living thing that moveth upon the earth.[12]

Adam surely believed that he was created in the image and likeness of God.[13] This was not figurative, as Adam relates in Genesis 5:1–3, for his son Seth was described to be in Adam's image and likeness in the same way that God described Adam. Thus to Adam, God was not a spirit without form, but was in the image and likeness of a man. If we were describing Adam's religion, this would be the first tenant of it—that God is in the form of a man.

Next, God gave Adam dominion over the earth and its creatures. The vegetation and animals were for his benefit.[14] But for what purpose? Why was God elevating Adam above all other creations? As Adam would soon find out, mankind and its dominion over this planet has a central role in God's plan that would play an important part of Adam's religion. But Adam was alone.[15]

> And the Lord God caused a deep sleep to fall upon Adam, and he slept: and He took one of his ribs, and closed up the flesh instead thereof;
>
> And the rib, which the Lord God had taken from man, made he a woman, and brought her unto the man.
>
> And Adam said, This is now bone of my bones, and flesh of my flesh: she shall be called Woman, because she was taken out of Man.
>
> Therefore, shall a man leave his father and his mother, and shall cleave unto his wife: and they shall be one flesh.[16]

Marriage and procreation became an essential tenant of Adam's religious faith, because man was commanded to be fruitful and multiply and replenish the earth.[17] It should be noted that at this time Adam and Eve lived in the Garden of Eden in the presence of God. Hence, they were immortal beings and could not die so long as they stayed in the Garden and continued to partake of the fruit of the tree of life.[18] We will not deal with the great theological debate about how or why the Fall of Adam took place except to suggest that Adam and Eve were given a commandment by God to multiply and replenish the earth, meaning to bear children. Something that apparently could not be accomplished while they remained in the Garden of Eden.

The biblical story of Adam and Eve commences with being tempted by the serpent, eating of the fruit of the tree of knowledge of good and evil, and ultimately being cast out of the Garden of Eden into the mortal world.[19] They became fallen and subject to mortality and sin.[20] Following their banishment from the Garden of Eden, Adam and Eve began to seek direction from God. According to James Ussher, it is 4004 BC.[21]

> And Adam and Eve, his wife, called upon the name of the Lord, and they heard the voice of the Lord from the way toward the Garden of Eden, speaking unto them, and they saw him not: for they were shut out from his presence.
>
> And he gave unto them commandments, that they should worship the Lord their God, and should offer the firstlings of their flocks for an offering unto the Lord. And Adam was obedient unto the commandments of the Lord.
>
> And after many days an angel of the Lord appeared unto Adam, saying: Why dost thou offer sacrifices unto the Lord? And Adam said unto him: I know not, save the Lord commanded me.
>
> And then the angel spake, saying: This thing is a similitude of the sacrifice of the Only Begotten of the Father, which is full of grace and truth.
>
> Wherefore, thou shalt do all that thou doest in the name of the Son, and thou shalt repent and call upon God in the name of the Son forevermore.
>
> And in that day the Holy Ghost fell upon Adam, which beareth record of the Father and the Son, saying: I am the Only Begotten of the Father from the beginning, henceforth and forever, that as thou hast fallen thou mayest be redeemed and all mankind, even as many as will.[22-23]

ELOHIM AND JEHOVAH

Here, we must temporarily depart from our story of Adam in order to investigate the contents of what the Angel had instructed Adam; namely, that he was to "do all that thou doest in the name of the Son (Jehovah), and thou shalt repent and call upon God (Elohim) in the name of the Son (Jehovah) forevermore." Thus, Adam's future interaction with God the Father (Elohim) would be through the Son (Jehovah).

The Old Testament begins with the words "breshit bara Elohim." Hebrew scholars have long disputed the origins of *Elohim*. While most agree that it refers to the God of Israel, the confusion arises from the use of "Yahweh" ("Jehovah" in Latin) to also describe God in the Old Testament. Are the uses of these two names for God synonymous or are we talking about two different divine beings? Biblical scholars suggest that these are one and the same God, just differentiated from each other by varying traditions in the region. These are referred to as the "E" and "J" traditions. The name of Elohim was typically used in the Kingdom of Israel (the Northern Kingdom), which was under the leadership of the tribe of Ephraim. While Jehovah was utilized in the Kingdom of Judah (the Southern Kingdom) under the banner of the tribe of Judah. As one may recollect from history, the twelve tribes of Israel, which occupied the Land of Canaan in the tenth century BC, split into two kingdoms as the result of internal divisions over taxes under the rule of Solomon's son, Rehoboam. Consequently, the traditions diverged over time, giving rise to differing names for the same Deity. In fact, it is reported that Elohim was a derivative of the Canaanite pagan god "El," the patriarchal creator god or father god. Elohim would then be the plural form and indicate a polytheistic belief in multiple Gods or perhaps the "sons of El," the father god. Over time, with a Judaic turn toward monotheism, it was eventually replaced with "Yahweh" or Jehovah, a singular God. However, other biblical scholars point to the use of Elohim not as multiple gods, but as one supreme father god with many attributes. To avoid confusion, Protestant scholars in the King James Version of the Bible replaced "Elohim" with "God" and "Jehovah" with "Lord."[24]

So which is it? Are *Elohim* and *Jehovah* one and the same or do they refer to different divine entities? It is of some import that the Apostle John noted that God (Elohim) created heaven and earth in and through the Word, who he identified as Jesus Christ (Jehovah).[25] Jesus Christ constantly referred to His Father in Heaven—Elohim. In fact, he prayed to Elohim, His Father, for support in the Garden of Gethsemane and, while suffering on the cross, asked Elohim to "forgive them for they know not what they do."[26] Finally, Christ referred to himself as Jehovah. "Before Abraham, I am."[27]

Of most significance is Christ's reference to himself as "the Son of Man." Elder James E. Talmage discussed this concept in detail in his book *Jesus the Christ*.

> In applying the designation to Himself, the Lord invariably uses the definite article. "The Son of Man" was and is, specifically and exclusively, Jesus Christ. While as a matter of solemn certainty He was the only male human being from Adam down who was not the son of a mortal man, He used the title in a way to conclusively demonstrate

that it was peculiarly and solely His own. . . . There is . . . a more profound significance attaching to the Lord's use of the title "the Son of Man"; and this lies in the fact that He knew His Father to be the one and only supremely exalted Man, whose Son Jesus was both in spirit and in body—the Firstborn among all the spirit children of the Father, the Only Begotten in the flesh—and therefore, in a sense applicable to Himself alone, He was and is the Son of the "Man of Holiness," "Elohim," the Eternal Father. In His distinctive titles of Sonship, Jesus expressed His spiritual and bodily descent from, and His filial submission to, that elected Father. As revealed to Enoch the Seer, "Man of Holiness" is one of the names by which God the Eternal Father is known; "and the name of his Only Begotten is the Son of Man, even Jesus Christ." We learn further that the Father of Jesus Christ thus proclaimed Himself to Enoch: "Behold, I am God; Man of Holiness is my name: Man of Counsel is my name; and Endless and Eternal is my name, also." (Moses 6:57; 7:35). "The Son of Man" is in great measure synonymous with "The Son of God," as a title denoting divinity, glory, and exaltation; for the "Man of Holiness," whose Son Jesus Christ reverently acknowledges Himself to be, is God the Eternal Father.[28]

The designation of the "Son of Man" is used some forty times in the New Testament. It is mentioned specifically to reference Christ in Acts 7:56, Revelation 1:13 and Revelation 14:14. Prior to Christ's birth, Daniel references the visit of Christ, the Son of Man, to the Ancient of Days (Adam) at Adam-ondi-Ahman in Doctrine and Covenants 49:6, 58:65, 65:5 and 122:8. What is of interest is that all ninety specific references in the Old Testament to the "son of man" are in lower case and denote mortal man. Jehovah uses such a title to address the Prophet Ezekiel. Hence, only Jehovah is referred to as the capitalized "Son of Man."

Thus, it appears clear: Elohim is God the Father and Jehovah is God the Son. It is only logical that Adam and Enoch referred to God as Elohim, but the Hebrews began referring to God as Jehovah, because there came a time when Jehovah exclusively became the spokesman to the Hebrews on behalf of His father, Elohim.

This leads to an important and quintessential question: who or what is Elohim? Adam knew him to be in the image of a man, Man of Holiness, for he is an exalted man.

Mankind and the Gospel

In Genesis, as we have already discussed, God says that he created man in his own image. Throughout the scriptures, both Elohim and Jehovah refer to us as spirit children. In fact, mankind is referred to as either the "children of God" or as the "sons and daughters of God" some twenty-seven times in the Old and New Testaments (King James Version). Is this figurative? Or is it literal? Certainly Adam and the Hebrews viewed it as literal.

If it is literal, that would mean that we are members of an elite race. God's race. A race of creators. "As man is God once was; as God is now, man may become."[29] Are we really to believe such a thought. Is that what Adam believed? For just as a cub grows up not to be a dog, but a bear, and a kitten grows to be a cat, so we grow to be like our Father in Heaven, Elohim. Is that possible?

After being cast out of the Garden, Adam no longer spoke directly with God the Father; rather, his interactions were with the Son, Jehovah. In seeking guidance from Jehovah, Adam and Eve learned of the importance of prayer; namely that they could communicate directly with Elohim.[30] They learned that they should worship Elohim and follow His commandments in order that they might return to His presence at the conclusion of their mortal lives. Obviously, they also fully understood that as fallen human beings they would sin (violate Elohim's commandments) and that would prevent them from returning to Elohim; for "no unclean thing can dwell with God."[31] It is this predicament that dictated the need for a Savior, one who could take upon Himself the sins of mankind so that all, including Adam and Eve, would have the opportunity to return to the presence of Elohim.[32] Consequently and most important, Adam learned of Jesus Christ and the role Christ would play in redeeming all mankind from the Fall of Adam. In fact, this central event was so important that Adam was commanded to make a sacrificial offering to Elohim and this offering was in similitude of the offering that would be made by the Son of God, Jesus Christ.[33]

> Adam said to Seth, his son, you have heard, my son, that God is going to come into the world after a long time, (he will be) conceived of a virgin and put on a body, be born like a human being, and grow up as

a child. He will perform signs and wonders on earth, will walk on the waves of the sea. He will rebuke the winds and they will be silenced. He will motion to the waves and they will stand still. He will open the eyes of the blind and cleanse the lepers. He will cause the deaf to hear, and the mute to speak . . . [The Messiah said to me] For your sake I will be born of the Virgin Mary. For your sake I will taste death and enter into the house of the dead. For your sake I will make a new heaven, and I will be established over your posterity. And after three days, while I am in the tomb, I will raise up the body I received from you. And I will set you at the right hand of my divinity.[34]

So Adam was the first Christian.

It is of some consequence that we learn through the holy scriptures that Adam knew of Christ through the power of the Holy Ghost. Thus he understood that the Holy Ghost is a testator who bears witness of the Father and the Son, Jesus Christ. With this knowledge, Adam understood the nature of the Godhead: God the Father, Jesus Christ, and the Holy Ghost.

Obviously, Adam also knew that Satan was in the world—the antagonist to God the Father. He knew this from his dealings with Satan in the Garden of Eden.[35]

Adam began to preach these things he had learned, which he termed the *gospel*, to his children.[36]

And a book of remembrance was kept, in the which was recorded in the language of Adam, for it was given unto as many as called upon God to write by the spirit of inspiration.[37]

Thus, the birth of holy scripture. Unfortunately, Adam's record-ings do not survive to this day; otherwise, we would have much more of what Adam believed directly from his own hand.

Adam also spoke in Moses 6:7 of having some form of the priest-hood; the power of God to act in His name on earth—for example, the power to perform sacred ordinances prescribed by God. We certainly know that such sacred ordinances were performed.[38]

And it came to pass, when the Lord had spoken with Adam, our father, that Adam cried unto the Lord, and he was caught away by the Spirit of the Lord, and was carried down into the water, and was laid under the water, and was brought forth out of the water.

> And thus he was baptized, and the Spirit of God descended upon him, and thus he was born of the Spirit, and became quickened in the inner man.
>
> And he heard a voice out of heaven, saying: Thou art baptized with fire, and with the Holy Ghost. This is the record of the Father, and the Son, from henceforth and forever.[39]

So Adam was baptized and received the Holy Ghost.[40] Central to Adam's understanding of the mortal world was the principal of "agency" or "free will"—that man was free to choose for himself his own destiny, whether that be for good or evil.[41]

Obviously, there was more to the religion of Adam than this, but this is what has been recorded. Mormons believe that Adam had the "fulness of the gospel," which would have included many more tenants than those I have listed here.

So what happened to this ancient religion after Adam?

Remember the concept of "dispensationalism." At the close of a dispensation or period of time when the gospel of Jesus Christ is upon the earth, there occurs an apostasy. According to Christian scholar Scott R. Petersen, an apostasy has four main characteristics: (1) rejection of living prophets, (2) loss of divine authority, (3) loss of pure doctrines, and (4) loss of specific authority to perform sacraments and rites. The general consensus of biblical scholars have settled upon five significant dispensations occurring prior to the birth of Jesus Christ; those being Adam, Enoch, Noah, Abraham, and Moses.[42] Each new dispensation is commenced by the visitation of God to a prophet through whom a restoration of the gospel is accomplished.

DISPENSATION OF ENOCH

Of Enoch, Genesis only states that he "walked with God."[43] The year, 3317 BC.[44] Notwithstanding the absence of biblical information, through other sources we know that Enoch was ordained to the priesthood by Adam and that Enoch was visited by God who spoke with Him.[45]

> Enoch, my son, prophesy unto this people, and say unto them—Repent, for thus saith the Lord: I am angry with this people, and my fierce anger is kindled against them; for their hearts have waxed hard, and their ears are dull of hearing, and their eyes cannot see afar off.

And for these many generations, ever since the day that I created
them, have they gone astray, and have denied me, and have sought their
own counsels in the dark.[46]

It certainly appears that an apostasy had occurred. Enoch was
called by God to restore the gospel. As recorded in Moses 6:37, Enoch
preached the gospel to the inhabitants of the land, telling them to
(1) have faith in Jesus Christ who would come into the world in the
"meridian of time," (2) repent of their sins, (3) be baptized in the name
of this Christ, and (4) receive the gift of the Holy Ghost.[47] Enoch himself was baptized.[48] Enoch further taught about the nature of Christ.
He stated that Christ existed before this mortal life in a premortal
existence.[49] There he was referred to as the "Son of Man."[50]

Enoch became one of the Lord's great prophets, inspiring an entire
people to live together in harmony and righteousness. In due time,
Enoch and his people were taken from the earth into heaven: "Therefore I now took away Zion, to visit the world in its own time more
speedily." The wicked who remained behind did not repent of their
sins, nor did they refrain from perverting the true gospel.[51]

DISPENSATION OF NOAH

By the time of Noah, approximately 2349 BC,[52] the Old Testament
teaches us that the descendants of Adam had fallen into apostasy
again; namely, that "God saw that the wickedness of man was great in
the earth, and that every imagination of the thoughts of his heart was
only evil continually."[53]

And the Lord said, I will destroy man whom I have created from the
face of the earth: both man, and beast, and the creeping thing, and the
fowls of the air; for it repenteth me that I have made them.[54]

"But Noah found grace in the eyes of the Lord."[55] Once again,
following an apostasy, God appears to a prophet to usher in a new
dispensation. This time, God commanded Noah to build an ark and
save his family and various assorted animals. Such flood stories appear
in nearly every culture (including ancient cultures) the world over.
Following the flood, Noah built an alter and offered animal sacrifice
to the Lord—just as Adam had done before him.[56] Also just as Adam
and Enoch before him, Noah was baptized.[57-58] The pattern that had

been established of an apostasy followed by a new dispensation where a restoration occurred was continuing through Noah.

Noah's sons then spread out over the earth. It is regarded that Japheth went to Europe (Britain, France, Germany, Russia, Greece, and Italy), that Shem cultivated the Middle East (Babylon, Sumaria, Palestine, and Persia), and Ham founded Africa (Egypt). It was some years later that the Tower of Babel was constructed (approximately 2242 BC),[59] supposedly by Nimrod, a descendent of Ham, and the languages of the earth were confounded.[60]

> Since we cannot here treat them individually, we must be content to note that the archetype of all usurpers is Nimrod, who claims kingship and priesthood by right of "the cosmic garment of Adam," which his father Ham stole from Noah. . . . Early Jewish and Christian traditions report that it was Nimrod who built the Tower of Babel, the first pagan temple, in an attempt to contact heaven; it was he who challenged the priesthood of Abraham; it was he who built the first city, found the first state, organized the first army, ruling the world by force; he challenged God to an archery contest and, when he thought he had won, claimed to be no less than God's successor.[61]

Once again, an apostasy had occurred at the time of the Tower of Babel, and with the confounding of the languages and migration throughout the world, the religion of Adam was taken here and there and spread throughout the known world. Is it any wonder that you find similarities in all religions of ancient origin and those of modernity? The commonality lies in a time of migration, for they all sprung from the same tree trunk, that of Adam. Hence, when we read about common religious beliefs or historicity between the Mayan and Egyptian civilizations, we are reading about something that is older than either one.

> The same comparative studies that discovered the common pattern in all ancient religions—a phenomenon now designated as "pattern-ism"—have also demonstrated the processes of diffusion by which that pattern was spread throughout the world—and in the process torn to shreds, of which recognizable remnants may be found in almost any land and time. It would now appear that the early [Christian] fathers were not far from the mark in explaining the resemblances [between all religions]: the rites do look alike wherever we find them; however,

modern Christians may insist on denying the fact, for they all come from a common source. The business of reconstructing the original prototype from the scattered fragments has been a long and laborious one, and it is as yet far from completed.[62]

DISPENSATION OF ABRAHAM

Abram means "exalted father." He is the founding patriarch of the Israelites (Hebrews), Ishmaelites (Arabs), Edomites (descendants of Esau, son of Isaac, which had its principal stronghold at Petra), as well as the Midianites (descendants of Median, son of Abraham's wife Kitura). Judaism, Christianity, and Islam are sometimes referred to as the "Abrahamic religions" because of the progenitor role that Abraham plays in their religious traditions. In both the Jewish tradition and the Quran, he is referred to as "our Father," for he is considered the father of their various races. This naturally follows from the name "Abraham," which means "father of many nations." For Jews and Christians, this Abraham is their father through his son Isaac, by his wife Sarai; for Muslims, he is a prophet of Islam and the ancestor of Muhammad through his other son Ishmael, born to him by Sarai's handmaiden, Hagar.

Terah, a direct descendant of Noah through Shem, fathered Abram, one of three sons in the City of Ur of the Chaldees. Abram married Sarai, his half sister. Terah is reported to have been a crafts-man in the art of manufacturing idols for king Nimrod, the same who built the famed Tower of Babel. Following the death of one of Terah's sons, Abram left Ur with his father heading toward Canaan, but instead settled in Haran with another of his brothers, where Terah died at the age of 205.[63]

When Abram was seventy-five years old, God told him to leave the land of his birth and go "to the land that I will show you," where Abram would father a great nation. So Abram left Haran with Sarai, Lot (his nephew), and all of their followers and flocks. They settled in Canaan, where God gave the land to Abram and his descendants. After some time, there was a famine in the land and Abram traveled west to Egypt for food with his wife Sarai, who was purported to be a great beauty. Abram knew that the Egyptian aristocracy would attempt to court Sarai due to her beauty. If they knew that Abram was her husband, his life would be in danger. Consequently, Abram and Sarai pretended to be brother and sister, which was true as Sarai was Abram's stepsister. However, when Pharaoh attempted to marry Sarai, Abram came forward and told Pharaoh the truth. Instead of killing Abram, Pharaoh compensated Abram with great wealth for having disgraced Abram by courting his wife. By today's standards, the term would be "hush money."[64]

Following the period spent in Egypt, Abram, Sarai, and his nephew Lot return to Canaan where due to a dispute over grazing rights, Abram and Lot separated. Lot took the land lying east of the Jordan River and near to Sodom and Gomorrah, while Abram lived in Canaan, moving south to Hebron.[65]

It is here in 1921 BC[66] that Abram is called of God. He is visited by Jehovah and enters into a covenant with Him.[67] Sound familiar? In that covenant, God promises Abram that (1) Christ would come through his lineage, and that (2) his posterity would be given the land of Canaan upon which to live.[68] Additionally, Abram was given the promise of eternal increase; namely, that after this life he would continue to have seed in the eternities, which is referred to as celestial or eternal marriage.[69] Abram and his posterity were further called by God to preach this gospel to all nations.[70] Of particular interest, is that Abram, whose name was changed by Jehovah to Abraham, paid tithes,[71] was given revelations,[72] prophesied,[73] was a polygamist and had many wives,[74] entertained angels,[75] and was commanded by Jehovah to sacrifice Isaac in order to test his faithfulness, ultimately being stopped by an angel.[76]

Abraham prophesied and was a prophet.[77] As were his progeny, Isaac, Jacob, and Joseph.[78] In furtherance of his calling as a Prophet of Jehovah, Abraham used the Urim and Thummim, which are seer stones, to receive revelations.[79] A higher priesthood, called the Melchizedek Priesthood, after Melchizedek, king of Salem, who was a High Priest after the Order of the Son of God, was bestowed upon Abraham.[80] Through this priesthood, Abraham was able to perform ordinances and give blessings to his family. As part of Abraham's leadership, he ordained other men to be patriarchs in the priesthood of God,[81] he taught that missionary work was vital in order to preach the gospel to all nations,[82] and he instituted the prayer circle as an appropriate way to speak with Elohim through Jehovah.[83] Ultimately, circumcision was given by Jehovah to Abraham as a sign of the covenant, which is referred to as the Abrahamic covenant.[84]

This covenant was then passed from Abraham to Isaac and then to Jacob. Thereafter, the pattern continues as another apostasy occurs following the death of Joseph, Jacob's son who was sold into Egypt by his brothers.

DISPENSATION OF MOSES

For four hundred years, the Hebrews (the children of Israel) were slaves to the Egyptians.[85] Moses was born in 1571 BC.[86] He is called of God from a burning bush.[87] He becomes a great prophet of God and attempts to restore the Adamic religion to the Hebrews after freeing them from Pharaoh. But when he returns from Mount Sinai the first time, the Hebrews are worshiping a golden calf—they are not ready to live the gospel in its fulness as practiced by Adam, Enoch, Noah, and Abraham. Instead, they are given a second set of commandments, because Moses destroys the first set.[88] This second set is referred to as the "law of Moses," and it is separate and apart from the Abrahamic covenant and the sign of that covenant, circumcision. Often the two have been confused.

According to the Apostle Paul, the law of Moses was to be a schoolmaster to the Jews in preparation for the fulness of the gospel, the religion of Adam, which would be given to them in a yet future setting by the Messiah.[89] The Hebrews believed that a new covenant would come to replace the old. "Behold, the days come, saith the Lord, that I will make a new covenant with the house of Israel, and with the house of Judah."[90] Little did they know that although to them it would be a new covenant, to history, it is very old. It is the first set of tablets that Moses received.

The law of Moses, the Ten Commandments, were instituted as the law ("Torah") and Moses built the first temple, a traveling one at that, to house the ark of the covenant, the throne of God on earth. To ensure the continued adherence to the Torah and provide a historical backdrop, Moses authored the Pentateuch, which composes the first five books of the Old Testament. In it, Moses recites the history of the world from Adam to Abraham (Genesis), and describes the exodus of the Hebrews from Egyptian captivity (Exodus), as well as a handbook for the Levitical priests (Leviticus) and a history of the wanderings of the children of Israel in the Sinai desert (Deuteronomy). Moses also instituted a governing council of twelve men who were chosen to represent each of the twelve tribes (notice the similarity with establishment in the meridian of time of Christ's Twelve Apostles).[91] In remembrance of their exodus, Moses instituted the Passover, which not only signified their deliverance by Jehovah, but also was in similitude of Christ's future sacrifice and became the functional equivalent of the Christian sacrament of the Lord's Supper.[92]

Following their release from captivity, the Hebrews conquered Canaan, the land of their inheritance according to the Abrahamic covenant. Thereafter, they divided into tribal areas, with each tribe representing one of the sons of Jacob (whose name had been changed by God to "Israel"). The Hebrews continued to worship Jehovah, the name of God that Moses received while he stood on holy ground next to a burning bush on Mount Sinai.[93] Notice that the name of God is no longer "Elohim" or "Man of Holiness," as revealed to Adam and Enoch, but is "Jehovah," who has become the God of the Old Testament. One aspect of Hebrew belief with respect to God and the creation of this earth was a belief in a Council of Gods (more than Elohim and Jehovah) who created the world.[94] Hence, although it is commonly understood that the Israelites were monotheists (namely; the belief in one God), there were always elements of polytheism (the belief in multiple Gods). To the Hebrews, this belief system recognized a Father God and then a hierarchy of lesser Gods, which is consistent with their doctrinal acceptance of deification, as will be discussed later.

Just as Abraham paid tithes, so the Israelites continued this tradition.[95] The Hebrews instituted a strict health code[96] and continued in their traditional spiritual fasts.[97] The Hebrews also looked to Jehovah to perform miracles for their benefit.[98]

The nation of Israel ventured through three kings: Saul, David, and Solomon. Solomon built the first permanent temple. "A temple, good or bad, is a scale-model of the universe. The first mention of the word *templum* is by Varro, for whom it designates a building specifically designed for interpreting signs in the heavens—a sort of observatory where one gets one's bearings on the universe."[99] It is the temple where the ancients could make contact with God and other worlds. Hence, the notion that temples were the dwelling places of the Gods is a false notion. These were communication centers, not divine habitations.[100]

This is perhaps the reason that temples generally resembled mountains because the original communication center used by the ancients to contact God was on a mountain. Nibley notes a long list of holy mountains utilized for this purpose.[101] One such example is Moses, who spoke with God at Mount Sinai. It is in these sacred temples that a ritual drama was played out before the Hebrews.[102] Obviously, the temple was important enough that Moses had the tabernacle (temple) carried during their wanderings in the Sinai.[103] Once a more permanent location was identified, Solomon's temple was built.[104] It is of some interest to note that a baptismal font placed on twelve oxen was built inside the temple,[105] for the Israelites still believed in the importance of baptism.[106] Ordinances such as ritual washings and anointings were also practiced,[107] as were vicarious ordinances for the dead to assure their salvation in the afterlife.[108]

It was the Levite priests who were given the sacred duty to officiate in the temple.[109–110] The priesthood of God was exercised by the Levites.[111] Individual Levitical priesthood offices included three ranks: Nethinim, Levite, and Priest.[112] Additionally, there appear to be three other offices in the priesthood: high priest,[113] Seventy,[114] and elder.[115] The Hebrew temple ceremony (Jewish initiation rite) required the wearing of ritual clothing (sacred garments).[116] An important aspect to temple worship was a belief in the bodily resurrection.[117] As a natural corollary to that was the tradition of a pre-existence.[118] The resurrection required that the human be immortal—living as spirits before the world was created, coming to a mortal sphere, and then being resurrected after mortal death to live forever, which leads into a discussion of the afterlife; the Hebrews believed in three degrees of glory in the afterlife.

> For an Israelite example we need only turn to a document known as the Testament of the Twelve Patriarchs. Within this text, the "Testament of Levi" purports to report the words of Levi who was the head of one of the twelve tribes of Israel. This document states that Levi ascended through three heavens, accompanied by an angel of the Lord. The lowest or "first heaven" was "dark" because it "sees all the injustices

of humankind." The "second heaven" was much brighter and more lustrous than the first. Finally, Levi ascended to "the uppermost heaven" which was even "more lustrous and beyond compare." In this place, which the angel called "the Holy of Holies," Levi saw God seated upon His throne. [119]

Prophets who communed with Jehovah helped to guide the successive monarchs because the Hebrews believed that prophets acted as spokesmen for Jehovah and, therefore, could provide essential guidance to the leaders of their nation.[120] The belief in direct revelation between God and man was an essential element to their religious underpinnings.[121] Israelite prophets cited an instrument called the Urim and Thummim as a device used to translate and receive prophesy.[122] Prophets, like Moses, and Hebrew scribes recorded their histories and dealings with Jehovah in many diverse and numerous scrolls or sticks, so called because the leather or papyrus, which could be as long as one hundred feet, was wound around a wooden stick for ease in use. These scrolls comprised the learnings of the Israelite culture.

One key component of the culture, as discussed by Isaiah, was a belief in a Messiah, a Savior of the chosen people of God. This Savior would be the fulfillment of the Abrahamic covenant.[123] Some scholars believe that the Israelites simply adopted this concept of a Messiah from the Persians, who were practicing adherents of Zoroaster. Zoroastrians believed in multiple messiahs, one at the beginning of civilization, another in the meridian of times, and the last before the end of the world. It is for this reason that most scholars agree that the wise men from the east who visited the baby Jesus some two years after his birth were Zoroastrian priests who recognized the sign in the night sky (as Zoroastrians practiced star gazing) of the coming of the Messiah in the meridian of time.[124] Thus to some, the resultant Hebrew belief in a messiah.[125]

Eventually the twelve tribes divided into two nations: the Northern Kingdom retained the name of Israel and was governed by descendants of Ephraim, Joseph's son who was given the birthright (the "higher priesthood"); the Southern Kingdom was named Judah, after the main tribe residing in the region. Of note is the catalyst that sparked the separation of the two nations. During the final years of king Solomon's reign, he began heavily taxing his people. After Solomon's death, his son, Rehoboam, ruled in his stead. Because Rehoboam continued with the same policy of heavy taxation, the northern ten tribes rebelled, forming their own nation. In 750 BC, the Assyrians from the north came and conquered Israel, carrying away the northern tribes, who became known to history as the "lost ten tribes of Israel." Some of these northern tribesmen escaped south to Judah.[126]

It was during this dispensation that the Hebrews began referring to themselves as the sons and daughters of God, in a literal, not figurative sense.[127] Thus the belief in deification—the idea that the Hebrews, as the chosen people of Jehovah, could become gods, like Elohim.[128–129] The Israelites understood Jehovah to be a glorified and perfected man who naturally was married to a glorified and perfected woman. "From our Old Testament alone we should never have guessed that Israel associated a goddess with Yahweh, even popularly, but the conclusion is irresistible, and we are justified in assuming that she played her part in the mythology and ritual of Israel."[130] To the Hebrews this was only natural, after all, didn't God say that man was created in His form and image (male and female)? Isn't it logical that Eve was created in the form and image of a female goddess, the wife of God? For this reason, marriage was considered a sacred covenant between a man and a woman. What's more, the Hebrews preached the concept of eternal marriage (that is, marriage that survives this mortal life).[131] This practice is historically shown in the coronation rites of ancient Near Eastern royalty.[132]

By 284 BC, the written record of the Jews had become unmanageable and to many Jews living at Alexandria unreadable, as Greek had become the common language to the masses. By tradition, it is said that seventy-two elders (Jewish scholars) were sent to Alexandria from Jerusalem and made a Greek translation of the most important scrolls in seventy days. This compilation became known as the "Septuagint." It included not only what is in our present day Old Testament, but also many texts that we refer to today as the "Apocrypha." For example, the First and Second Books of Esdras, the Book of Tobit, the Book of the Wisdom of Solomon, and Bel and the Dragon.[133] The Israelite Prophet Ezekiel, in the late sixth century BC, foresaw not only the Septuagint (Old Testament), but also the full Bible (Old and New Testaments together). He referred to this Bible as the stick of Judah, which would come forth in the meridian of time. However, he also spake of another Stick, the Stick of Joseph, which would come forth in the last dispensation of the fulness of times.[134]

So what is the meaning of writing upon a "stick"? Evidence from the period suggests that the Babylonians "wrote upon wax-filled writing boards or wooden tablets. These tablets were hinged on one edge so that two or more of them could be connected together and folded shut." Hence the "sticks" may refer to these wax-filled writing boards that are hinged together forming our equivalent of books. "In the verses that follow this passage the Lord explains that the 'sticks' of Joseph and Judah represent the divided kingdoms of Israel ('stick of Joseph'—Northern Kingdom; 'stick of Judah'—Southern Kingdom). The Lord states in verses 21 and 22 of Ezekiel 37 that the joining together of the inscribed 'sticks' is symbolic of the gathering together of Israel's scattered children and their reunification as 'one nation.'"[135]

Already known to Ezekiel at the time of this prophecy was the destruction of the Northern Kingdom of Israel. In 722 BC, the Northern Kingdom of Israel was taken captive by the Assyrians and, as has already been discussed, became the lost ten tribes.[136] That left the Southern Kingdom—Judah, which was in the grip of widespread apostasy. In fact, the Old Testament confirms a "four hundred year gap in Jewish history (between Malachi and John the Baptist) when no prophecy is recorded and when the Lord gave stewardship to no recognized prophets upon the earth." This is further corroborated by the text of 1 Maccabees 4:46. The Jewish temple had been sacked and desecrated following the Babylonian captivity, the altar having been used for pagan ritual sacrifice. Hence, after the reoccupation of the area by the Jews, the temple needed to be rededicated to Jehovah and more specifically, the desecrated altar needed to be destroyed and, thereafter, rebuilt and rededicated. However, Judas Maccabaeus, who lived in the second century BC, reports that this rededication could not be accomplished because there was no authorized representative of Jehovah (a prophet) upon the earth to perform the ceremony. Hence, the rededication had to wait.[137]

One hundred and fifty years after the carrying away of the Northern Kingdom, in around 600 BC, the Babylonians captured Judah and sacked Jerusalem and its temple. It is during this time of unrest that Mormons believe that a small party of Hebrews from the tribes of Ephraim and Manasseh crossed the Arabian desert and ultimately went to the Americas. Their experiences and history is documented in the Book of Mormon. As for the Jews, they were subsequently incorporated into the Persian Empire when Cyrus conquered Babylon. Thereafter, Darius allowed the Jews to return to their homeland of Canaan and rebuild their temple. With the conquest of Persia by Alexander the Great, Canaan and the Jews came under the jurisdiction of the Greeks. Upon Alexander's untimely death, his southern general, Ptolemy, who had become sovereign of Egypt, took control of Jerusalem in 301 BC. A century later in 198 BC, Antiochus III of Syria, defeated the Egyptians in a battle near Caesarea Philippi and occupied Palestine. This set the scene for the Maccabean War, where the Jews revolted against the Seleucid Dynasty in Syria and set up the Hasmonean Dynasty under Mattathias ben Johanan. It was due to a power struggle within the Hasmonean Dynasty and the invitation by Hyrcanus II to the Romans to assist him in regaining the throne from the Syrians that ultimately led to the occupation of Palestine by the Romans in 63 BC. Although the rule of kings would continue through Herod the Great (37–4 BC), the Jews were again under the rule of another foreign empire.[138] They had again fallen into apostasy.[139]

Obviously, there are many other doctrines contained in the Old Testament that are not addressed here. However, I have attempted to illustrate the kinds of doctrines that were taught. Once the prophets were gone, Malachi being one of the last, Israel was without spiritual leadership. Some years later, the Jews began in earnest to seek for their deliverer, the Messiah, who would save them from the Romans.

THE MERIDIAN OF TIME

Jesus of Nazareth was born in Bethlehem at the meridian of time (Ussher approximates this to be around 5 BC).[140] He called twelve Apostles and preached the "Goods News," the gospel of Jesus Christ. Who is Jesus of Nazareth? He is the promised Messiah, the Christ. But more than that, he told the Jews, "verily, verily, I say unto you, Before Abraham was, I am."[141] Christ proclaimed that he was none other than Jehovah himself, the great "I am" of the Old Testament. What was the response of the Jews to this declaration? "Then took they up stones to cast at him."[142] It was blasphemy!

Notwithstanding heavy opposition by the Sanhedrin, Christ proceeded to preach in the tradition of the rabbis and set up His Church upon the earth. Of utmost importance to understand, this gospel was the same restored religion that Jesus Christ, as Jehovah, had given to Adam four millennia earlier.

THE ORIGINAL CHURCH

During the earthly ministry of Jesus of Nazareth, the Apostles appeared at times like a group of school boys vying for the attentions of their teacher and mentor. In like manner, they also appeared somewhat dense to the doctrines and lessons that Christ had taught them and showed varying degrees of faith in their divine calls. They were certainly not ready to lead Christ's Church.

Following Christ's crucifixion, the Apostles were in disarray and appeared to be on the brink of desertion. However, things changed after the Resurrection of the Savior and His subsequent forty day ministry. The Apostles appeared to have gained a stronger testimony of the divinity of Christ. Additionally, they were privileged to learn privately from the Master the mysteries of the kingdom of God.

After Christ's ascension, the Apostles waited for the Comforter, whom Christ promised would come and teach them all things that they should do. That Comforter, the Holy Ghost, did come—on the day of Pentecost. Thereafter, the Apostles embarked on their missions to spread the gospel of Jesus Christ to all the world. They went from city to city preaching the gospel, baptizing with water and conferring the gift of the Holy Ghost on those who accepted the gospel, and setting up small congregations throughout the Roman Empire. The Church, under the direction of the senior Apostles (Peter, James, and John), grew at a remarkable pace.

The main body of the church remained at Jerusalem until at least AD 50, when the Jerusalem Council was held. Thereafter, Peter and John departed to Antioch, in modern-day Turkey, there to set up a new headquarters of the Church. Ultimately, Peter would go on to Rome a decade later and be martyred, while John would spend his days in Ephesus (with a detour courtesy of Rome to the prison colony at the Isle of Patmos).

Christian scholars from all faiths agree that following Peter's death up until the third century AD, the history of Christ's Church is sketchy at best. Through the writings of some of the Apostolic Fathers, Heresy Hunters, and Apologists, we obtain most of our knowledge.[143] One thing is certain, however, the Church splintered into three general groups within the whole.

It is irrefutable fact that the first Christians were Jewish Christians, and consequently their theology made use of Jewish thought forms and Jewish categories. . . . The Jews of the diaspora provided the initial basis for church growth during the first and early second centuries. However, by the mid-second century we can speak of three major movements within Christianity: Jewish Christianity, Hellenistic or Gentile Christianity, and Gnosticism.[144]

These three distinct sects within the Christian movement are said to have had their origins in the specific teachings of the Apostles. The Jewish or Hebrew Christians were said to have been adherents of the head Apostle Peter, as well as of the Apostle James the Just, the bishop of Jerusalem, while Hellenistic or Pauline Christians were followers of the Apostle Paul (Saul of Tarsus). The Gnostics looked to the Apostle John.[145] It will be important to our understanding of the fate of Christianity to fully comprehend who each of these groups were and what they believed before going into what happened to them and to Christianity.[146]

NOTES

1. Acts 10
2. Galatians 3:8.
3. 1 Corinthians 10:1–5.
4. Hebrews 4:2.
5. Ignatius, Magnesians 8 in Alexander Roberts and James Donaldson, *Ante-Nicene Fathers*, 10 vols (Peabody, Massachusetts: Hendrickson Publishers, 1994) (hereinafter, "ANF"), 1–62.
6. Theophilus, Theophilus to Autolycus 3:29; in ANF, 2:120–121; Tatian, Address to the Greeks 31 in ANF, at 2:77; Eusebius, *Ecclesiastical History* (Grand Rapids, MI: Baker Books, 1995), 1–4, 6–10; Eusebius, *The Proof of the Gospel* 1:5, vol. 1 25–26
7. Athanasius, De Decretis Nicaena Synodi 5, in Scott R. Petersen, *Where Have All the Prophets Gone?* (CFI, Springville, UT: 2005), 39, citing J.P. Migne, *Petrologiae Graedae* (Paris: 1857).
8. Galatians 3:19.
9. Eusebius, *Ecclesiastical History*, 1:26–28, quoted in Petersen, *Where Have All the Prophets Gone?*, at 37–38.
10. Petersen, *Where Have All the Prophets Gone?*, 18.

11. In deciding how to address the historicity of Adam's religion and the general lack of information found in the Bible, I have decided to use all available resources, including the canonized scriptures of The Church of Jesus Christ of Latter-day Saints, Apocrypha, and Pseudepigrapha.
12. Genesis 1:26–28.
13. Adam believed in the premortal life of man. (Genesis 2:4–5).
14. Genesis 1:19.
15. Genesis 1:20.
16. Genesis 2:21–24.
17. Genesis 1:28.
18. Genesis 3:22.
19. Genesis 3.
20. Sacred garments were given to Adam and Eve; namely, animal skins to clothe their nakedness (Genesis 3:21).
21. James Ussher, *The Annals of the World* (Green Forest, Arkansas: Larry and Mario Pierce, Master Books, 2003), 17.
22. Moses 5:4–9.
23. Adam was taught and protected by three visitors from God. Nibley, *Mormonism and Early Christianity* (Salt Lake City, UT: Deseret Book, 1987), 69, citing the Book of Adam.
24. See generally, Bruce R. McConkie, *Mormon Doctrine* (Salt Lake City, UT: Deseret Book, 1979), 224.
25. John 1:1–3, 14.
26. John 17; Luke 23:34.
27. John 8:58.
28. James E. Talmage, *Jesus the Christ*, (Salt Lake City, UT: Deseret Book, Salt Lake City, 1916), 108.
29. Quote of Lorenzo Snow, President, The Church of Jesus Christ of Latter-day Saints.
30. See also "Conflict of Adam and Eve with Satan," 26:18–19 in Rutherford Platt, *The Forgotten Books of Eden* (New York: Alpha House, 1927), 18.
31. 1 Nephi 10:21.
32. Moses 6:59.
33. See also "Conflict of Adam and Eve with Satan," 68–69 in Platt, *The Forgotten Books of Eden*, 47–49.
34. Petersen, *Where Have All the Prophets Gone?*, 23, quoting Testament of Adam 3.1–4. See also "Conflict of Adam and Eve with Satan," 14, 42, 49 in Platt, *The Forgotten Books of Eden*, 13, 28, 33.
35. Genesis 3:1–13.
36. Moses 5:58.
37. Moses 6:5.
38. "Adam finding he needed help, solicited divine assistance with prayers and sacrifices. . . . That was the beginning of the ordinances of God." Clementine Recognitions IV, 11, in Nibley, *Mormonism and Early Christianity*, 65.
39. Moses 6:64–66.
40. See also Apocalype of Adam 8.9–11, 17, cited in Petersen, *Where Have all the Prophets Gone?*, 22 and in James Charlesworth, *Old Testament Pseudepigrapha and the New Testament*, 2 vols (Harrisburg, Pennsylvania: Trinity Press International, 1998) (hereinafter, "OTP"), 1:719.
41. 2 Enoch 30:12–15 in OTP, 1:152; Epistle of the Apostles 39; Petersen, *Where Have all the Prophets Gone?*, 24–25.

42. Petersen, *Where Have All the Prophets Gone?*, 19–21.

43. Genesis 5:22, 24.

44. Ussher, *Annals of the World*, 18.

45. Doctrine and Covenants 107:48–49.

46. Moses 6:27–28.

47. Moses 6:52, 62.

48. Moses 7:11.

49. 1 Enoch 48:3 in OTP, 1:35.

50. Ibid., 37–71.

51. Petersen, *Where Have All the Prophets Gone?*, 30.

52. Ussher, *Annals of the World*, 19.

53. Genesis 6:5.

54. Genesis 6:7.

55. Genesis 6:8.

56. Genesis 8:20.

57. Moses 8:23–24.

58. An interesting tale told anciently was that Canaan, the son of Ham, stole Adam's sacred garment given to Noah. (Nibley, *Mormonism and Early Christianity*, 366).

59. Ussher, *Annals of the World*, 22.

60. Genesis 11:1–9.

61. Nibley, *Mormonism and Early Christianity*, 366.

62. Ibid., 366–67.

63. Genesis 11.

64. Genesis 12.

65. Genesis 13.

66. Ussher, *Annals of the World*, 25.

67. Genesis 12:1–9.

68. Genesis 17; 22:15–18; Galatians 3.

69. Doctrine and Covenants 132:29–50; Abraham 2:6–11.

70. Matthew 3:9, Abraham 2:9–11.

71. Genesis 14:20, 28–30.

72. Genesis 15:1.

73. Genesis 15:13.

74. Genesis 16:1–4; Genesis 25:1–10; Genesis 29:23–35; Genesis 30:3–4, 8–9; 2 Chronicles 13:21; 1 Kings 11:1–3; 2 Samuel 2:2; 2 Samuel 12:7–8; Genesis 16:1–3, 25:1–10.

75. Genesis 18.

76. Genesis 22.

77. Genesis 20:1–7.

78. Genesis 26:2–3, 24; Genesis 32:24–30; Genesis 35:1; Genesis 37:5–10; Genesis 41:16–40.

79. Abraham 3:1–4.

80. Genesis 14:18–20; Hebrews 7:11–12; Petersen, *Where Have all the Prophets Gone?*, 33.

81. Genesis 49:1; Genesis 27:27–30. There has been wide speculation that this Melchizedek was none other than Shem, the son of Noah, who would not die until 1846 BC. Ussher, *Annals of the World*, 27.

82. Matthew 3:9; Abraham 2:9–11.

83. "Apocalypse of Abraham," chapter 12 in OTP, 1:695; The Testament of Job 46:1–5,

in H. F. P. Sparks, *The Apocryphal Old Testament* (Oxford: Clarendon Press, 1984), 644–46.

84. Genesis 17:17–27; 22:15–18.
85. Exodus 1.
86. Ussher, *Annals of the World*, 34.
87. Exodus 3:4–6.
88. Exodus 20.
89. Galatians 3:24.
90. Jeremiah 31:31–33; Ezekiel 37:21–28.
91. Numbers 1:4–16, 44; Joshua 4:4.
92. Exodus 12:12–14.
93. Exodus 3:14.
94. Psalm 82:1; Job 15:8; Job 25:14; Proverbs 3:32; Psalm 111:1; Jeremiah 6:11; Jeremiah 15:17; Ezekiel 13:9; Psalm 55:14; Psalm 83:3; Psalm 89:5–7; Proverbs 15:22; Jeremiah 23:18, 22; Psalm 64:2.
95. Leviticus 27:30–34; Deuteronomy 12:5–6; Deuteronomy 14:22–23; Deuteronomy 26:12–14; Malachi 3:3–10; Proverbs 3:9–10.
96. Numbers 6:1–4, 8; Judges 13:13–14; Leviticus 10:8–11; Daniel 1:8.; Leviticus 11:1–47; Deuteronomy 14:2–21; Isaiah 5:11–12; Isaiah 28:7–8.
97. Isaiah 58:3–7; Psalm 35:13; Nehemiah 9:1–3.
98. Genesis 41:16–40; Exodus 7–12; Exodus 14:21–27; Joshua 3:9–17; Joshua 6:1–27; Joshua 10:12–14; 1 Kings 18:21–40; Numbers 16:28–33; 2 Kings 1:9–12; 2 Kings 2:6–8, 11–12, 14; 2 Kings 4:3–7, 20–36; 2 Kings 5:1–14; Daniel 2; Daniel 3:16–27; Daniel 6.
99. Nibley, *Mormonism and Early Christianity*, 358.
100. Ibid., 359.
101. Ibid., 360.
102. Ibid., 362.
103. Exodus 25:8–9; 35:21; 40:30–38.
104. 1 Kings 6.
105. 1 Kings 7:21–25; 2 Chronicles 4:2–4; Jeremiah 52:20.
106. Isadore Singer and Cyrus Adler, *Jewish Encyclopedia* (New York: Funk & Wagnalls, 1901–1906), 2:499.
107. Exodus 40:12, 15.
108. Psalm 16:9–11; Isaiah 24:21–22; Obadiah 1:21; Malachi 4:5–6.
109. 1 Chronicles 6:10.
110. Hebrew temples: (1) Moses's tabernacle (Sinai); (2) Solomon's temple (ark of the covenant in the temple, built 1005 BC by king David and destroyed 600 BC by Nebuchadnezzar); (3) Zerubabel's temple (built around 500 BC, ark no longer present); (4) Herod's temple (rebuilt Zerubabel's temple around 1 BC and destroyed by Titus AD 60).
111. Exodus 29:9.
112. Matthew B. Brown, *All Things Restored* (American Fork, UT: Covenant Communications, 2006), 78.
113. Ezra 7:5.
114. Exodus 24:1,9; Numbers 11:16; Ezekiel 8:11.
115. Deuteronomy 31:9; Joshua 8:33.
116. Testament of Job 46–51; Exodus 28:1–4; 29:29, 45; 31:10; 35:19–21; 39:27–29; 40:12–15; Leviticus 16:4; 1 Chronicles 15:27; Daniel 7:9.

117. See 1 Samuel 2:6; Job 14:14, 19:26; Isaiah 25:8, 26:19; Ezekiel 37:12; Daniel 12:2; Hosea 13:14.

118. See Numbers 16:22, Job 38:7, Ecclesiastic 12:7, Jeremiah 1:5, Zechariah 12:1; Wisdom of Solomon 8:19–20.

119. Brown, *All Things Restored*, 123.

120. See Amos 3:7; Numbers 11:29; Exodus 3:1–4; 7:1; Deuteronomy 18:15–21; Joshua 1:1–9; Judges 6:8–24; 1 Samuel 3:20–21; 2 Chronicles 35:18; 2 Samuel 7:2; 1 Kings 12, 14:2, 16:7, 18:22; 2 Kings 2:14, 6:12, 14:25, 19:2, 20:1, 11:14; 2 Chronicles 12:5, 15, 13:22, 15:8; Ezra 5:1–6; 1 Haggai 1:1–3, 12; 2 Chronicles 36:12; Jeremiah 28:1; Zechariah 1:1–7; Daniel 1:17; Joel 1:1; Obadiah 1; Micah 1:1; Habakkuk 1–3; Malachi 1–4.

121. Numbers 11:29, 12:6; Proverbs 29:18; Amos 3:7.

122. Exodus 28:30–31; Leviticus 8:7–8; Numbers 27:21; Deuteronomy 33:8; 1 Samuel 28:5–8; Nehemiah 7:65; Ezra 2:62–63.

123. Ernest A. Wallis Budge, *Coptic Martyrdoms* (British Museum 1914, New York: AMS, 1977), 482; William G. Braude, Pesikta Rabbati, Yale Judaica Series, 18 vols (Yale University Press, 1968), 2:677–679.

124. Mary Boyce, *Zoroastrians: Their Religious Beliefs and Practices* (London: Routledge & Kegan Paul, 1979), 42–43, 74–75.

125. Budge, *Coptic Martyrdoms*, 482; Braude, *Yale Judaica Series*, 2:677–679.

126. See 1 Kings 12.

127. See Job 1:6, 38:7, Psalm 82:6, Isaiah 45:11, Hosea 1:10, Numbers 16:22, Deuteronomy 14:1, Malachi 2:10.

128. See Genesis 1:26, 3:22; Leviticus 19:2; Psalm 8:6, 82:6.

129. "In an early Jewish document the concept of deification can be found." Brown, *All Things Restored*, 124. God the Father is a "God of gods, and Lord of lords." Deuteronomy 10:17; Joshua 22:22; Psalm 136:2–3.

130. Theodore Robinson, "Hebrew Myths," *Myth and Ritual* (Oxford University Press 1933), 185. See also Margaret Barker, *The Great Angel* (Westminster: John Knox Press, 1992), 52, 57.

131. Genesis 2:18, 21–24; Ezekiel 16:8, 10–13; Isaiah 61:10.

132. Matthew Brown, *The Gate of Heaven: Insights on the Doctrines and Symbols of the Temple* (American Fork, UT: Covenant Communications, 1999), 135–38, 160, n. 153.

133. The Church of Jesus Christ of Latter-day Saints, Bible Dictionary (Salt Lake City, 1989), 771.

134. Ezekiel 37:15–20.

135. Brown, *All Things Restored*, at 187–88.

136. 2 Kings 17:6.

137. Petersen, *Where Have All the Prophets Gone?*, 37.

138. S. Kent Brown & Richard Neitzel Holzapfel, *The Lost 500 Years*, (Salt Lake City, UT: Deseret Book, 2006), 35–74.

139. Deuteronomy 9:7,25; 29:25; 30:15–19; Judges 3:7; 1 Kings 11:2; 14:22; 2 Kings 17:7; 21:2; Psalm 106:36; Isaiah 2:8; 39; 24:5; 29:13–14; 59:2; Jeremiah 2:17; 7:11; 35:11; Ezekiel 2:3; 11:12; 22:26; Hosea 4:6; 17; Amos 8:11; Micah 3:11; Matthew 13:15; 15:9

140. Ussher, *Annals of the World*, 779.

141. John 8:58.

142. John 8:59.

143. Apostolic Fathers: Clement (AD 30–100), bishop of Rome from AD 90–100. Ignatius (AD 30–108), bishop of Antioch from AD 80–108, Polycarp (AD 69–155), bishop of Smyrna from AD 100–155. Apologists (defended the faith against outsiders): Justin Martyr (AD 100–165), Tatian (AD 110–180), Tertullian of Carthage (AD 150–225), Cyprian bishop of Carthage (AD 249–58), Eusebius bishop of Caesarea (AD 325). Polemicists (defended the faith against heresies): Irenaeus of Lyons (AD 140–202), Hippolytus (AD 165–235), Clement of Alexandria (AD 155–220), Origen of Alexandria and Caesarea (AD 185–254).

144. Barry Bickmore, *Mormonism in the Early Jewish Christian Milieu* (FAIR Conference 1999). Jewish Christian teaching was the "first form of Christian theology."

145. Stephen L. Harris, *Understanding the Bible* (Palo Alto: Mayfield, 1985), cited in http://en.wikipedia.org/wiki/Early_Christianity.

146. When referring to the Apostolic Fathers, I am referring to various authoritative figures in the early Church. These include the three bishops immediately following the Apostles: Clement, bishop of Rome; Ignatius, bishop of Antioch; and Polycarp, bishop of Smyrna. Additionally, there are Justin Martyr, the First Apologist; Irenaeus, bishop of Lyons; Clement of Alexandria; Tertullian of Carthage; Origen of Alexandria and Caesarea; Cyprian, bishop of Carthage; Eusebius, bishop of Caesarea. Richard Lloyd Anderson, "Clement, Ignatius, and Polycarp: Three bishops between the Apostles and the Apostasy," *Ensign,* Aug. 1976.

CHAPTER 2

THE HEBREW CHRISTIANS

WHO WERE THE HEBREW CHRISTIANS?

The Hebrew Christians were the Jews at Jerusalem and those of the diaspora (at the time of Christ) who remained orthodox Jews untainted by the philosophies of the Greeks.[1] These were the original followers of Christ.[2] Their religious foundations and traditions are those found in the Old Testament and Talmud. They are the children of Abraham, Isaac, and Jacob. These were the Jews who looked forward to the coming of a Messiah, the son of David. It was to this group that Matthew wrote his Gospel, convincing them that the promised Messiah had come in the man Jesus of Nazareth, the son of a carpenter.

> Christianity arose on Jewish soil; Jesus and the Apostles spoke Aramaic, a language related to Hebrew. . . . As the New Testament writings show, they were firmly rooted in the Old Testament and lived in its world of images. Shortly after the death of the Founder, however, the new religious communities centre of gravity shifted into the Greek-speaking Hellenistic world, and after the year 70, the community was severed finally from its motherland: Christianity has been the religion of Europeans ever since. It is significant, however, that despite their absolute authority the words of Jesus were preserved by the Church

only in the Greek language. Not only are these two languages [namely; Aramaic and Greek] essentially different, but so too are the kinds of images and thinking involved in them. This distinction goes very deeply into the psychic life; the Jews themselves defined their spiritual predisposition as anti-Hellenic. Once this point is properly understood, it must be granted completely.[3]

These original Christians believed that Jesus did not come to form a new religious order, but rather to restore the traditions of their fore-fathers. To them, the teachings of Christ were a mere extension of Judaism. As we discussed in Chapter 1, there had been a four-hundred-year gap since a prophet of Jehovah had lived upon the earth, Malachi being the last. Judas Maccabaeus in the second century BC had given voice to the popular sentiment that without a prophet upon the earth, the rebuilt temple alter at Jerusalem could not be rededicated. Christ fulfilled the need for a prophet to these Jews. Consequently, "Jewish Christian teaching was the first form of Christian theology."[4]

After the Savior's ascension, the main body of Hebrew Christians remained at Jerusalem, although a good number apparently went with Peter and John to Antioch after the Jerusalem Council. The beliefs of these early Christians has been extensively documented in both the Old and New Testaments, as well as by various outside sources. Originally the gospel was preached only to the Jews.[5]

Then it was taken to the Gentiles, Cornelius being the most nota-ble.[6] The Jerusalem Council was held around AD 50 as a result of this missionary effort to the Gentiles. The Council was asked to determine whether the converted Gentiles needed to follow the law of Moses and be circumcised.[7] According to Eusebius, the first fifteen bishops of Jerusalem were "of the circumcision";[8] meaning that they were identi-fied as being Hebrew Christians who had followed the law of Moses.

Hence, it was during the time of the Jerusalem Council that a group, referred to by Paul as "Judaizers," demanded that all new converts to Christianity adhere to the law of Moses. Paul opposed the Judaizers. It is from this confrontation that Hellenized Christians would adopt Paul as their champion. However, the historical record clarifies that it was Peter, the chief Apostle, and not Paul, who at the Jerusalem Council, declared that the law of Moses was fulfilled through the Atonement of Jesus Christ and that the sign of the covenant, circumcision, would no longer be a requirement among Christians. Rather Christians would instead summit to baptism with a broken heart and a contrite spirit as a witness to God of their desire to serve and follow the Son of Man.

Still, a small contingent of Judaizers persisted in the Church thereafter. Some biblical scholars are insistent that Judaizers and Hebrew Christians were one in the same, but they were not and the historical record is clear on this. Some also suggest that Hebrew Christians are Messianic Jews—this is also untrue; for the Messianic Jews of today consider themselves to be fully Jewish and in no way associated with the Christian Church.

After the Jerusalem Council, Peter sent Paul to the Gentiles to preach that Jesus fulfilled the law of Moses and that circumcision was no longer required.[9] It is primarily due to this Jerusalem Council that most Romans considered the early Christians to be nothing more than "apostate Jews."[10]

The Book of Acts (AD 61–63), written by Luke, physician and historian, and traveling companion to Paul, illustrated the infant Church's progress from its center at Jerusalem to its new headquarters at Antioch in Syria and then beyond to Rome.

WHAT DID THE HEBREW CHRISTIANS BELIEVE?

The Hebrew Christians were not influenced by Greek philosophy and attempted to keep the doctrine pure, adhering to the original teachings of Jesus Christ. However, there is a strong overlay of Old Testament traditions and philosophies within those original doctrines.

ANTHROPOMORPHIC GOD AS A GLORIFIED AND PERFECTED MAN

To the Hebrew Christians, God was not a mere spirit; He was a glorified man. The Jews had long believed this concept.[11] "The Hebrews . . . pictured the God whom they worshiped as having a body and mind like our own, though transcending humanity in the splendor of his appearance, in his power, his wisdom, and the constancy of his care for his creatures."[12]

Consequently, those that converted to Christianity held on to that belief in God.[13]

The God of the Hebrews and the early Christians had passions and attributes.[14] This made him comprehensible.

Christ himself serves as a good example of the anthropomorphic nature of God the Father. Jesus teaches that he was with the Father in the beginning. According to John, Jesus was the "Word" and the "Word was with God, and the Word was God."[15] Yet Jesus was born into this world as the Only Begotten of the Father. He lived a mortal life and died. He was then resurrected and received a perfected and immortal body. We know for a surety that it was a physical body of flesh and bones, because when he showed himself to the Apostles he made it a point to state that he was not a spirit.[16] Consequently, today, Christ has the same perfected and immortal body that he was given by the Father at the Resurrection. Doesn't it then go to reason that the Father must have the same type of body as His Only Begotten Son? After all, according to the Apostle John, Christ only does what he sees the Father do.[17] Under that reasoning the Father must also be a resurrected being. In furtherance of this concept, Christ taught that He was in the "express image" of the Father's person.[18] Since the Hebrews knew that Christ was in the image of a man as he toiled in mortality and thereafter had a resurrected body, they also knew that God the Father had a resurrected body as well.

According to professor Edmond Cherbonnier of Trinity College, "in short, to use the forbidden word, the biblical God is clearly anthropomorphic—not apologetically so, but proudly, even militantly."[19]

> In John 8:17–18 Jesus Christ clearly states that his Father is a man. In these verses we read "It is also written in your law, that the testimony of two men is true. I am one that bear witness of myself, and the Father that sent me beareth witness of me." In the 1611 edition of the King James Bible, Mark 10:18 reads: "And Jesus said unto him, Why callest thou me good? There is no man good, but one, that is God." The phrase "no man" was removed from every subsequent printing of the King James Bible even though the same Greek word that underlies the 1611 rendition [oudeis] is also translated as "no man" in Revelation 7:9 and 14:3.[20]

Hence, in the original version of Mark 10:18, God is defined as a "man." Even the Dead Sea scrolls, which were thought to be the work of the Essenes (a right wing Jewish contingent who lived in a separatist colony at Qumran), identify God as a "glorious man."[21]

YAHWEH WAS JESUS CHRIST

The Hebrews believed that the God of the Old Testament was Yahweh or Jehovah.[22] In John 8:58, Christ makes an explicit statement that he is Yahweh.

> This is as blunt and pointed an affirmation of divinity as any person has or could make, "Before Abraham was I Jehovah." That is, "I am God Almighty, the Great I AM. I am the self-existent, Eternal One. I am the God of your fathers. My name is: I AM THAT I AM. . . ." That the Jews understood Jesus's plainly stated claim to Messiahship is evident from their belligerent attempt to stone him—death by stoning being the penalty for blasphemy, a crime of which our Lord would have been guilty had not his assertions as to divinity been true.[23]

The Christian Apologist of the second century Justin Martyr also taught that Jesus Christ was Jehovah.[24] So did the Christian Heresy Hunter Irenaeus,

> all who have known God from the beginning, and have foretold the advent of Christ, have received the revelation from the Son himself. . . . The Son . . . [is] that God who spake in human shape to Abraham, and again to Moses.[25]

As did Eusebius, the great Church Historian in his *History of the Church*, "it is obvious that [the patriarchs] knew God's Christ Himself, since He appeared to Abraham, instructed Isaac, spoke to [Jacob], and conversed freely with Moses and the prophets who came later."[26]

THE TRINITY

The Hebrews believed that the Father, Son, and Holy Ghost were separate and distinct individuals and rejected any notion that they were one in person. At the baptism of Jesus, it is noteworthy that Matthew, who is preaching to the Jews in his Gospel, denotes the differentiation between Father, Son, and Holy Ghost. Jesus is baptized, his Father glorifies him, and the Holy Ghost rests upon him in the form of a dove.[27] Luke recounts Stephen's martyrdom, "I see the heavens opened, and the Son of man standing on the right hand of God."[28] These two accounts demonstrate what the Hebrew Christians believed.

Further proof can be found throughout the New Testament. Jesus is the Only Begotten Son of the Father.[29] Jesus often comments about doing the will of His Father, who he calls God.[30] Christ states that the Father is greater than the Son.[31] There is but one God the Father and one Lord Jesus Christ.[32] Christ does his Father's work.[33] Christ prayed to the Father.[34] The Father spoke to Jesus.[35] Obviously, Jesus was not speaking to himself. Christ speaks of the Holy Ghost being different than himself.[36] Christ further teaches that he and the Father are one in purpose, but not in personage.[37]

This concept was not lost on the Apostolic Fathers. As Hippolytus taught,

> if, again, he allege His own word when He said, "I and the Father are one," let him attend to the fact, and understand that He did not say, "I and the Father am one, but are one." For the word "are" is not said of one person, but it refers to two persons, and one power.[38]

Justin Martyr calls Christ the "second God."[39] Clement of Alexandria taught that Jesus was the "Second Cause."[40] Tertullian taught that Christ is "second to the Father."[41] Even Origen spoke of Christ as a "second God."[42] Eusebius compared the Godhead to the three degrees of glory in 1 Corinthians 15:40–42.[43] "At the Council of Nicaea, the majority party [Hebrew Christians] believed "that there are three divine hypostases [or 'persons'], separate in rank and glory but united in harmony of will."[44]

A corollary to this is the concept of subordination—that the Son is subject to the Father and the Holy Ghost is subject to the Son and Father.[45] Both Apostolic Fathers Hippolytus and Irenaeus agreed with this concept.[46]

"Indeed, until Athanasius began writing, every single theologian, East and West, had postulated some form of Subordinationism. It could, about the year 300, have been described as a fixed part of catholic theology."[47] "Subordinationism is pre-Nicene orthodoxy."[48] Even the early Christian Apologist Justin Martyr thought of Christ and the Holy Ghost as angels, who were subordinate to the Father.[49]

In any case, the Hebrews certainly believed that Christ was our advocate with the Father,[50] and was subordinate to the Father's will.[51] After all, Christ actively taught that the doctrine He preached was not of Himself, but was that of His Father who sent Him.[52]

THE PREMORTAL LIFE OF MAN

Both the Apostles John and Peter clearly taught that Christ lived with the Father prior to the creation of this earth.[53] The early Apostolic Fathers taught similarly. For example, Origen preached the premortal life of man in the early Church.[54] In commenting on Jeremiah 1:5, Clement of Alexandria agreed.[55] As did Justin Martyr.[56] RG Hammerton-Kelly, professor of the New Testament, at McCormick Theological Seminary has noted that

> one is impressed by the ease with which the idea of pre-existence is assumed as the background for certain aspects of Paul's theology, especially for his doctrines of Christ and the Church.[57]

In fact, Apocrypha books like the Gospel of Thomas preach of the pre-existence of mankind.[58] Christian scholar Hammerton-Kelly recounts that "the idea that certain things pre-exist in the mind of God or in heaven has a long history in the biblical and early Jewish traditions."[59]

It was clearly an historical Hebrew tradition.[60] In the Wisdom of Solomon, king Solomon makes reference to the pre-existence of souls.[61]

Certainly, the Apostles believed in the premortal life of souls, as was seen in John 9:2, when they asked Jesus about a blind man and whether he had sinned in the premortal life to warrant his current situation in this mortal life.[62]

Further, the Hebrew Christians believed that men and women were foreordained (not predestined) in this premortal life to do things in mortality.[63] Mortality on this earth was looked at as a testing ground for men,[64] because one of the purposes of this life was to obtain a mortal body and learn to govern it.[65]

THE OFFSPRING OF GOD

One of the hallmarks and most controversial of Hebrew Christian beliefs was the doctrine of deification or theosis.[66]

> According to Acts 17:28–29 "we are the offspring [genos] of God." The Greek word "genos" is related to the Latin word "genus" which means "race." Hence, mankind is of the same "race" [as] God.[67]

The Apostle John speaks in Revelation 3:21 of sitting with Christ on His throne. "To sit someone on your throne, in the ancient world, indicates an equality of authority, as it was with Jesus in relation to the Father."[68] John even goes so far as to quote Christ on this very issue.[69] The Apostle Paul, as well, clearly taught this doctrine of deification to the Romans. Said Paul, "the Spirit itself beareth witness with our spirit, that we are the children of God; and if children, then heirs; heirs of God, and joint heirs with Christ."[70] To the Corinthians, Paul further referred to "gods many and lords many, but to us there is but one God, the Father."[71] Peter preached it in 2 Peter 1:3–10, referring to mankind as being "partakers of the divine nature."

The Jews traditionally believed such a doctrine.[72] This belief was also held by many of the Apostolic Fathers in the second century—for example, Irenaeus,[73] Justin Martyr,[74] and Clement of Alexandria.[75-76] Even Origen interpreted 1 Corinthians 8:5–6 to mean the future existence of men as gods.[77] Taught Origen,

> and thus the first-born of all creation, who is the first to be with God, and to attract to Himself divinity, is a being of more exalted rank than the other gods beside Him, of whom God is the God, as it is written, "The God or gods, the Lord, hath spoken and called the earth." It was by the offices of the firstborn that they became gods, for He drew from God in generous measure that they should be made gods, and He communicated it to them according to His own bounty. The true God, then, is "The God," and those who are formed after Him are gods, images, as it were of Him the prototype. . . . Now it is possible that some may dislike what we have said representing the father as the one true God, but admitting other beings besides the true God, who have become gods by having a share of God. They may fear that the glory of Him who surpasses all creation may be lowered to the level of those other beings called gods. We drew this distinction between Him and them that we showed God the Word to be to all the other gods the minister of their divinity. . . . As then, there are many gods, but to us there is but one God the Father, and many Lords, but to us there is one Lord, Jesus Christ.[78]

Clearly Origen understood that the Father will always be the Father to us all, but that we have the potential to be like Him—gods in our own right.[79] Hippolytus taught, "and thou shalt be a companion of the Deity, and a co-heir of Christ, no longer enslaved by lusts or passions, and never again wasted by disease. For thou hast become God . . . thou hast been deified, and begotten to immortality."[80]

Christian scholar G. L. Prestige has concluded that deification was commonly taught in the ancient church.[81] Irenaeus stated "do we cast blame on him [God] because we were not made gods from the beginning, but were at first created merely as men, and then later as gods?"[82]

Athanasius later wrote, "The Word was made flesh in order that we might be enabled to be made gods. . . . Just as the Lord, putting on the body, became a man, so also we men are both deified through his flesh, and henceforth inherit everlasting life."[83] Even Augustine, the standard bearer for orthodoxy, stated, "but he himself that justifies also deifies, for by justifying he makes sons of God. 'For he has given them power to become the sons of God' [John 1:12] If then we have been made sons of God, we have also been made gods."[84] Clement of Alexandria states of the afterlife, "and they are called by the appellation of gods, being destined to sit on thrones with the other gods that have been first put in the places by the Saviour."[85] And according to Tertullian, "for we shall be even gods."[86]

But this is not all! Deification was also taught by early Christians Gregory Nazianzen, Heraclitus, Cyprian of Carthage, Novation, Maximus the Confessor, Cyril of Jerusalem, John Chrysostom, Jerome, and the Persian Aphrahat of Syria.[87]

> What makes this all most interesting is that this doctrine of deification was taught by both heterodox and orthodox Christians alike, with little variation of wording between the various groups before the fourth century. Further, the doctrine was so geographically widespread through the Church at such an early date that it stands to reason that the doctrine had to have been advanced very early in Christian history, and accepted by the mass of Christians throughout the farthest reaches of the Church. The doctrine is found in the writings of fathers in regions from what is now known as Lyons, France, to Carthage, a city in Africa.[88]

Hence, Church Fathers from across the Roman Empire agreed.

> Athanasius, the great Bishop of Alexandria, the head of the Church in Egypt, summarized the Christian doctrine of salvation in the words, ' God became man so that we may become God." The goal of salvation is deification, and Athanasius invokes in this context the words of Jesus: "Be ye therefore perfect, even as your Father which is in heaven is perfect."[89]

45

As a result of the belief that mankind are God the Father's children, the Hebrew Christians rejected any notion of original sin.

> But Jesus said, Suffer little children, and forbid them not, to come unto me: for of such is the kingdom of heaven."[90]

Clement of Alexandria agreed.[91] In fact, the original catechetical lectures did not preach the doctrine of original sin at all.[92] That came much later.

THE DOCTRINE OF CHRIST: FAITH, REPENTANCE, BAPTISM, AND THE RECEIPT OF THE GIFT OF THE HOLY GHOST

The Apostle Paul taught to the Jewish members of the Church, "let us go unto perfection; not laying again the foundation of repentance from dead works and of faith toward God. Of the doctrine of baptisms, and of laying on of hands."[93] This simply echoed Peter's instruction on the Day of Pentecost, "men and brethren, what shall we do?—Repent, and be baptized every one of you in the name of Jesus Christ, for the remission of sins, and ye shall receive the gift of the Holy Ghost."[94]

FAITH AND WORKS

Faith that Jesus Christ has the power to save mankind and bring us into His kingdom is essential to following Him and His teachings.[95] Those who have faith in Christ will do the works of Christ and live their lives in conformity with His teachings.[96] In fact, the Apostle Barnabas preached being "zealous in . . . works."[97] Clement preached the same.[98] As did the Pastor of Hermas,[99] and Irenaeus, the bishop of Lyons.[100] Hence, faith leads to works for "faith without works is dead."[101]

> The New Testament records 541 scriptural statements by over sixteen different biblical personalities that pertain directly or indirectly to the way salvation is achieved. The preponderance of evidence is clearly in favor of statements that indicate that man will be held accountable and judged on the basis of his works, deeds, acts, fruits, obedience, and so forth. Of the 541 New Testament scriptural statements, 418 (or 77 percent) are supportive of works as a criterion in final judgment.[102]

Christ stated, "for the Son of Man shall come in the glory of his Father with his angels; and then he shall reward every man according to his works."[103] Hence, belief alone, without more, is simply not sufficient for salvation.[104] Clement of Rome certainly preached this.[105] The Eastern Orthodox Church has always practiced works and faith. "Eastern Orthodox Christians emphasize a unity of faith and works. For the Orthodox, being conformed to the image of Christ . . . includes a response of our faith and works."[106]

REPENTANCE

Repentance is the process by which men and women become better Christians. It is the process of perfecting themselves by following Christ's perfect example.[107]

BAPTISM

Baptism is the capstone of Christianity. Cyril, bishop of Jerusalem, wrote in the fourth century, "If any man receive not Baptism, he hath not salvation."[108] Through baptism, the Atonement of Christ is implemented in one's life, which enables mankind to return to their Father in Heaven.[109] It is a sacred covenant between men and God. In exchange for your commitment to God the Father, Christ promises to cleanse you of your sins and imperfections. This gives you entrance into the kingdom of God.[110] Hence, Hebrew Christians believed that they were saved through a covenant relationship with God the Father and Jesus Christ.[111]

The Apostolic Fathers agreed.[112] Christ himself commanded his disciples to baptize,[113] and also was baptized in order to show his followers an example.[114] Jesus spoke of this covenant at the last supper, which was the Passover meal, wherein He performed the sacrament of the Lord's Supper/Eucharist,[115] which is a symbolic retaking of the new baptismal covenant[116] in remembrance of Christ,[117] as it was practiced by early Christians.[118]

> What did Jesus mean by this "new covenant"? The background, to be sure, was the Exodus from Egypt and the formation of Israel as a nation at Mount Sinai. But Jesus had in mind more than this reminder of the obvious. He spoke of the "new covenant" in his own blood. His words

were an echo of the prophet Jeremiah who had promised a day when the covenant on tablets of stone would be replaced by a covenant written on the hearts of men. "This is the covenant which I will make with the house of Israel after those days, says the Lord: I will put my law within them, and I will write it upon their hearts; and I will be their God, and they shall be my people . . . for I will forgive their iniquity, and I will remember their sin no more."(Jeremiah 31:33–34).[119]

Further, this baptism of which the Hebrew Christians spoke was by immersion, not sprinkling or dipping.[120] "In the primitive Church, and down to the fourteenth century, the ordinary mode of baptism was by the immersion of the whole body in water. The original term 'baptizo' conveys the meaning of immersion, and no other. On this point we have most valuable testimony from the Fathers of the Church and other ecclesiastical writers."[121] Additionally, infant baptism was not practiced.[122] However, baptism for the dead was practiced. The Apostle Paul recognized the doctrine of performing vicarious ordinances for those who died without receiving such.[123] Peter's preaching was consistent with this doctrine as he taught the importance of preaching the gospel to the dead.[124] Matthew 16:18–19 is also consistent with it, as what is bound on earth is bound in heaven. Thus the saving ordinances are performed in mortality and are given effect in the eternal worlds beyond.

Scholars also uniformly agree that vicarious baptism was practiced in early Christianity.[125] According to Nibley, even in New Testament times, when the Apostles were still upon the earth, as well as in the days of the Apostolic Fathers in the second and third centuries, there were lingering doubts by members of the church about the reality of the physical resurrection. Consequently, it should come as no surprise "that the doctrine of salvation for the dead, so closely bound with the economy of the resurrection, should also be a matter of doubt and confusion."[126]

In the Clementine Recognitions when Clement asks Peter, "Shall those be wholly deprived of the kingdom of heaven who died before Christ's coming?" he receives a cautious answer: "You force me, Clement, to make public things that are not to be discussed. But I see no objection to telling you as much as we are allowed to." He tells him of the spirits of the dead "retained in good and happy places" but refuses to explain how they are to be redeemed.[127]

Belief in the salvation of the dead was fairly widespread in the Hebrew Christian world.[128] Matthew 16:17–19 discusses how the "gates of hell" shall not prevail against the gospel of Christ. This had a specific meaning, which had nothing to do with the Church of Christ never falling into apostasy, which is the way the Catholic Church views it today. Instead, Jewish tradition speaks of the gates of hell being where the dead reside. It is sometimes thought of as "the realm of Satan." Christ opened those gates to hell by preaching the gospel and authorizing baptism to free the dead from their prison as is explained by the Apostle Peter in 1 Peter 3:18–20 and 1 Peter 4:6. The key is vicarious baptism, which was given to the Apostles.[129] Hence the true meaning of Matthew 16 is that the gates of hell will not prevail against the dead who accept the gospel of Christ. The Pastor of Hermas records,

> these apostles and teachers . . . went down therefore with them into the water and came up again, but the latter went down alive and came up alive, while the former, who had fallen asleep before, went down dead but came up alive. Through them, therefore, they were made alive, and received the knowledge of the Son of God.[130]

Thus, Christ preached to the dead following His death and before His Resurrection.[131] This is consistent with the Hebrew belief in a spirit world where the dead reside between death and judgment.[132] There, those spirits wait to be freed through vicarious baptism.

THE GIFT OF THE HOLY GHOST

The receiving of the gift of the Holy Ghost after baptism was practiced by the laying on of hands.[133] The Holy Ghost sanctifies those who receive the gift and endure to the end, becoming new creatures in Christ.[134] Through the spirit, Hebrews came to know whether they were on the correct path.[135] They liken the reception of the Holy Ghost to a baptism of fire.[136] Apostolic Fathers widely practiced this ordinance of the laying on of hands,[137] including bishop Cornelius of Rome.[138]

THE RESURRECTION OF THE BODY

The physical, as opposed to spiritual, resurrection was an essential doctrine as taught by the Apostles.[139] Christ had a resurrected body of "flesh and bones."[140]

Heresy Hunter Ignatius believed in a physical resurrection.[141]

And so in his letter to the Trallians, Ignatius warns against those who claim that Jesus "only appeared to suffer" and insists, in response, that Jesus "was truly born, both ate and drank; was truly persecuted at the time of Pontius Pilate, was truly crucified and died . . . and was also truly raised from the dead." So, too, in the letter to Smyreneans, Ignatius attacks those who claimed that Jesus's passion was a sham, that he was not an actual flesh-and-blood human being who really suffered. Ignatius again denies that such persons are "believers" and warns his readers not even to meet and talk with them. In opposition to their views, he insists that Jesus was "actually born" and was "actually crucified . . . in the flesh" and he "genuinely suffered" and "genuinely raised himself." Even after his resurrection he was "in the flesh," as evidenced by the fact that his disciples touched him and observed him eating and drinking."[142]

Justin Martyr also believed in the physical resurrection,[143] as did other Apostolic Fathers like Irenaeus,[144] Tatian,[145] and Tertullian.[146] Clement comments on the physical resurrection as well.[147] Athenagora went so far as to preach that the resurrected body had no blood.[148]

When Paul preached the physical resurrection to the Greeks, they mocked him.[149] Later, Clement of Rome reflected that a major problem at Corinth at around AD 96 was the denial of the bodily resurrection.[150]

In later years, Ignatius taught,

and I know that He was possessed of a body not only in His being born and crucified, but I also know that He was so after His resurrection, and believe that He is so now. When, for instance, He came to those who were with Peter, He said to them, "Lay hold, handle Me, and see that I am not an incorporeal spirit." "For a spirit hath not flesh and bones, as ye see me have." And He says to Thomas, "Reach hither thy finger into the print of the nails, and reach hither thy hand, and thrust it into My side"; and immediately they believed that He was Christ. Where Thomas also says to Him, "My Lord, and my God." And on this account also did they despise death, for it were too little to say, indignities and stripes. Nor was this all; but also after He had shown

Himself to them, that He had [raised] indeed, and not in appearance only, He both ate and drank with them during forty entire days. And thus was He, with the flesh, received up in their sight unto Him that sent Him.[151]

It was thus apparent in the early years of the Church that the Apostles were fighting the idea of docetism, which was taking hold in some areas of the Church; that is the doctrine that suggests that the resurrection was simply that of the spirit and not the physical body. This became a standard tenant of the Gnostic Christians, who we will discuss in a later chapter. The Apostles made no bones about the fact that Jesus had come in the flesh and was physically resurrected, and those who denied it were called by them "Anti-Christs."[152]

THE PRIESTHOOD

The priesthood is best defined as the power of God given to man to act in His name. Christ gave this priesthood to His Apostles who would act with "power and authority" from on high.[153] The Hebrews always believed in the necessity of the priesthood by specific ordination.[154] Clement of Rome spoke of the Apostles ordaining leaders to the local church.[155]

Hippolytus noted the ordaining of bishops, elders, and deacons to the church.[156] Peter told Simon Magus that the power of the priesthood could not be "purchased with money,"[157] and Ignatius stated that without the priesthood, "there is no Church."[158] Carrying on in the tradition of the Hebrews, the priesthood of God was called the priesthood after the order of Melchizedek.[159] In sum, one must be called of God, as was Aaron, and claim divine authority to officiate in the Church.[160] The power was given by the laying on of hands, as the Apostles did to the seven who would minister to the temporal affairs of the early church (Stephen was one of them and did "great wonders and miracles"—Acts 6:8).[161] Christ, himself, went to John the Baptist to be baptized because it was John who held legitimate priesthood authority. He received that authority from his father, Zacharias, who was a temple priest. As I shall shortly discuss, this has great significance, because John was not just of the lineage of the tribe of Levi, but was from the actual direct line of Levite priests, which went back to Aaron.

Thus he was truly "a priest after the order of Aaron."[162]

As a consequence of the issue over proper priesthood authority, the laity was prohibited from performing any of the duties of the priesthood offices (for example, baptism, laying on of hands, blessings) in the early church without having been called of God and having a bishop confer upon him the priesthood by the laying on of hands; "for no man taketh this honor unto himself, but he that is called of God."[163]

The Levitical Priesthood can be traced back to Levi, the son of Jacob. Aaron, Moses's brother, as well as Moses himself, were of the tribe of Levi. Under the Mosaic law, Levites were authorized to perform ordinances under the Levitical Priesthood. When Christ fulfilled the law of Moses, as Paul states in the Book of Hebrews, the Levitical Priesthood did not suddenly vanish. Rather, it continued, but its exclusivity to the tribe of Levi ended. Instead, all worthy male followers of Christ could be ordained to this priesthood. It, however, remained a lesser priesthood to that of Melchizedek, just as the law of Moses was a lesser version of the law to that of the gospel of Jesus Christ. Moses records the following concerning the conferring of the Levitical or Aaronic Priesthood:

> And take thou unto thee Aaron thy brother, and his sons with him, from among the children of Israel, that he may minister unto me in the priest's office, even Aaron, Nadab and Abihu, Eleazar and Ithamar, Aaron's sons.[164]

Thus, Aaron was literally called of God by divine revelation to receive the priesthood and administer the affairs of His Church. This is the pattern of God. The Apostles were called in the selfsame manner. Records Luke:

> And it came to pass in those days, that he [Jesus] went out into a mountain to pray, and continued all night in prayer to God.
> And when it was day, he called unto him his disciples: and of them he chose twelve, whom also he named apostles.[165]

These newly called Apostles were then ordained by Jesus using the Old Testament pattern of the laying on of hands.[166] States Jesus, "ye have not chosen me, but I have chosen you, and ordained you."[167] This ordination was one of priesthood authority as seen by the power conveyed to them.

And when he had called unto him his twelve disciples, he gave them power against unclean spirits, to cast them out, and to heal all manner of sickness and all manner of disease.[168]

PRIESTHOOD OFFICES

By the early second century, local Christian churches had two levels of leaders. According to Shelley, the top level group were men called "elders or Presbyters (from the Greek for 'elders')." It is from these men that "bishops (overseers) and pastors (shepherds)" were chosen to lead congregations. The lower level group consisted of "deacons." According to Ignatius, he speaks of "a single bishop (or pastor) in each church, a body of presbyters, and a company of deacons."[169] It was the bishop that became the undisputed leader of local church congregations by the end of the second century.[170]

The office of bishop and deacon are not new to the original church because they were part of the ancient Jewish faith. Clement of Rome admits as much.[171] As such, the office of bishop could not be the highest office in the Church as it came from the lower law, the law of Moses.[172] "While it is obvious enough that the apostles appointed bishops and presbyters, . . . it is not less clear that the functions of an apostle were quite different from those of a presbyter or bishop, and that functionally the apostle is akin to the prophet, not to the presbyter."[173]

> If we ask who were the most important people in the Christian church in the first generation, the answer undoubtedly is, the Apostles and Prophets. If we go on farther, and ask who was the most important person in the church at Rome at the end of the second century, the answer unquestionably is that it was the Bishop. But the difficulty comes when we inquire how this change took place; for that is precisely the problem to which no undoubted or unquestionable answer can be given.[174]

According to Duchesne, once the apostles were gone, the natural tendency was to revert back to the old Jewish system, that being the bishop, priest, and deacon.[175] It may be for this reason that Tertullian stated that the church grew up "in the shadow of the synagogue."[176]

BISHOP

The Apostolic Constitutions teach that the bishop should follow the Jewish pattern of being a common judge over his congregation.[177] And further, that bishops should be financially supported by the congregation just like the Levites.[178]

There has been some confusion about James the Just, the brother of the Lord. He apparently became an Apostle, but was also the bishop of Jerusalem. Hence, he exercised unique authority. However, his was not superior to Peter's, the lead Apostle. Instead, James appears to have served in a capacity as a presiding bishop over the other bishops because they made reports to him. Nevertheless, this position in the early church also appears to have died when James the Just was killed in AD 67. Of particular interest, as noted earlier, is the belief by some scholars that the office of bishop is one of Jewish origin under the law of Moses and hence part of the Levitical Priesthood. Since that priesthood passed only in a patriarchal fashion through family lines, James the Just was the heir to such priesthood through his father Joseph and ultimately from his ancestor king David. As a result of this reasoning, none other than a literal descendent of Jesus could have been ordained to that office over Jerusalem.[179] "This close tie-in of the office of bishop with the office and blood of Aaron was a permanent heritage in the church—vague and confused as the traditions all became, it nevertheless keeps turning up in every age."[180]

The office of bishop was that of local church administer. It was not a spiritual calling, but one to minister to the temporal affairs of the church members. The bishop was initially called and ordained by the Apostles. Their local congregations then sustained them by uplifted hand. They were not originally elected by those congregations or the college of presbyters.[181] According to Ignatius, the office of bishop was a principal officer in the church since Paul's day. The job of a bishop was to lead individual Christian communities.[182] The bishop, as an office in the Levitical Priesthood, was regarded as the president of the priests. The purpose of the Levitical Priesthood revolved around the performance of temporal functions, while the Melchizedek Priesthood (which will be discussed later) was to care for spiritual matters. Yet, when the law of Moses was fulfilled in Jesus Christ, it did not mean the end of the Levitical Priesthood; rather, as Paul points out in Hebrews, it meant a change in status.

Christ held the Melchizedek Priesthood and was not of the tribe of Levi. Under the Levitical Priesthood, only those of the tribe of Levi held the priesthood—deacons and teachers. Descendents of Aaron were the priests and direct descendants of Aaron's firstborn (patriarchal order) were the high priests. So when Christ fulfilled the law of Moses, the result was that others (non-Levites) could then hold the priesthood, both the higher priesthood of Melchizedek and the lower priesthood of Aaron. This lower priesthood appears to have consisted of the offices of deacon,[183] teacher,[184] priest,[185] and bishop.[186]

ELDER

As was noted earlier, in the early second century, local Christian churches or congregations were led by a group of priesthood holders, which have been referred to as "elders." These individuals appear to have been ordained to the office of elder, a status affiliated with the higher priesthood, that of Melchizedek.[187]

SEVENTY

The office in the high priesthood of Seventy, named for the seventy missionaries sent out by the Savior himself in Luke 10:1, is really a more ancient office than the one that existed in the meridian of time, first appearing over one thousand years earlier at the time of Moses in Numbers 11:16–25. Eusebius claims that the Seventy operated in the early Christian church of the second century AD as general authorities.[188]

HIGH PRIEST

A high priest after the order of Melchizedek was also an office in this higher priesthood, although it was not well defined in the New Testament.[189] It is differentiated from the Levitical High Priest, the direct descendant of Aaron's firstborn.

PATRIARCH

A patriarch was an office that existed in ancient days, as well as in the meridian of time. A patriarch seems to be an ordained Melchizedek priesthood holder who was authorized to bestow specialized blessings upon individuals. These blessings tell about God's plan for the recipient in this mortal life (some would call this blessing a "foreordination" or a "patriarchal blessing").[190]

APOSTLE

Many studies have shown the name *apostle*, when specifically applied to the Twelve, to mean more than a mere messenger, emissary, or missionary—it meant a "special delegate" or "witness." "There were many "apostles," as we read in the Didache, but the Twelve, "the perfect year of the Lord," were something very special. "At the present time," says Peter in the Clementine Recognitions, "do not look for any other prophet or apostle except us. There is one true prophet and twelve apostles."[191]

The apostolic office was an ordained office.[192] When an apostle died, another was chosen and ordained to take his place.[193] As has been noted, an apostle is a special witness of Christ. "From the beginning, wrote Lietzmann, 'the Twelve appear as a compact group in which only three men stand out as individuals. These were . . . Peter, James, and John, the pillars of the primitive church.' . . . While we see in the church a definite local organization, wrote Eduard Meyer, 'the highest authority was held by the Twelve, and at their head was Peter.'"[194]

Harnack's thorough study of non-Christian sources regarding Peter showed that he was far and away the most important man in the church. After he and James were dead for at least twenty-four years, Eusebius specifically states that "John the beloved returned from Patmos and continued to govern the churches."[195]

Plainly the apostles had a kind of authority that none of their successors had. They were conceived of as the twelve judges of Israel and so were limited to that number.[196]

But on one thing all are agreed: the apostles were traveling general authorities, "essentially itinerant," "a nomadic apostolate," a fraternity officiating in the establishment of a worldwide institution, forming itself everywhere into identical Christianities, cooperating among themselves, having the same faith, the same cult, the same authorities.[197]

PROPHETS

Paul declared that Christ's Church needed apostles and prophets in order to function properly.[198] In Old Testament times, the Prophet Amos declared that "God will do nothing but reveal his will to his servants, the prophets."[199]

> A long time ago there lived certain men—much older than any of those so-called philosophers we have been talking about; blessed and righteous men, beloved of God. And they spoke by the Holy Spirit, foretelling those very things which are now coming to pass. They are called prophets. They are the only men who have ever seen the truth of things and told it to men without making any timid concessions to public opinion, without seeking to make an impression on people, and without being in the least influenced by concern for what other people might think of them. But, being filled with the Holy Ghost, they simply reported those things which they had seen and heard. The writings of those men survive to this day, and anyone can derive the greatest benefit from them, and learn from them about the beginnings and endings of things, and all such matters as philosophers are supposed to know. For it was not their wont to build up a case by formal argument, but simply to report the truth as reliable witnesses, without any disputations at all.[200]

THE AFTERLIFE

The Hebrew Christian belief in an afterlife is best defined as a belief in varying degrees of heaven.[201] Paul taught:

> There are also celestial bodies, and bodies terrestrial; but the glory of the celestial is one, and the glory of the terrestrial is another. There is one glory of the sun, and another glory of the moon, and another glory of the stars; for one star differeth from another star in glory. So also is the resurrection of the dead.[202]

Origen interpreted this to mean that resurrected bodies have differing glories.[203] Apostolic Father Irenaeus states that this view of 1 Corinthians was taught by the "elders who knew the Apostles."[204] Clement of Alexandria boldly taught that those in the "celestial" glory would become gods.[205]

Those who are deemed worthy of an abode in heaven shall go there, others shall enjoy the delights of paradise, and others shall possess the splendor of the city. . . . [They say moreover], that there is this distinction between the habitation of those who produce an hundredfold, and that of those who produce sixtyfold, and that of those who produce thirtyfold: for the first will be taken up into the heavens, the second will dwell in paradise, the third will inhabit the city. . . . The elders, who were] the disciples of the apostles, affirm that this is the gradation and arrangement of those who are saved.[206]

Apostolic Father bishop Papias of Hieropolos (AD 140) went further in explaining,

But that there is a distinction between the habitation of those who produce an hundred-fold, and that of those who produce sixty-fold, and that of those who produce thirty-fold; for the first will be taken up to the heavens, the second class will dwell in Paradise, and the last will inhabit the city; and on this account the Lord said, "In my Father's house are many mansions": for all things belong to God, who supplies all with a suitable dwelling-place, even as His word says, that a share is given to all by the Father, according as each one is or shall be worthy.[207]

The Hebrew tenants of a final judgment of man are shored up in not only the need for faith in a Savior, but in individual works; thus invoking the teachings of James the Just, the brother of Jesus, who wrote,

What doth it profit, my brethren, though a man say he hath faith, and have not works? Can faith save him?

If a brother or sister be naked, and destitute of daily food,

And one of you say unto them, Depart in peace, be ye warmed and filled; notwithstanding ye give them not those things which are needful to the body; what doth it profit?

Even so faith, if it hath not works, is dead, being alone.

Yea, a man may say, Thou hast faith, and I have works: shew me thy faith without thy works, and I will shew thee my faith by my works.

Thou believest that there is one God; thou doest well: the devils also believe, and tremble.

But wilt thou know, O vain man, that faith without works is dead?

Was not Abraham our father justified by works, when he had offered Isaac his son upon the alter?

Seest thou how faith wrought with his works, and by works was faith made perfect?

And the scripture was fulfilled which saith, Abraham believed God, and it was imputed unto him for righteousness: and he was called the Friend of God.

Ye see then how that by works a man is justified, and not by faith only.

Likewise also was not Rahab the harlot justified by works, when she had received the messengers, and had sent them out another way?

For as the body without the spirit is dead, so faith without works is dead also.[208]

The implications are clear. Hebrew Christians believed that their place or status in the afterlife was inextricably connected with their good or bad works that they performed in mortality.

REVELATION

Hebrew Christians, as their forefathers before them, believed in the importance of continuous revelation, of prophesy—that Jehovah still speaks with men, the cannon of scripture is, therefore, not closed.[209] As the Apostle John reminded, "Worship God; for the testimony of Jesus is the spirit of prophecy."[210] The Apostle Paul counseled the Ephesians, "that the God of our Lord Jesus Christ, the Father of glory, may give unto you the spirit of wisdom and revelation in the knowledge of him."[211] Paul further spoke to the Thessalonians "Quench not the spirit. Despise not prophesying."[212] According to Petersen:

The one principle that has guided every dispensation is continuing revelation, a doctrine and practice that joins man and God and ensures that God's will is performed over man's desires. Although Christianity in general holds that revelation ceased with the death of the apostles, this presumption cannot be supported by religious history, because it supposes that revelation was no longer necessary. The Old Testament affirms that God revealed His will to man through revelation; the Gospels contain the revelations of the Father to the Son and the apostles; the remainder of the New Testament provides an account of the Church being guided by revelation from God through direct administration and by the Holy Ghost. Other than the foreboding prophecies of apostasy, nothing in the New Testament foreshadows that the heavens would be silent following the apostolic ministry. To the contrary, the post apostolic vision, the Shepherd of Hermas, was broadly recognized by the early Church as inspired and authentic scripture.[213]

However, the Hebrews went beyond a belief in revelation through holy men or prophets, they also believed in the development of a personal relationship with their God, for they practiced the specific doctrine of personal revelation. This doctrine holds that God may direct the personal affairs of individuals who seek him.[214]

> Clearly the Scriptures—originally the Old Testament, and eventually the books that came to form the "New" Testament—were ultimate authorities for the proto-orthodox Christians. *But doesn't God speak in other ways as well, apart from these written texts?* Ignatius appears to have thought so. Again, in his letter to the Philadelphians, he indicates that he himself was a direct recipient of a revelation from the Spirit of God, a revelation that confirmed his own convictions about the importance of bishop.[215]

According to Ehrman, Ignatius was following in the footsteps of other Apostolic Fathers and leaders before him in receiving revelations through the Holy Spirit.[216] These communications with God were all received after the Revelation of John the Divine, which later would become the closing book of the Bible.

The most famous of the "prophetic movement" Christian sects are the "Montanists," whose most famous convert was the Apostolic Father and scholar Tertullian. The movement was ultimately marginalized as critics challenged direct revelation that contradicted written scripture.[217]

ESOTERIC DOCTRINES

The Hebrews long believed in various esoteric doctrines; namely, the concept that there are certain mysteries of the kingdom of God, which are reserved only for the most devout of followers. Since the details of what was taught is not well known, as the Savior spoke only to His Apostles concerning these matters, these doctrines have been referred to as "secret" teachings. A better term would be "sacred" teachings. As the Apostle Peter taught Clement,

> Let such a one then hear this: The teaching of all doctrine has a certain order, and there are some things which must be delivered first, others in the second place, and others in the third, and so all in their order; and if these things be delivered in their order, they become plain; but

if they be brought forward out of order, they will seem to be spoken against reason.[218]

Consequently, the reason for secrecy had more to do with the readiness of the overall church than it did any attempt to hide the truth. As Peter had taught, these sacred teachings would be imparted in the correct order. For example, the teachings that Christ gave to His Apostles during the forty days following His resurrection probably encompass the doctrines Christ had put off telling them because the Apostles were not yet ready. As Jesus had previously mentioned to His Apostles, "I have yet many things to say unto you, but ye cannot bear them now."[219] He further told them, "These things have I spoken unto you in proverbs: but the time cometh, when I shall no more speak unto you in proverbs, but I shall show you plainly of the Father."[220] In the Clementine Homilies, Peter is reported to have stated, "Wherefore also He [meaning Jesus] explained to His disciples privately the mysteries of the kingdom of heaven."[221] Far from being abnormal, as some Christian scholars suggest,[222] the practice of having secret or sacred doctrines was common in early Christianity.[223] Biblical scholars generally agree that there was restricted knowledge reserved only for the most faithful. "Many references to sacred rites and ordinances have been preserved in the apocryphal writings, the sheer volume of which demonstrate their existence and implies their importance to early Christians."[224]

PARABLES

During His mortal ministry, Christ spoke in parables, not unlike many oriental teachers of His time, so that only those who were ready could understand the deeper principles of the gospel—the secrets if you will.[225] Parables had their origins in Greek culture. It was a way of teaching complex topics by comparing them to commonly understood images. Today, we would call them analogies. Consequently when Christ taught, to some, the stories were simply morality tales that were enjoyable to listen to, but to others they held deeper meaning concerning the doctrine. Mark 4:34 states that during His Galilean ministry, Christ taught exclusively in parables.

> Therefore speak I to them in parables: because they seeing see not; and hearing they hear not, neither do they understand.

And in them is fulfilled the prophecy of Esaias, which saith, By hearing ye shall hear, and shall not understand; and seeing ye shall see, and shall not perceive.[226]

In his book *Trial Notebook*, James McElhaney discusses the use of analogies and states that the analogy is

perhaps the most powerful form of argument we know. . . the greatest weapon in the arsenal of persuasion is the analogy, the story, the simple comparison to a familiar subject. Nothing can move [a person] more convincingly than an apt comparison to something they know from their own experience is true. Analogies are effective, and it is worth knowing why. The answer is simple. Analogies work for two related reasons. First, good stories command the attention of the audience. They want to find out what happened. Second, analogies challenge an audience to test their appropriateness to the point made. When someone tells a story to prove a point, it is almost impossible to resist testing it to see if it fits the situation. What is the net effect? . . . The audience, in testing the aptness of a comparison, reasons the problem through and reaches the conclusion on its own. . . . Analogies—whether simple allusions or detailed stories—are a distinguishing mark of outstanding . . . arguments. They lead [people] to draw their own conclusions, which they believe more fervently than if they had merely been told what conclusion to reach.[227]

The Apostle Matthew reports that Christ secretly took His Apostles to the Mount of Olives just days before He was to be crucified. There, He taught them through the use of parables the last, and perhaps most important, principles of His Gospel prior to His death and atoning sacrifice. Notice the final two parables that Christ imparted during His mortal ministry, which were told during this most sacred meeting.

THE PARABLE OF THE TEN VIRGINS

Then shall the kingdom of heaven be likened unto ten virgins, which took their lamps, and went forth to meet the bridegroom.
And five of them were wise, and five were foolish.
They that were foolish took their lamps, and took no oil with them:
But the wise took oil in the vessels with their lamps.
While the bridegroom tarried, they all slumbered and slept.
And at midnight there was a cry made, Behold, the bridegroom cometh; go ye out to meet him.

Then all those virgins arose, and trimmed their lamps.

And the foolish said unto the wise, Give us of your oil; for our lamps are gone out.

But the wise answered, saying, Not so; lest there be not enough for us and you: but go ye rather to them that sell, and buy for yourselves.

And while they went to buy, the bridegroom came; and they that were ready went in with him to the marriage: and the door was shut.

Afterward came also the other virgins, saying Lord, Lord, open to us.

But he answered and said, Verily I say unto you, I know you not.

Watch therefore, for ye know neither the day nor the hour wherein the Son of man cometh.[228]

Traditional Jewish marriage ceremonies require a marriage contract or formal betrothal followed by the equivalent of a one year engagement. On the marriage day, the bridegroom and the children of the bride chamber (who are the friends of the couple) begin a procession at dusk from the bridegroom's home to that of the bride. The procession carries torches and lamps so that all additional invitees to the wedding may join the processional. Once at the home of the bride, a marriage deed is signed and then a marriage supper or feast begins. Thus marks the celebration of the marriage. The parable of the ten virgins is the tale of one such wedding. However, this one is of particular importance. It is the wedding of Christ (the bridegroom) to His Church (the bride).[229] The invited guests and friends of the bride chamber included these ten virgins. The procession, which is to be led by Christ as the bridegroom, occurs at around midnight (symbolizing the end of the world).[230] However, none of the bride chamber know exactly when the procession (or end of the world) will commence. Each waits and prepares. Notice how each of the virgins is initially equipped with a lamp full of oil. They are ready for the Christ. They are worthy to be in the processional and enter the home of the bride (the temple) to view the wedding and participate in the marriage feast (kingdom of God). The lamps with oil may thus symbolize the faith of these virgins in the bridegroom and His kingdom. However, over time, five of the virgins lose their faith, they run out of oil and are not prepared at His coming. They must find additional stores. They try to borrow some from the other five virgins, but they cannot give them from their own, as faith is a personal journey. One cannot rely upon another's faith. We must each stand on our own. The five unprepared virgins quickly sought oil from various merchants, but by the time they had acquired the necessary oil, the processional had departed and when they arrived at the bride's home, the bridegroom no longer recognized them as part of the bride chamber. Christ's parable was one of warning of tough times ahead to His Apostles and to those who would join His Church—it was also one of counsel, to keep the faith and await His return.

THE PARABLE OF THE MARRIAGE OF THE KING'S SON

Christ's last parable is termed the Marriage of the King's Son and gave some additional final insights to His Apostles.

And Jesus answered and spake unto them again by parables, and said,

The kingdom of heaven is like unto a certain king, which made a marriage for his son,

And sent forth his servants to call them that were bidden to the wedding: and they would not come.

Again, he sent forth other servants, saying, Tell them which are bidden, Behold, I have prepared my dinner: my oxen and my fatlings are killed, and all things are ready: come unto the marriage.

But they made light of it, and went their ways, one to his farm, another to his merchandise:

And the remnant took his servants, and entreated them spitefully, and slew them.

But when the king heard thereof, he was wroth: and he sent forth his armies, and destroyed those murderers, and burned up their city.

Then saith he to his servants, The wedding is ready, but they which were bidden were not worthy.

Go ye therefore into the highways, and as many as ye shall find, bid to the marriage.

So those servants went out into the highways, and gathered together all as many as they found, both bad and good: and the wedding was furnished with guests.

And when the king came in to see the guests, he saw there a man which had not on a wedding garment:

And he saith unto him, Friend, how camest thou in hither not having a wedding garment? And he was speechless.

Then said the king to the servants, Bind him hand and foot, and take him away, and cast him into outer darkness; there shall be weeping and gnashing of teeth.

For many are called, but few are chosen.[231]

Here, the king is clearly Elohim, the Father. His Son who is to be married is none other than the prince of peace, Jesus Christ or Jehovah. Through Elohim's servants, His prophets on the earth, invitations are given to His chosen people, Israel, to come to the wedding of His Firstborn Son. However, Israel killed the messengers, the prophets. Consequently, Elohim sent messengers to the highway to collect all travelers there (the Gentiles), both good and bad, and bid them to the wedding. However, when these arrived and one was found not to be wearing the appropriate wedding garment, he was cast out. This parable is to represent two things: first, it signifies the coming apostasy of Israel; and second, it demonstrates the efforts made by Elohim to bid all to come to Him and the gospel, both bond and free, young and old, good and evil. However, once you accept the invitation, you are expected to live the gospel, for if you are found without the appropriate attire, notwithstanding the invitation, you will be cast out. Thus, "many are called, but few are chosen." The Apostles needed to remain true to the gospel and bring others who would remain true as well.

According to biblical scholars, other esoteric doctrines that Christ did not teach openly during His mortal life included: His Messiahship, prediction of his crucifixion, and signs of the end times.[232] All were taught through parables.

THE ESOTERIC TRADITION

Following His Resurrection, Christ taught the Apostles for an additional forty days—yet there is no account of what he taught them, except for Luke's generalized description that He spake "of the things pertaining to the kingdom of God."[233] These teachings would appear to be doctrines that Christ did not teach prior to His death. As Christ formerly said to the Apostles during His mortal ministry, "I have yet many things to say unto you, but ye cannot bear them now."[234] The secrets to what He imparted to the Apostles may be gleaned from the Epistles of Paul, for according to Paul, he was to be a steward over the mysteries of God.[235]

One can readily see how Paul fulfilled that stewardship; because as Paul preached the gospel, he did so in increments, so that those he taught would hear only as much as they could accept at the time. He kept back much of the meat of the gospel until they could accept it and follow it—"I have fed you with milk, and not with meat: for hitherto ye were not able to bear it, neither yet now are ye able."[236] Perhaps this explains why Christ did not impart all of the doctrines openly to His followers—they were simply not ready to hear them. Christ taught, "give not that which is holy unto dogs, neither cast ye your pearls before swine, lest they trample them under their feet, and turn again and rend you."[237] So the highest and holiest doctrines were reserved for mature disciples. According to Peter,

> We remember that our Lord and Teacher, commanding us, said, "Keep the mysteries for me and the sons of my house." Wherefore also He explained to His disciples privately the mysteries of the kingdom of heaven. But to you who do battle with us, and examine into nothing else but our statements, whether they be true or false, it would be impious to state the hidden truths.[238]

The esoteric tradition is not new to Christianity, it originated with the Jews.[239] Clement preached that there were hidden truths taught by Christ that the Apostle Peter purposely kept back for only the mature members of the gospel.[240] According to Bickmore, Tertullian "chided certain heretics, not for having esoteric teachings, but for making the higher teachings available to everyone."[241] Many of the early Church leaders revealed that there were mysteries taught in the "tradition of the Apostles."[242]

So what other esoteric teachings did Christ impart during His forty-day ministry? According to Clement, these esoteric doctrines had to do with the creation of the earth and the nature of God.[243] Bickmore states "the esoteric teachings attributed to the Apostles by the Apocrypha and the traditions of the elders who knew the Apostles had primarily to do with the 'celestial voyage' or the journey from earth to heaven."[244] Ignatius reports that the sacrament or Eucharist was one of these mysteries. The apocrypha appear to suggest that Christ taught the Apostles about where he went after the Resurrection; that being the spirit world to teach the gospel to the kindred dead and to other peoples in other lands.[245] Clement of Alexandria boasts that he was passed down secret knowledge that came from Christ to Peter, James and John during the forty-day ministry, but does not say what it was.[246]

THE PRAYER CIRCLE

Among the traditions that are said to be among the secrets and mysteries of the gospel was the ring dance or prayer circle.[247] "The actual performance of such a rite is described in a very old text, attributed to Clement of Rome and preserved in a seventh century Syriac translation entitled 'The Testament of our Lord Jesus Christ as delivered orally by him to us the Apostles after His Resurrection following his death.'"[248] Scholar Hugh Nibley recounts the "Round Dance" or "Prayer Circle." Priests and deacons with "authorized widows" and deaconesses stand in a circle around the bishop. All give the "sign of peace." Anyone with ill feelings toward another or the doctrines is asked to be reconciled or withdraw from the circle. The bishop then begins the prayer with those in the circle repeating his words. A "diptych," which is a piece of paper or notebook with the names of people that the circle wished to remember in their prayer, was laid on the alter in the center of the ring.[249] "In the circle we pray for those who are sick and afflicted; in short, we pray for whoever is in need of help."[250]

THE TEMPLE AND ITS RITUALS

Christ called the temple at Jerusalem "my father's house."[251] Temple worship was discussed by Luke, Paul, and John in the New Testament.[252] Some have suggested that temple worship was abandoned following the rending of the veil of Herod's temple at the time of the crucifixion, signifying the end of the law of Moses. However, BYU professor William J. Hamblin wrote:

> Unfortunately for [critics] it is quite clear that the New Testament apostles continued to worship in the Jerusalem temple after Christ's ascension (Acts 2:46, Acts 3:1–10, Acts 5:20–42). Even Paul worshiped there (Acts 21:26–30, Acts 22:17, Acts 24:6–18, Acts 25:8, Acts 26:21). Paul is explicitly said to have performed purification rituals (Acts 21:26, Acts 24:18), and prayed in the temple (Acts 22:17, cf. Acts 3:1); he claims that he has not offended "against the temple," implying he accepts its sanctity (Acts 25:8). Indeed, Paul also offered sacrifice (prosfora) in the temple (Acts 21:26, cf. Num. 6:14–18), a very odd thing for him to do if the temple had been completely superceded after Christ's ascension. Finally, and most importantly, Paul had a vision of Christ ("The Just One" *ton dikaion*) in the temple (Acts 22:14–21),

paralleling Old Testament temple theophanies, and strongly implying a special sanctity in the temple, where God still appears to men even after Christ's ascension.[253]

Within the temple, ritual temple dramas would be played out. Historians agree that the temple rituals of the early Christians was similar to those of the Hittites, Egyptians, Greeks, and Hebrews.[254] These ritual dramas generally included (a) a recital of the story of the creation and of Adam and Eve, (b) the reception of sacred ordinances and covenants, and (c) the promise of special blessings.[255] As part of this temple ritual was the wearing of special white clothing,[256] in which there were washings and anointings[257] as well as secret passwords[258] and handclasps[259] for entrance. "After all allowances have been made, there remains a definite residue of early Christian ritual that goes far beyond anything known to later Christianity . . . the rites just mentioned all look to the temple and belong to the instructions of the 40 days."[260]

MARRIAGE

Marriage was instituted by God.[261] That it was encouraged is seen by Paul's direction to Timothy that bishops should be married.[262] In fact, the leading Apostle, Peter, was himself married.[263]

Notwithstanding the open encouragement of marriage, it was regarded in early Christianity among the Hebrews as an esoteric ritual.[264] Especially the idea that marriage continued beyond death. That this ritual was widely practiced is readily seen by Origen's complaint of those Christians who engaged in it.

> Certain persons . . . are of the opinion that the fulfillment of the promises of the future are to be looked for in bodily pleasure and luxury. . . . And consequently they say, that after the resurrection there will be marriages, and the begetting of children. . . . Such are the views of those who, while believing in Christ, understand the divine scriptures in a sort of Jewish sense, drawing from them nothing worthy of the divine promises.[265]

Clement of Alexandria disagreed with Origen's chastisement, instead stating that marriage "was good practice for life as a god."[266]

Biblical scholar Petersen has investigated the ancient practices in the Jewish temple of antiquity and has found it to be consistent with Christ's teachings.

> There were three buildings [within the temple] as places of offering in Jerusalem: the one which opens to the west was called "the holy"; another which opens to the south was called "the holy of holy"; the third which opens to the east was called the "holy of holies," where only the high priest might enter. Baptism is the "holy" house. The redemption is "holy of holy." "The holy of the holies" is the bridal chamber . . . The woman is united to her husband in the bridal chamber. . . . Those who have united in the bridal chamber can no longer be separated. . . . If the marriage of defilement is so secret, how much more is the undefiled marriage a true mystery! . . . If anyone becomes a son or daughter of the bridal chamber, he will receive the light. If anyone does not receive it while he is in the world, he will not receive it in the other place.[267]

That brings an interesting question to light: was Christ married? In Dan Brown's book *The DaVinci Code* the proposition is placed before its readers that Mary Magdalene was Jesus's wife. Certainly, Jewish tradition holds that rabbis or itinerant teachers, as Christ was, were married. It would indeed have been unusual that a man of thirty years of age was not married within the Jewish culture. Certainly, the Pharisees and the Sadducees, who looked to ridicule Christ throughout His life, would have attacked him for being unmarried, but the scriptures are silent on such a criticism. Mary Magdalene appears to be a possible choice, if for no other reason than the fact that she followed Christ faithfully, was at the crucifixion, and was the first to see the Resurrected Christ at the Garden Tomb. John's commentary of the conversation between Jesus and Mary at the tomb draws some raised eyebrows.

> But Mary stood without at the sepulchre weeping: and as she wept, she stooped down, and looked into the sepulchre,
>
> And seeth two angels in white sitting, the one at the head, and the other at the feet, where the body of Jesus had lain.
>
> And they say unto her, Woman, why weepest thou? She saith unto them, Because they have taken away my Lord, and I know not where they have laid him.
>
> And when she had thus said, she turned herself back, and saw Jesus standing, and knew not that it was Jesus.

Jesus saith unto her, Woman, why weepest thou? whom seeketh thou? She, supposing him to be the gardener, saith unto him, Sir, if thou have borne him hence, tell me where thou hast laid him, and I will take him away.

Jesus saith unto her, Mary. She turned herself, and saith unto him, Rabboni: which is to say, Master.

Jesus saith unto her, *Touch me not; for I am not yet ascended to my Father:* but go to my brethren, and say unto them, I ascend unto my Father, and your Father; and to my God, and your God.[268]

Was Christ telling his wife that she should not touch him in the way that a wife would offer herself to her husband? Gnostic texts appear to suggest this special relationship between Mary and Jesus.

However, Mary Magdalene is not the only candidate for a married Jesus. Mary, the sister of Martha and Lazarus, appears to have had a special relationship with Christ as well. Jesus often spent time with Mary and her family. He treated Lazarus, whom he raised from the dead,[269] with special attention—a relationship that might be akin to that of someone who is a member of the family. Mary lived in Bethany and Christ retired to her home, which she shared with her brother and sister, with frequency. In fact, if there is a place that Jesus could call home, it appears to have been in Bethany where Mary sat at Jesus's feet, as a wife might do.[270] Mary was also always at Christ's side and was present at the crucifixion.[271] Of import to the issue of marriage is Mary's anointing of Jesus with "spikenard," an oil, which means "to be committed to."

Then took Mary a pound of ointment of spikenard, very costly, and anointed the feet of Jesus, and wiped his feet with her hair: and the house was filled with the odour of the ointment.

Then saith one of his disciples, Judas Iscariot, Simon's son, which should betray him,

Why was not this ointment sold for three hundred pence, and given to the poor?

This he said, not that he cared for the poor; but because he was a thief, and had the bag, and bare what was put therein.

Then said Jesus, Let her alone; against the day of my burying hath she kept this.

For the poor always ye have with you; but me ye have not always.[272]

The act of anointing in such a manner among the Jews was the province of the wife.[273] Further, Christ gives reference to the fact that Mary would be the one to anoint his body after the crucifixion—again, an act traditionally done by the family of the deceased.

Was the marriage feast in Cana, referred to in John 2:1, the marriage of Jesus, as some gospel scholars have supposed? Mary, the mother of Jesus, is clearly the hostess. The marriage must be for one of her children. Is that child Jesus, who on this occasion performs his first recorded miracle, changing water into wine?

In the end, such is speculation, as the gospel writers are silent as to the marital status of Jesus.[274]

Polygamy also appears to have been allowed in early Christianity under certain conditions.[275] Augustine noted that polygamy would have been openly allowed in early Christianity, as it was in the days of the patriarchs, however, the laws and customs of Rome prohibited it.[276] It is of note that Christ and the Apostles speak of plural wives existing in Abram's bosom (paradise).[277] Justin Martyr, in defending polygamy during the early second century, noted it was an esoteric doctrine that was practiced in secret.[278] If Jesus was married, could he have been married to both Mary Magdalene and Mary, the sister of Martha?

In sum, the forty-day period following Christ's Resurrection was distinguished from other times as one in which secret doctrines meant only for the mature and faithful were taught. However, the contents of those most guarded secrets have never been made fully known to anyone not present during those teachings. That knowledge, or called by Nibley the "highest revelations," simply have not been passed down to us.[279]

THE APOSTASY

The Apostles predicted an apostasy after the resurrection and before the Second Coming of Christ.[280]

> Astonishing as it seems, then, the immediate second coming of Christ, which everyone seems to take for granted as the basic doctrine of the early church, is not only not proclaimed among its writings, but is definitely precluded by the expected rule of evil, which also rules out completely any belief in an immediate end of the world. There was to be an end, and that end was at hand, with the winter and the wolves closing in: "the night cometh, when no man can work." The modern Christian

theory is that such a night never came, but the Apostles knew better.[281]

Christ taught that His message would be rejected, like the prophets of old.[282] The Apostles would be "hated of all men" and killed.[283] The same fate was to befall the early Christian members.[284] Then comes the Apostasy.[285] The dispensation of Christ ends.[286]

"The Apostolic Fathers compare[d] the church to fallen Israel, and confirm their solemn warnings by citing the most lurid and uncompromising passages of scripture."[287] For example, "in the Visions of the Pastor of Hermas the church is represented as an old and failing lady. . . ."[288] It is the "Wintertime of the Just."[289]

Biblical scholars have always been puzzled by the unsympathetic and uncompromising positions that the Apostles took in their guise as missionaries in the service to Jesus Christ. The Apostles viewed the conversion process as short and so they never stayed long in any one place. They gave their warning message and left. Today's missionaries proselyte an area for long periods of time, ensuring a stable congregation before moving on, but not the Apostles of old.

> What strange missionaries! . . . The failure of the apostles to leave behind them written instructions for the future guidance of the church has often been noted and sadly regretted. It is hard to conceive of such a colossal oversight if the founders had actually envisaged a long future for the church. . . . No church buildings were constructed in the early church. . . . The strange indifference of the early martyrs to the future of a church for which later ages fondly believed they gave their lives has not received the comment it deserves.[290]

With the death of the Apostles and elders came a loss in the gifts of the spirit, power, and knowledge.[291] The New Testament itself predicts an apostasy before the Second Coming of Christ.

> And Jesus answered and said unto them [the Apostles], Take heed that no man deceive you,
>
> For many shall come in my name, saying, I am Christ, and shall deceive many . . .
>
> And many false prophets shall rise, and shall deceive many.[292]

In fact, there are many New Testament scriptures that indicate that the apostasy had already begun at the time of the Apostles.

I [the Apostle Paul] marvel that ye are so soon removed from him that called you into the grace of Christ unto another gospel: Which is not another; but there be some that trouble you, and would pervert the gospel of Christ.[293]

Hence, the apostasy was well known to the Apostles and the early Christians. They knew that they would suffer and be persecuted until death.[294] It was not until after this apostasy that Christ would return for His Second Coming and usher in His millennial reign.[295] Apostolic Fathers Irenaeus and Martyr preached of the Millennium in the second century, as a far future event.[296]

MISCELLANEOUS DOCTRINES

There were obviously many other doctrines held sacred by the Hebrew Christians, who referred to themselves as "saints."[297] They believed that with the priesthood came the power to bind on earth and heaven,[298] as well as the power to anoint and heal the sick.[299]

The Hebrews also believed and practiced the law of tithing and the fast.[300] The early Church believed that fasting and providing for the poor was part of what Christ commanded them to do.[301] Just as the ancient Hebrews, the Christian Hebrews also adhered to a strict code of health.[302]

They believed in miracles and the gifts of the spirit,[303] as well as missionary work.[304] All of the Apostles did missionary work,[305] the Apostle Paul being the most famous. Of interesting note, the Apostles did not go out alone, but they went out two by two.[306]

The Hebrews did not believe that the world was created out of chaos. "Nearly all recent studies on the origin of the doctrine of *creatio ex nihilo* have come to the conclusion that this doctrine is not native to Judaism, is nowhere attested in the Hebrew Bible, and probably arose in Christianity in the second century BC in the course of its fierce battle with Gnosticism. The one scholar who continues to maintain that the doctrine is native to Judaism, namely Jonathon Goldstein, thinks that it first appears at the end of the first century BC, but has recently conceded the weakness of his position in the course of debate with David Winston."[307]

Hebrews also had a historical belief that Elohim was married. In the lost Jewish Christian book, *The Gospel According to the Hebrews*, Christ apparently refers to his Mother in Heaven.[308]

> A biblical precedent for the Heavenly Mother doctrine can be found in Genesis 1:26–27 where God, addressing an unidentified audience, says, "Let us make man in our image, after our likeness . . . So God created man in his own image, in the image of God created He him; male and female created He them." In Genesis 5:1–2 we again read that "God created man, in the likeness of God made He him; male and female created He them." We may deduce from these scriptures that the "likeness of God" is "male and female."[309]

Even the Apostle Paul refers to a "family in heaven."[310] And according to Jewish scholar Peter Hayman, "many, perhaps the majority, of ancient Israelites, believed that God had a 'female consort.' Some Jews, during a much later age, held a similar view."[311]

The Hebrews have long believed that Lucifer or Satan was a son of God[312] and brother to Jehovah.[313] Catholic scholar Giovanni Papini confirms this understanding of the early Church and goes on to assert that Lucifer was the younger brother of the Christ.[314] Ultimately, Lucifer became a fallen angel who fought against God.[315] According to John the Divine,

> There appeared another wonder in heaven; and behold a great red dragon, having seven heads and ten horns, and seven crowns upon his heads.
>
> And his tail drew the third part of the stars of heaven, and did cast them to the earth: and the dragon stood before the woman which was ready to be delivered, for to devour her child as soon as it was born. . . .
>
> And there was war in heaven: Michael and his angels fought against the dragon; and the dragon fought and his angels,
>
> And prevailed not; neither was their place found any more in heaven.
>
> And the great dragon was cast out, that old serpent, called the Devil, and Satan, which deceiveth the whole world: he was cast out into the earth, and his angels were cast out with him.[316]

Satan obviously was a persuasive figure; a "Son of the Morning,"[317] for he convinced one third of all of God's children to follow him and revolt against the Father. That war that began in heaven, according to Hebrew Christianity, is continuing here on the earth.

Another important aspect of Hebrew Christianity included the gifts of the Spirit. In fact, Christ preached that these gifts "shall follow them that believe."[318] As the Apostle Paul explained

> Now there are diversities of gifts, but the same Spirit.
>
> And there are differences of administrations, but the same Lord.
>
> And there are diversities of operations, but it is the same God which worketh all in all.
>
> But the manifestation of the Spirit is given to every man to profit withal.
>
> For to one is given by the Spirit the word of wisdom; to another the word of knowledge by the same Spirit;
>
> To another faith by the same Spirit; to another the gifts of healing by the same Spirit;
>
> To another the working of miracles; to another prophecy; to another discerning of spirits; to another divers kinds of tongues; to another the interpretation of tongues;
>
> But all these worketh that one and the selfsame Spirit, dividing to every man severally as he will.[319]

The Hebrews did not believe in having a paid ministry,[320] nor did they believe that God changed. So His gospel would be the same in the past, present, and future.[321] Hebrews long believed in the literal scattering and gathering of Israel, to include the Jews and lost ten tribes.[322] It is of some interest that they strongly believed in the return of the Tribe of Judah to Jerusalem as outlined in Jeremiah 33:10–11 and Zechariah 2:12. However, this was not the return that the early Christians had in mind. For although the Jews did return and rebuild under the domination of the Persians, then the Greeks, and lastly the Romans at the time of Christ, this was not the foretold gathering. That would come later for in AD 66, Rome sacked Jerusalem, completely destroyed Herod's temple, and scattered the Jews once more. This is the prophesied "Abomination of Desolation" spoken of by Daniel the Prophet as quoted by Christ in Matthew 24:15–22, 29, 34–35.

> And now the ax was laid at the root of the rotted tree. Jerusalem was to pay the price. Daniel had foretold this hour when desolation, born of abomination and wickedness, would sweep the city (Daniel 9:27; 11:31; 12:11). Moses had said the siege would be so severe women

would eat their own children (Deut. 28). Jesus specified the destruction would come in the days of the disciples. And come it did, in vengeance, without restraint. Hunger exceeded human endurance; blood flowed in the streets; destruction made desolate the temple; 1,100,000 Jews were slaughtered; Jerusalem was ploughed as a field; and a remnant of a once mighty nation was scattered to the ends of the earth. The Jewish nation died, impaled on Roman spears, at the hands of Gentile overlords.[323]

Perhaps this is why the Gospel writers made plain that the gathering foretold in the Old Testament was still to come.[324]

The Hebrews made it a point to emphasize various other tenants of Christianity. For example, members were referred to as "saints,"[325] they honored the Sabbath day,[326] they believed in the importance of daily prayer[327] and the Atonement of Christ,[328] they took care of the welfare needs of the members of the Church,[329] and they used a device called the "Urim and Thummim" to translate and receive revelation.[330]

They also practiced the doctrine of foreordination. According to this doctrine, men and women were selected or "foreordained" in the premortal life to receive certain callings, responsibilities, obligations, blessings, and stewardships during their mortal sojourn. In a sense, each was given a specific mission to accomplish.[331]

Early Christian worship service (AD 161–180) also included the sacrament of the Lord's Supper administered by deacons (given only to those who had been baptized).[332] A change had been made previously that instead of worshiping on Saturday as was historical Hebrew practice, the day of Christ's resurrection, Sunday, should be the new worship day in which the sacrament was to be administered.

THE EBIONITES

No discussion of the Hebrew Christians would be complete without a discussion of a fringe Hebrew sect known as the Ebionites. Too often, scholars incorrectly refer to the Ebionites as the Hebrew Christians. They were not. In fact, these Jewish Christians, who believed that Jesus was the Jewish Messiah foretold in the Old Testament, also believed that to be a Christian, you first had to convert to Judaism. Some scholars maintain that these are the descendants of individuals spoken of by the Apostle Paul in Galatia, who demanded that gentiles convert to Judaism first and be circumcised. They did not believe in the virgin birth or the premortal life of Christ, as did the majority of the Hebrews. They did not even believe that Jesus was the Son of God. Rather they believed that Jesus was a mortal man who was chosen to fulfill a special mission by God—Jehovah, and that he died for the sins of the world and was resurrected to fulfill that mission. Notwithstanding this differing belief in Christ, they did believe that Jesus's sacrifice fulfilled the law of Moses requirement for burnt offerings. Hence, the practice was no longer adhered to by Ebionites. Yet they rejected the writings of Paul, who they believed to be a heretic because he taught that the law of Moses was fulfilled in Christ completely and that circumcision was no longer required. To the Ebionites, circumcision still signified the covenant relationship that the chosen people had with God.

Obviously, they adhered to the Old Testament as scripture, as well as to the Gospel of Matthew, although their Matthew was an altered version missing the first two chapters. They also are said to have adopted their own summarized version of the synoptic gospels, sometimes called the Gospel of the Ebionites.[333]

The Ebionites viewed themselves as Jews first and then Christians. These Christians concentrated more on the teachings of Peter and James the Just, which to them stood for the proposition that works are important, rather than simply the grace of Jesus, as preached by Paul. Thus many elements of the law of Moses remained paramount notwithstanding their belief that the law was satisfied in Christ. Obedience to the 613 specific regulations proffered by the Pharisees and scholars in order to adhere to the law of Moses was still essential to salvation. They also continued to keep Saturday as their Sabbath.

The fact that they did not believe Jesus to be divine demonstrated that the Ebionites had much more in common with the Gnostics, than they did with the Hebrews. Just as the Gnostics, who we shall discuss, believed that Christ exited the body of Jesus before the crucifixion, leaving the human Jesus to suffer alone, the Ebionites believed that Jesus was chosen by Jehovah to be the Messiah and was therefore adopted as His Son, the Son of God. To express the matter more fully, the Ebionites believed that Jesus was a real flesh and blood human like the rest of us, born as the eldest son of the sexual union of his parents, Joseph and Mary. What set Jesus apart from all other people was that he kept God's law perfectly and so was the most righteous man on earth. As such, God chose him to be his son and assigned to him a special mission, to sacrifice himself for the sake of others. Jesus then went to the cross, not as a punishment for his own sins but for the sins of the world, a perfect sacrifice in fulfillment of all God's promises to his people and to the Jews, as foretold in the holy scriptures. As a sign of his acceptance of Jesus's sacrifice, God then raised Jesus from the dead and exalted him to heaven.[334]

In sum, if there were apostates to Hebrew Christianity, they were the Ebionites. They are the ones that Paul was so concerned about. He wasn't concerned about the Hebrew Christians because Paul himself adhered to the belief structure of the Hebrews. It was Paul who referred to some Ebionites in the New Testament as "Nazareans." They were not Hebrew Christians and should not be confused as such, for it would be an insult to those early Christians.

NOTES

1.   "Strangely enough, most of the Jews in the days of the Apostles did not reside in Jerusalem or in its immediate vicinity. They lived in scattered communities throughout the Roman Empire and were part of what was known as the Diaspora, or the 'people of the dispersion.' Nearly every large city possessed sufficient numbers of these people to form a local synagogue; the same was true of many of the smaller cities. The work of scattering began in 721 BC under Sargon II of Assyria, who led away into captivity the inhabitants of Israel, the ten tribes of the northern kingdom of Palestine. Later, Nebuchadnezzar conquered Judah, the southern kingdom, and about 589 BC destroyed Jerusalem and carried its captives into Babylon. Some seventy years or so later, Cyrus, a benevolent king of Persia, permitted those exiled Jews to return to their native land and rebuild their sacred temple. All, however, did not return. Later, when Alexander the Great conquered the known world, further Jewish migrations from the Holy Land occurred. Many of those who took up residency in other lands later applied for and were granted the rights of Roman citizenship. . . . Unquestionably these scattered Jews, like some of their compatriots in Palestine, were influenced by the world around them. . . . These are sometimes referred to as Hellenistic Jews or Grecians because they adopted the Greek culture and language as their own. . . . Even in their scattered condition, however, the Jews, . . . continued to look upon Jerusalem as their spiritual home on earth. . . . Pilgrimages to the sacred temple, while not a yearly occurrence for those scattered in the further regions, were great events and eagerly anticipated. All faithful Jews continued to pay the half-shekel tax for maintenance of temple worship. Moreover, it would appear that the famed Sanhedrin of Jerusalem exercised at least token influence over the scattered Jewish communities throughout the empire." *The Life and Teachings of Jesus and His Apostles* (Salt Lake City, UT: Intellectual Reserve, 1978), 235–36.

2.   "Christians adopted as their Bible the Greek translation of the Jewish Scriptures

known as the Septuagint and later also canonized the books of the New Testament. . . . Christianity continued many of the patterns of Judaism, adapting to Christian use synagogue liturgical worship, prayer, use of Sacred Scripture, a priesthood, a religious calendar commemorating on certain days each year certain events and/or beliefs, use of music in worship, giving material support to the religious leadership, and practices such as fasting and almsgiving and baptism." http://en.wikipedia.org/wiki/Early_Christianity.

3.   Daniel C. Peterson, "What Has Athens to Do with Jerusalem?: Apostasy and Restoration in the Big Picture," (FAIR Conference 1999), quoting Thorleif Boman, Hebrew Thought Compared with Greek (Norton, 1970), 17.

4.   Bickmore, "Mormonism in the Early Jewish Christian Milieu" (FAIR Conference 1999).

5.   Acts 2:4,14,41; 11:19.

6.   Acts 10.

7.   Acts 15:1–29; Galatians 2:1–10. The Apostle Paul wrote his Epistle to the Hebrews (approximately AD 65) setting forth to the Jewish Christians that Christ fulfilled the law of Moses, just three years prior to Paul's death in AD 68.

8.   Eusebius, Ecclesiastical History, 4.5.3–4.

9.   S. Kent Brown, "Whither the Early Church," Ensign, Oct. 1988.

10. Ibid.

11. Genesis 32:30; Exodus 24:9–11, 33:11, 18–23, Ezekiel 1:26; Numbers 12:7–8 Deuteronomy 5:4, 34:10; Isaiah 6:1, 5; Genesis 1:26–27, 5:1–3; Exodus 33:21–30.

12. Christopher Stead, Philosophy in Christian Antiquity (Cambridge University Press, 1994), 120.

13. Acts 7:55–56 (Stephen sees Christ on the right hand of God the Father); Hebrews 1:1–5 (God the Father is in the express image of Jesus); James 3:8–11 (man made after the similitude of God); Revelation 22:3–6 (seeing the face of God); 1 Corinthians 11:7 (man in the image of God).

14. John 3:16 (Love); Jeremiah 4:8 (Anger); Jeremiah 44:4 (hate); Exodus 34:6 (long suffering and merciful); Romans 11:33 (wise); Matthew 19:26 (all powerful); Hebrews 1:8–12 (unchanging); Acts 15:18 (all knowing).

15. John 1:1.

16. Luke 24:36–43.

17. John 5:19.

18. Hebrews 1:3; Philippians 2:5–8.

19. Cherbonnier, "In Defense of Anthrophomorphism," Reflections on Mormonism: Judaeo-Christian Parallels (Provo, UT: Religious Studies Center, BYU, Bookcraft, 1978), 162, cited in Barry Bickmore, Restoring the Ancient Church: Joseph Smith and Early Christianity (Phoenix, Arizona: Cornerstone Publishing, 1999), chapter 3.

20. Brown, All Things Restored, 104.

21. Ibid., citing 1QM 12.2 and 1QM 19.

22. Psalm 110:1 and Acts 2:34–36; Isaiah 6 and John 12:40–41; Isaiah 54:5 and Matthew 11:27; Isaiah 43:11 and Luke 2:11; Deuteronomy 32:3–4 and 1 Corinthians 10:1–4; Exodus 3:14

23. Bruce R. McConkie, Doctrinal New Testament Commentary, 3 vols (Salt Lake City: Bookcraft, 1965), 1:464.

24. Martyr, Dialogue with Trypho 36, 113 in ANF 1:212–13, 1:255 ("it was Jesus who appeared to and conversed with Moses, and Abraham, and all the other patriarchs without exception, ministering to the will of the Father").

25. Irenaeus, Against Heresies 4.7.2, 4 in ANF 1:470.
26. Brown, *All Things Restored*, 111 quoting Geoffrey A. Williamson, Eusebius: *The History of the Church from Christ to Constantine* (Dorset Press, 1984), 47. See also Brown, *All Things Restored*, 11–12, for an extensive list comparing Jehovah and Christ.
27. Matthew 3:16–17.
28. Acts 7:56.
29. Mark 9:7; John 3:16, 9:35–37, 17:1, 20:17, 21, 31; Romans 15:6; Ephesians 3:14; Hebrews 1:6, 5:5.
30. Matthew 27:46; Mark 15:34; John 20:17; 2 Corinthians 11:31; Ephesians 1:3, 17; 1 Peter 1:3; Revelation 3:12.
31. John 14:28.
32. 1 Corinthians 8:4–6; Ephesians 4:5–7.
33. Luke 2:49–50; John 17:3–4.
34. Matthew 6:6–9, 26:39, 27:46; Luke 3:34; John 12:27–28, 16:26, 17:5–11.
35. Matthew 3:17, 17:5; Mark 1:11; Luke 3:22; John 12:28–30.
36. Mark 13:11; Luke 12:12; John 15:26.
37. John 17:11.
38. Hippolytus, *Against the Heresy of One Noetus* 7, ANF 5:226.
39. Edwin Hatch, *The Influence of Greek Ideas and Usages Upon the Christian Church*, (London: Williams & Norgate, 1890), 268.
40. Clement of Alexandria, Stromata 7:3, ANF 2:527.
41. Tertullian, *Against Praxeas* 7, ANF, 3:602.
42. Origen, Dial Heracl 2:3, quoted in Alan F. Segal, *The Two Powers in Heaven* (Leiden: E.J. Brill, 1977), 231.
43. Eusebius, *Preparation for the Gospel* 7:15, ANF, John 17:11, 21–24 (oneness of Godhead).
44. Barry Bickmore, *Doctrinal Trends in Early Christianity and the Strength of the Mormon Position* (FARMS, 2001), quoting J. N. D. Kelly, *Early Christian Doctrines,* revised edition (San Francisco: Harper, 1978), 247–48.
45. Henry Bettenson, *The Early Christian Fathers* (Oxford University Press, 1963), 330. See also John 14:28 (Father is greater than the Son); 1 Corinthians 15:24–28 (Christ is subject to the Father).
46. Hippolytus, Scholia on Daniel 7, ANF, 5:189; Irenaeus, *Against Heresies*, 2:27:8, ANF, 1:402; Matthew 26:39; Mark 13:32.
47. Richard Hansen, "The Achievement of Orthodoxy in the Fourth Century AD," *The Making of Orthodoxy: Essays in honour of Henry Chadwick* (Cambridge University Press, 1989), 153.
48. Bettenson, *The Early Christian Fathers,* 54.
49. Justin Martyr, Dialogue with Trypho 56 in ANF, 1:223.
50. Hebrews 7:25; 1 Timothy 2:5.
51. John 6:38.
52. John 7:16–18 (Christ's doctrine is His that sent Him); John 8:13–18 (Father sent the Son); John 8:25–29 (does what his Father taught Him).
53. John 1:1; 1 Peter 1:19–20; Clementine Recognitions 1:28, ANF, 8:85.
54. Origen, De Principiis 2:9:6, ANF, 4:292.
55. Clement of Alexandria, *The Instructor* 1:7, ANF, 2:224.
56. Martyr, Dialogue with Trypho 5, ANF, 1:197.
57. Bickmore, *Restoring the Ancient Church*, quoting Hammerton-Kelly, *Pre-existence, Wisdom and the Son of Man*, 156.

58. Gospel of Thomas 49, James M. Robinson, Nag Hammadi Library in English (Leiden: E. J. Brill, 1988).

59. Bickmore, *Restoring the Ancient Church*, chapter 3, note 2, quoting Hammerton-Kelly, *Pre-existence, Wisdom and the Son of Man*, 15.

60. Job 15:8; Apocalypse of Abraham 22 in Sparks, The Apocryphal Old Testament, 384; Origen, Commentary on John 2:25, ANF, 10:340–41; Secrets of Enoch 23:2, 30:12–13, Platt, *Forgotten Books of Eden*, 89; 1 Enoch 39:4–7, 40:5, 61:12 in Rabbi Nissim Wernick, *A Critical Analysis of the Book of Abraham in Light of Extra-Cannonical Jewish Writings* (BYU, 1968), 23.

61. David Winston, *The Wisdom of Solomon* (Doubleday, 1982), 26, 197–98.

62. See also Ephesians 1:3–6 (before the foundation of the world); Titus 1:1–2 (before the world began); Acts 17:26–29 (pre-determined status of birth); Revelation 12:7–12 (premortal war in heaven); Jude 6 (talks about those who kept not their first estate); 2 Peter 2–4 (some angels sinned before earth life); Mark 3:11–12 (devils recognized Christ).

63. John 9:1–3; Jeremiah 1:5; Titus 1:2; Ephesians 1:4.

64. James 1:12; 1 Peter 1:7; Judges 2:21–22; 2 Corinthians 5:6–7.

65. 1 Corinthians 3:16; Matthew 8:28–32.

66. Job 38:7; John 10:34–36; 2 Corinthians 3:18; Galatians 4:1–7; Revelation 21:7 (inherit all things that the Father has); John 17:20–23 (become one with Christ just as He is one with the Father); Philip 3:21 (resurrected body like Christ); 1 John 3:2 (be like resurrected Christ); Revelation 1:6 (kings and priests unto Christ and His Father); Hebrews 12:9–10 (spirit children of God and partakers of His holiness); 1 Peter 5:6 (exalted); Matthew 5:48 (be perfect like Father).

67. Brown, *All Things Restored*, 114.

68. Pyle, "I have said, 'Ye Are Gods': Concepts conducive to the Early Christian doctrine of Deification in Patristic Literature and the Underlying Strata of the Greek New Testament Text" (FAIR Conference, 1999).

69. John 10:34.

70. Romans 8:16–18.

71. 1 Corinthians 8:5–6.

72. Genesis 3:22 ("Behold, the man is become as one of us, to know good and evil."); Deuteronomy 10:17; Joshua 22:2; Psalm 136:2; Psalm 82:6 ("Ye are gods; and all of you children of the most High"); Segal, *Paul the Convert: The Apostolate and Apostasy of Saul the Pharisee* (Yale 1960), 22, 34–71; Testament of Adam 3:2–4 quoted in Petersen, *Where Have all the Prophets Gone?*, 90 ("Adam, Adam do not fear. You wanted to be a god; I will make you a god, not right now, but after a space of many years. . . . And I will set you at the right hand of my divinity, and I will make you a god just like you wanted").

73. Irenaeus, Against Heresies 4:38:4, ANF, 1:522.

74. Martyr, Dialogue with Trypho 124, ANF, 1:262.

75. Clement of Alexandria, Stromata 7:10, ANF, 2:539; The Instructor 3:1, ANF, 2:271.

76. A Medieval Armenian text commenting on Genesis has stated it thusly: "When Adam departed and was walking around in the garden, the serpent spoke to Eve and said, "Why do you taste of all the trees, but from this one tree which is beautiful in appearance you do not taste?" Eve said, "Because God said, 'When you eat of that tree, you shall die.' But the serpent said, "God has deceived you, for formerly God was man like you. When he ate of that fruit, he attained this great glory. That is why he told you not to eat, lest eating you would become equal to God." W.

Lowndes Lipscomb, *The Armenian Apocryphal Adam Literature*, Armenian Texts and Studies 8 (University of Pennsylvania, 1990) 262–264. Jewish tradition has the same type of context: "It is only out of jealousy that God has said this, for He well knows that if you eat thereof your eyes will be opened, and you will know how to create the world just as He." Moses Gaster, *The Chronicles of Jerahmeel*; or, *The Hebrew Bible Hostoriale* (Ktav, 1971), 47. See also M. Rosenbaum and A. M. Silbermann, *Haphtaroth and Rashi's Commentary* (Silvermann Family, 1973), 1:13; H. Freedman and Maurice Simon, *Midrash Rabbah*, 5 vols (Socino Press, 1961) Genesis vol. 1:150–51.

77. Origen, Commentary on John 2:3, ANF, 10:324–25; see also Origen, Commentary on John 2:2, ANF, 9:323–24.

78. Origen, Commentary of the Gospel of John 2:2–3, ANF, 9:323–24; 10:324–25.

79. Origen, Commentary on the Gospel of John, ANF ("Men should escape from being men, and hasten to become Gods").

80. Hippolytus, Refutation of All Heresies 10:30, ANF, 5:153.

81. Prestige, *God in Prestistic Thought* (London: Oxford University Press, 1956), 73, cited by Bickmore in Restoring the Ancient Church, chapter 3.

82. Irenaeus, Against Heresies 4:38, ANF, 1:522; Arthur Cushman McGiffert, *A History of Christian Thought, vol. 1—Early and Eastern* (New York: Charles Scribner's & Sons, 1932), 141, quoted by David Waltz in his critique of Bickmore's *Restoring the Ancient Church* ("Participation in God[hood] was carried so far by Irenaeus as to amount to deification 'we are not made gods in the beginning,' he says, 'but at first men, then at length gods.' This is not to be understood as mere rhetorical exaggeration on Irenaeus' part. He meant the statement to be taken literally.").

83. Athanasius, *Against the Arians*, 1:39, 3:34, in Alexander Roberts and James Donaldson, *The Nicene and Post-Nicene Fathers*, 14 vols (Peabody, MA: Hendrickson Publishers, 1999) (hereinafter "NPNF"), 2:4:329, 412–13.

84. Augustine, On the Psalms, 50:2, NPNF, 1:8:178.

85. Clement of Alexandria, The Stromata 4.14, ANF, 2:426.

86. Tertullian, Against Hermogenes V, ANF, 3:479–80.

87. John A. Tvedtnes, "The King Follett Discourse in the Light of Ancient and Medieval Jewish and Christian Beliefs," (FAIR Conference, 2004).

88. Pyle, "I have said, 'Ye are Gods': Concepts conducive to the Early Christian Doctrine of Deification in Patristic Literature and the Underlying Strata of the Greek New Testament Text."

89. Ernest W. Benz, "Imago Dei: Man in the Image of God," *Reflections on Mormonism: Judeao-Christian Parallels* (Bookcraft, 1978), 215–216.

90. Matthew 19:14.

91. Clement of Alexandria, Stromateis 4:25 in ANF at 2:439–41.

92. Cyril of Jerusalem, Catechetical Lectures 4:19 in NPNF at 2:7:23–24.

93. Hebrews 6:1–2.

94. Acts 2:37–39.

95. John 3:16–18; Mark 9:23; Romans 10:16–17; Romans 1:16–17; 2 Corinthians 5:7; James 1:5–6; 1 Peter 1:9; Hebrews 11:6; Ephesians 2:8–9; Galatians 2:16; Romans 3:22–25; John 14:6.

96. James 2:14–26; Ephesians 2:8–10; Galatians 5:6, 19–26; 1 John 5:1–4; Romans 14:23; Romans 2:5–11, 13–16; Hebrews 5:5–10; James 1:22–25; Matthew 7:15–23, 16:27; Revelation 22:12–15; Luke 6:46–49; John 14:15–21; Acts 10:34–36; Titus 3:8; Galatians 5:20–23; Matthew 24:13.

97. Epistle of Barnabas 19, ANF, 1:148.
98. Clement 3–4, ANF, 7:518.
99. Pastor of Hermas, Vision 3:1, ANF, 2:13.
100. Robert M. Grant, *Second Century Christianity* (London: Society for Promoting Christian Knowledge, 1946), 80.
101. Revelation 20:12; James 2:14–26.
102. Brown, *All Things Restored*, 120, quoting Michael D. Adair, "The Doctrines of Salvation by Grace vs. Works: A New Look at an Old Controversy," *A Symposium on the New Testament* (The Church of Jesus Christ of Latter-day Saints, 1980), 28–33.
103. Matthew 16:17.
104. Matthew 7:21–23, 15:7–9, 24:13; Mark 13:13; Luke 12:36–48; James 4:17; Matthew 7:20.
105. Werner Jaeger, *Early Christianity and Greek Paideia* (Cambridge: Harvard University Press, 1961), 12, 15–16. See also Justo L. Gonzales, *A History of Christian Thought*, 3 vols (Nashville: Abingdon, 1970), 1:89.
106. W. G. Rusch, "Getting to Know the Orthodox," *The Luthern* (April 2, 1986), 12.
107. Acts 2:37–39; 2 Corinthians 7:10; Acts 17:30, 26:19–20; Luke 13:1–5; Matthew 4:17; 2 Peter 3:9.
108. Cyril of Jerusalem, Catechetical Lectures 3:10; 21:5, NPNF, 2:7:148–51.
109. Mark 10:13–16; Romans 5:1–21, 18–19; Ephesians 2:8–10; Hebrews 9:14–18, 28; 1 John 2:2–5, 4:10, 1:29; 2 Corinthians 5:15–18; 1 Peter 3:18; 1 Corinthians 15:20–27; John 12:32–36; 1 Peter 2:21–25; Revelation 5:9–10; John 15:13; 1 John 3:16; Matthew 20:28; Galatians 1:4; 1 Peter 1:18–19; 1 Corinthians 6:17–20; Hebrews 10:10–14; Hebrews 2:7–11; Ephesians 5:26; Matthew 1:21; John 11:51–52; 1 Peter 3:18–19; 2 Peter 2:1–5; Jude 6; Acts 5:31.
110. Mark 16:15–16; John 3:4–5; 1 Peter 3:21; Acts 2:37–39; Titus 3:5; Matthew 3:1–2, 11–17, 28:19–20; Luke 7:29–30; Galatians 3:27; John 14:12; Acts 5:30–32; Matthew 19:13–15; Mark 10:13–16; Acts 10, 9:17–18, 22:7–16; Hebrews 6:1–6; 1 Corinthians 10:1–6; Luke 13:24–30; Acts 2:37–39.
111. Hebrews 8:1–13, 10:9.
112. Martyr, First Apology 61, in *Ancient Christian Writers* (Mahwah, New Jersey: Paulist Press, 1948) (hereinafter "ACW"), 1:183; Clementine Homilies 11:25–26 in ANF at 8:289–90; Apostolic Constitutions 6:15, ANF, 7:456–57.
113. Matthew 28:19.
114. Matthew 3:11–16.
115. Luke 22:19.
116. Matthew 26:22, 24–25; Leslie Barnard, *St. Justin Martyr: the First and Second Apologies* (Paulist Press, 1997), 71, cited in Brown, *All Things Restored*, at 90–91.
117. Luke 22:15–20; 1 Corinthians 11:24–25.
118. Acts 2:46–47, 20:7; 1 Corinthians 11:27–30.
119. Shelley, *Church History*, 10.
120. Matthew 3:5–6, 13–16; John 3:2–6, 23; Romans 6:4; Mark 1:5, 9–10; Acts 8:36–39; Colossians 2:12; 1 Peter 3:20–21.
121. Wolfred N. Cote, *The Archeology of Baptism* (Yates and Alexander: 1876), 16. See also Rev. Charles Callan, *The Epistles of St. Paul* (New York: Kessinger Publishing: 2006). ("Baptism in the early Church was generally administered by immersion; and this form of giving the sacrament quite aptly represented the death, burial and resurrection of Christ. The complete plunge into the water was at once an image of Christ's death and burial, and of the Christians death to sin; while the emersion

from the water signified the Resurrection of Jesus and the Christian's birth to the new spiritual life of grace.")

122. Mark 10:13–16; Matthew 19:13–15; Acts 8:12; 1 Corinthians 7:14.

123. 1 Corinthians 15:29; Hebrews 11:40.

124. 1 Peter 3:18–20; 1 Peter 4:6.

125. NIV Study Bible, 1757. See also Pastor of Hermas 9:16, in *The Apostolic Fathers*, 2 vols (Cambridge, Massachusetts: Harvard University Press, 1960), 2:263; Epistle of the Apostles cited in Bickmore, *Restoring the Ancient Church*, chapter 4; Friedrich, *Theological Dictionary of the New Testament* (Grand Rapids, MI, Eerdmans Publishing: 1992), 8:512–13; Nibley, *Mormonism and Early Christianity*, at 121–135; Origen, Homily on Luke 24, cited in Nibley, Mormonism and Early Christianity, 124; Tertullian, On the Resurrection 48, ANF, 3:584.

126. Nibley, *Mormonism and Early Christianity*, 140.

127. Nibley, *Mormonism and Early Christianity*, 77, citing Clementine Recognitions 1:52.

128. Martyr, Dialogue with Trypho 45, 80, ANF, 1:216–17; 1:239; Irenaeus, Against Heresies 4:22:2, ANF, 1:494; Nibley, *Mormonism and Early Christianity*, 115–18.

129. Nibley, *Mormonism and Early Christianity*, 105–109.

130. Pastor of Hermas 9:5–7, in Bart D. Ehrman, *Lost Scriptures* (New York: Oxford University Press, 2003), 256.

131. 1 Peter 4:6; Nibley, *Mormonism and Early Christianity*, at 118–121; Tertullian, On the Soul, 55, ANF, 3:232; Hippolytus, On Christ and the Antichrist, 44–45, ANF, 5:214.

132. Luke 23:43, 16:22, 23, 26; 1 Peter 3:18–20, 4:6; Matthew 27:52; Martyr, Dialogue with Trypho 5, ANF, 1:197; Irenaeus, Against Heresies 5:31, ANF, 1:560–61; Tertullian, On the Soul 7, 55, 58, ANF, 3:232–35; and Origen, De Principiis 2:11:6, 4:1:23, ANF, 4:299, 4:373.

133. Acts 2:1–4, 8:12–23, 19:1–6; Hebrews 6:1–2.

134. 2 Corinthians 5:17, 3:18; Romans 12:2; 1 Corinthians 6:9–11; 1 John 3:9; Matthew 5:48; 2 Corinthians 13:9–11; 2 Peter 1:10.

135. 2 Corinthians 1:21–22, 5:5; Ephesians 1:13–18; 1 John 3:24.

136. Matthew 3:11; Luke 3:16, 13:24–30.

137. Tertullian, On Baptism 12, 6, 8, ANF, 3:672, 674–75; Cyprian Epistle 72:9; 71:1, ANF, 5:381, 5:378.

138. Eusebius, *Ecclesiastical History* 6:43.

139. Acts 24:15.

140. Luke 24:36–39; John 20–21; Job 19:25–26; 1 Corinthians 15:35–55.

141. Ignatius, Smyrnaeans 3, ANF. 1:87.

142. Ehrman, *The Lost Christianities*, 152, quoting Ignatius, Letter to the Trallians and Letter to the Smyreneans.

143. Martyr, First Apology 18, ACW, 1:169.

144. Irenaeus, Against Heresies 4:18:5, ANF, 1:486.

145. Tatian, Address to the Greeks 6, ANF, 2:67.

146. Tertullian, On the Soul 56, ANF, 3:232.

147. Clement 9, ANF, 7:519.

148. Bickmore, *Restoring the Ancient Church*, chapter 4.

149. Acts 17:32.

150. Clement 24–27, Ehrman, *Lost Scriptures*, 167–184.

151. Ignatius, Epistle to the Smyrnaeans 3, ANF, 1:87.

152. 1 John 4:1–3; 2 John 1:7; John 1:14.

153. Luke 9:1; Matthew 10:1; Mark 6:7.

154. Exodus 28:41; Numbers 27:22–23; Mark 3:14; John 15:16; 1 Timothy 4:14; Hebrews 5:4 (must be called of God, as was Aaron).

155. Clement 42 in Ehrman, *Lost Scriptures*, 167–184.

156. Hippolytus, The Apostolic Tradition 2, 8–9, 2–3, 13–17, cited in Bickmore, *Restoring the Ancient Church*, chapter 5.

157. Acts 8:13, 18–20.

158. Ignatius, Trallians 3, ANF, 1:67.

159. Psalm 110:4; Genesis 14:18; Hebrews 7:26–27.

160. Hebrews 5:4–10.

161. Acts 6:5–6.

162. Brown, *All Things Restored*, 88.

163. Apostolic Constitutions 3.10, ANF, 7:429.

164. Exodus 28:1.

165. Luke 6:12–13.

166. Petersen, *Where Have All the Prophets Gone?*, 55.

167. John 15:16 (emphasis added).

168. Matthew 10:1.

169. Shelley, *Church History*, 70.

170. Ibid., 71.

171. Clement 42:5, in Ehrman, *Lost Scriptures*, 167–184.

172. Tertullian, De Pudicitia 21 cited in Hugh Nibley, *Apostles and Bishops in Early Christianity* (Salt Lake City, UT: Deseret Book, 2005), 18, 31, 37.

173. Kirsopp Lake, "The Shepherd of Hermas and Christian Life in Rome in the Second Century," Harvard Theological Review 4 (1911), 38.

174. Ibid., 37.

175. Louis Duchesne, *Origines du Culte Chretien: Etude sur las Liturgie Latine Avant Charlemagne*, 5th ed. (Paris: de Boccard, 1925), 7–9, cited in Nibley, *Apostles and Bishops in Early Christianity*.

176. Tertullian, The Apology 21, ANF, 3:33–36.

177. Apostolic Constitution 2.16.1–4, cited in Nibley, *Apostles and Bishops in Early Christianity*, 47–48.

178. Ibid., 2.25–2.26.1.

179. Nibley, *Apostles and Bishops in Early Christianity*, chapter 1.

180. Ibid., 46.

181. Ibid.

182. Ehrman, *The Lost Christianities*, 140–41

183. Shelley, *Church History*, 70.

184. Ephesians 4:11; Acts 13:1; 1 Corinthians 12:28–29.

185. Acts 6:7.

186. Ephesians 4:11; 1 Timothy 3:1–10; Philippians 1:1; Titus 1:5–9.

187. Acts 14:23; Titus 1:4–5; James 5:14; 1 Peter 5:1; Philippians 1:1; 1 Timothy 3:8, 10, 12–13.

188. Eusebius, *Ecclesiastical History* 1:13.

189. Hebrews 5:1–10.

190. Genesis 49:1; Genesis 27:27–30; Ephesians 4:11.

191. Nibley, *Apostles and Bishops in Early Christianity*, 8.

192. Mark 3:13–15; John 15:16; Luke 6:12–16.

193. Acts 1:21–26 (Matthias ordained an Apostle); Acts 13:1–4, Romans 11:13,

2 Corinthians 11:5, 1 Corinthians 15:9, 1 Timothy 2:7 (Paul ordained an Apostle); Acts 14:14 (Barnabas ordained an Apostle); Galatians 1:19 (James the Just, the Lord's brother, ordained an Apostle).

194. Nibley, *Apostles and Bishops in Early Christianity*, 9, quoting Lietzmann.

195. Ibid., 9–10.

196. Ibid., 10.

197. Ibid., 11–12.

198. Ephesians 4:11; Acts 13:1–4; Ephesians 2:20; 1 Corinthians 12:28.

199. Amos 3:7.

200. Justin Martyr, Dialogue with Trypho, 7, ANF, 1:198.

201. John 14.2; Revelation 20:12–15; 1 Corinthians 12:2–4 (Paul's vision of "the third heaven").

202. 1 Corinthians 15:40–42.

203. Origen, De Principiis 2:10:2, ANF, 4:294; Commentary on John 2:3, ANF, 10:324–325. John Chrysostom also viewed this scripture as pertaining to differing glories in the afterlife. Chrysostom, Homilies on 1 Corinthians 41:4, NPNF, 1:12:251.

204. Irenaeus, Against Heresies 5:36:1–2, ANF, 1:567.

205. Clement of Alexandria, Stromata 6:14, ANF, 2:506.

206. Irenaeus, Against Heresies 5.36.1–2, ANF, 1:567.

207. Fragments of Papias 5, ANF, 1:154.

208. James 2:14–26.

209. Acts 4:5–19, 27:23, 9:3–8; John 15:26–27, 16:7–15; Matthew 7:7–8; Acts 1:1–2, 2:38–39; 1 Corinthians 14:26–33; Galatians 1:11–19; 1 Corinthians 2:10, 13; Acts 11:27–28; James 1:5–6; 2 Peter 1:20–21; Acts 13:1–4, 21:10–11; 1 Corinthians 12:8; John 14:25–26; Revelation 2:7.

210. Revelation 19:10.

211. Ephesians 1:15–17.

212. 1 Thessalonians 5:19–28.

213. Petersen, *Where Have All the Prophets Gone?*, 63.

214. 1 Corinthians 14:6; 2 Corinthians 12:1; Ephesians 1:17, 3:1–5.

215. Ehrman, *The Lost Christianities*, 148–49 (emphasis added).

216. Ibid.

217. Ibid., 150–151.

218. Clementine Recognitions 3:34, ANF, 8:123.

219. John 16:12.

220. John 16:25.

221. Clementine Homilies 19:20, ANF, 8:336.

222. R. P. C. Hanson, *The Early Christian Fathers* (London: Oxford University Press, 1956), 27–35 (arguing that there are no esoteric doctrines in the early Christian church).

223. Ignatius, Epistle to the Trallians 5, ANF, 1:68; Hippolytus, Apostolic Tradition, 23:14, R. P. C. Hanson, *Tradition in the Early Church*, (London: SCM Press, 1962), 32.

224. Petersen, *Where Have All the Prophets Gone?*, 85.

225. Matthew 13:9–13.

226. Matthew 13:13–14.

227. McElhaney, James, *Trial Notebook*, (American Bar Association, 2005), 503–504.

228. Matthew 25:1–13.

229. Doctrine and Covenants 88:92; 133:10, 19; Ephesians 5:22–32.

230. Doctrine and Covenants 45:56–57.

231. Matthew 22:1–14.

232. Joachim Jeremias, *The Eucharistic Words of Jesus* (Fortress Press, 1977), 125–130.

233. Acts 1:1–3.

234. John 16:12.

235. 1 Corinthians 4:1, 2:6–7 (Paul speaks of the "wisdom of God as a mystery, even the hidden wisdom . . .").

236. 1 Corinthians 3:2.

237. Matthew 7:6.

238. Clementine Homilies, 19:20, ANF, 8:336.

239. Guy G. Stroumsa, *Hidden Wisdom: Esoteric Traditions and the Roots of Christian Mysticism* (E. J. Brill, 1996), 41 quoted by Bickmore, *Restoring the Ancient Church*, chapter 6. Origen taught that other religions have esoteric doctrines too, not just Christianity. Origen, Against Celsus 1:7, ANF, 4:399.

240. Clementine Homilies, 19:20, ANF, 8:336; Clementine Recognitions 2:4, 3:1, ANF, 8:98, 8:117.

241. Bickmore, *Restoring the Ancient Church*, chapter 6, citing to Tertullian, *Prescription Against Heretics*, 41.

242. Basil of Caesarea, Treatise De Spiritu Sancto 27, NPNF, 2:8:40–42.

243. Clement of Alexandria, Stromata, 4:1, ANF, 2:409.

244. Bickmore, *Restoring the Ancient Church*, chapter 6, citing Stroumsa, *Hidden Wisdom*, 43.

245. Ibid., 15–17, 43.

246. Johann Mosheim, *Historical Commentaries on the State of Christianity*, 2 vols. (S. Converse, 1854), 1:375–76.

247. Bickmore, *Restoring the Ancient Church*, chapter 6, citing Eugene Backman, *Religious Dances in the Christian Church and in Popular Medicine* (Greenwood Press, 1977), 22, 24–25; Cyril of Jerusalem, Catechetical Lecture 23: 4–10, NPNF, 2:7:153–54; 2 Jeu 54, 66–67, in Nibley, *Mormonism and Early Christianity*, 142 (Christ in prayer circle with the Apostles and their wives to teach them secret ordinances that are necessary for eternal progression).

248. Nibley, *Mormonism and Early Christianity*, 47–48.

249. Ibid., 75–76.

250. Dissertatio de Vita Sancti Cyrilli, 1, 16, quoted by Nibley, *Mormonism and Early Christianity*, 79.

251. John 2:16.

252. Acts 21:26–30, 24:17–18; 1 Corinthians 9:13; Revelation 7:15.

253. William J. Hamblin, "Temples Obsolete after Christ" (FAIR 2006).

254. Theodore Gaster, *Thespis: Ritual, Myth, and Drama in the Near East* (New York: Schuman, 1950).

255. Brown, *The Gate of Heaven: Insights on the Doctrines and Symbols of the Temple*, 6–8, 118, 123–24, 133–35, 138–39, 186–89.

256. Backman, *Religious Dances in the Christian Church and in Popular Medicine*, 18; Pastor of Hermas 9, in *The Apostolic Fathers*, 217–297; Origen, Homilies on Leviticus 9:1:3, cited in Gary W. Barkley (Washington, D.C.: The Catholic University of America Press, 1990), 6:2:7; Barker, *The Great Angel*, 125; Cyril of Jerusalem, Catechetical Lecture 22:8, NPNF, 2:7:153. See also Brown, *The Gate of Heaven: Insights on the Doctrines and Symbols of the Temple*, 80–88, 127–31, 185–88; Matthew 22:1–14 (wedding garment); Revelation 3:4–5, 18, 6:11, 15.

257. Clement of Alexandria, Stromata 5:26:5, quoted in Stroumsa, *Hidden Wisdom* 113; Secrets of Enoch 22:7–8, Platt, *Forgotten Books of Eden*; Cyril of Jerusalem, Catechetical Lectures 20–21, 23:22, NPNF, 2:7:146–156; Revelation 1:6, 5:10. See also Brown, *The Gate of Heaven: Insights on the Doctrine and Symbols of the Temple,* 78–80, 126–27, 184–85.

258. Bickmore, *Restoring the Ancient Church,* chapter 6; Hatch, *The Influence of Greek Ideas and Usages Upon the Christian Church,* 298.

259. The Gospel of Nicodemus, 8–9, M. R. James, *The Apocryphal New Testament* (Oxford: Clarendon Press, 1924); 1 Enoch 71:3, OTP 1:49.

260. Brown, *The Gate of Heaven,* 17.

261. Genesis 1:26–28, 2:18, 21–24; Ecclesiastes 3:14; Matthew 19:3–8; 1 Corinthians 11:11–12; Hebrews 13:4; 1 Timothy 5:14, 4:1–5.

262. 1 Timothy 3:1–12.

263. Luke 4:38.

264. Grant, *After the New Testament* (Fortress Press, 1967), 184; 1 Corinthians 1:11; Ephesians 5:22–33.

265. Origen, De Principiis 2:11:2, ANF, 4:297.

266. Walter Wagner, *After the Apostles,* (Augsburg: Fortress Publishers, 1994), 180.

267. Petersen, *Where Have All the Prophets Gone?* 105, quoting from the Gospel of Philip, in Schneemelcher, New Testament Apocrypha, 1, vv. 76–77, 79, 122a, 127, 197–98, 204, 206.

268. John 20:11–17 (emphasis added).

269. John 11:1–45.

270. Luke 10:39, 42.

271. Luke 10:38–42.

272. John 12:3–8; Mark 14:3–5.

273. Song of Solomon 1:2; 4:13–14.

274. Christians are exhorted to follow the example of Jesus. He is called the Exemplar. Followers of Jesus were baptized because Jesus was baptized. They prayed after the manner that Jesus taught and tried to emulate him in their lives. Jesus taught of the importance of marriage in Matthew 19:4–9 and Mark 10:2–12, wherein he preaches that a man shall "leave father and mother, and shall cleave to his wife: and they twain shall be one flesh." He concludes that what "God hath joined together, let not man put asunder." Marriage appears to be as essential to the gospel as baptism. Therefore, isn't it logical that Jesus should be married so as to demonstrate by his example what his followers should do?

275. Tertullian, Exhortation to Chastity, 6, ANF, 4:53.

276. Augustine, Reply to Faustus, 22:47, NPNF, 1:4:288..

277. Luke 16:19–31.

278. Martyr, Dialogue with Trypho, 141, ANF, 1:270.

279. Nibley, *Mormonism and Early Christianity,* 14.

280. Nibley, *Mormonism and Early Christianity,* 135–149, 168–194; Didache 16:3–8 in Ehrman, *Lost Scriptures,* 217; 2 Timothy 4:3–4; Galatians 1:6; 2 Cement 5 translated by J. B. Lightfoot (Athena Data Products, 1990).

281. Nibley, *Mormonism and Early Christianity,* 139.

282. Matthew 17:12, 21:37–39, 23:31–37; Mark 12:6–8; Luke 17:25; John 1:5, 10–11, 3:11–12, 19,32, 5:38, 40–47, 7:7, 8:19, 23–24, 37–38, 40–47, 15:22–25.

283. Matthew 10:16–22, 28, 24:9; Mark 3:9; Luke 10:3; John 16:1, 2, 33; 1 Corinthians 4:9.

284. James 5:10–11; 1 Peter 1:6–7, 24, 4:12–14; Romans 8; 1 John 3:1; 1 Peter 5:1; John 17:25; Matthew 16:24–26; 2 Corinthians 4:8–16; Philippians 3:1–21; Luke 12:22–34. The gospel of Christ would be rejected. Jude 4–11, 16–19; Matthew 13:13–30; Romans 1:16–32; 2 Corinthians 11:3–4; 2 Thessalonians 2:7–12; 1 Timothy 4:1–3, 6:20–21; 2 Timothy 4:3–4; 2 Peter 2:1–22.

285. Acts 20:29; 2 Timothy 4:2–4; 2 Thessalonians 2:9–12; Romans 1:21–31.

286. Matthew 24:14.

287. Nibley, *Mormonism and Early Christianity*, 173, citing Clement, First Epistle to the Corinthians 3–7; Apostolic Constitutions 7:32, ANF, 7:471–72; Lactantius, Divine Institutes VII, 17, cited in Brown, *All Things Restored,* 116.

288. Nibley, *Mormonism and Early Christianity*, 174.

289. Pastor of Hermas, Similitudes 3, ANF, 2:32–33.

290. Nibley, *Mormonism and Early Christianity*, 174–80.

291. Martyr, Dialogue with Trypho, 82, ANF, 1:240; Origen, Against Celsus II, 8, ANF, 4:432–33.

292. Matthew 24:4–5, 11. See also 1 Timothy 4:1–2; Hebrews 13:20; Acts 20:29–30; Matthew 7:15; 2 Timothy 3:1–8; 2 Peter 3:3–7; Jude 18; 2 Timothy 4:3–4; 2 Peter 2:1–3; Jude 16; 2 Peter 2:18; Matthew 24:4–12, 24:23–28; 2 Timothy 3:12–13; John 12:43, 16:1–4; 2 Thessalonians 2:3–4; Revelation 13:4, 13:7–8, 12:4–6; Matthew 21:41–46; Luke 20:9–18; 2 Peter 1:19–21.

293. Galatians 1:6–7. See also Colossians 2:22; Romans 10:2–3; Titus 1:10; Jude 4; Galatians 2:4; 1 Timothy 1:6–7; 2 Timothy 2:18; 1 Corinthians 1:3–5, 1:11–13; 1 John 2:18–19; Titus 1:16; 2 Corinthians 11:13; John 3:19; Revelation 1:11–20, 2, 3, 17, 18; Hebrews 2:3; Ephesians 4:4–5; 2 Timothy 1:15; 2 Corinthians 11:12–15; 1 Corinthians 12:12–31; 2 Corinthians 4:4, 3:14.

294. John 15:19; 2 Timothy 3:12.

295. Revelation 20:1–6; Matthew 24:44–51; Malachi 4:1–3; Isaiah 2:1–4.

296. Norman Cohn, *Cosmos, Chaos and the World to Come* (Yale University Press, 1993), 199; Martyr, Dialogue with Trypho, 80, ANF, 1:239.

297. Matthew 27:52; Romans 1:7; Ephesians 2:19, 4:12, 5:3; 1 Corinthians 1:1–2, 6:1–2, 14:33; 2 Corinthians 8:4; Philippians 4:21–22; Jude 1:3.

298. Matthew 18:18, 16:19.

299. James 5:14–15; The Apostolic Constitutions 8:29, ANF, 7:493.

300. Malachi 3:8, 10; Matthew 23:23; Luke 11:42; Hebrews 7:4–9; Apostolic Constitutions 2:25; ANF, 7:408–410; Isaiah 58:6–7.

301. J. G. Davies, *The Early Christian Church,* (London: Weidenfeld & Nicholson, 1965), 108–09. See also Barnabas 3, ANF, 1:138; Luke 2:37; Matthew 17:19–21; Mark 9:28–29; Acts 13:2–3, 14:23, 27:33; 1 Corinthians 7:5; Pastor of Hermas 3:5:1–3, ANF, 2:33–34.

302. 1 Corinthians 6:10; Ephesians 5:18; 1 Timothy 3:2–3; Titus 1:7; Galatians 5:21; Acts 10:9–16; 1 Corinthians 12:7–8, 3:16–19.

303. Matthew 11:5; Ephesians 1:17; Revelations 19:10; Mark 16:17–18; 1 Corinthians 12:27–28, 12:1–11, 14:1,39; 1 Thessalonians 5:19–20; Acts 3:2–16, 4:16–22, 5:15–16, 8:5–8, 14:8–11, 28:3–9, 6:8, 15:12, 19:11, 20:9–12.

304. Matthew 28:18–20; Mark 16:15.

305. Mark 3:14–15.

306. Luke 10:1; Mark 6:7.

307. Peter Hayman, "Monotheism—A Misused Word in Jewish Studies?" *Journal of Jewish Studies,* 42 (1991), 1–15, quoted in Brown, *All Things Restored,* 114. Wisdom

of Solomon 11:17 ("your all-powerful hand . . . created the world out of formless matter"); Clement of Alexandria, *The Instructor* 3.12, ANF, 2:296 ("the universe" was created out of "shapeless matter"); Justin Martyr, First Apology 10, ACW, 1:165 ("in the beginning [God] . . . create[d] all things out of unformed matter").

308. Origen, Commentary on John 2:6, ANF, 10:329–30.

309. Brown, *All Things Restored*, 113.

310. Ephesians 3:15.

311. Brown, *All Things Restored*, 114.

312. Job 1:6; Job 38:4–7; Zechariah 3:1–2.

313. Brown, *All Things Restored*, 116, citing Lactanius, Divine Institutions, 2.9 .

314. Brown, *All Things Restored*, 116, citing Giovanni Papini, The Devil (E. P. Dutton, 1954), 81–82.

315. Isaiah 14:12–17; Luke 10:18–20; 2 Corinthians 11:14–15; 2 Peter 2:4; 2 Thessalonians 2:4; Jude 6.

316. Revelation 12:4, 7–12.

317. Isaiah 14:12–15.

318. Mark 16:17–18.

319. 1 Corinthians 12:4–11. See also 1 Corinthians 13:28 (speaking in tongues); 1 Corinthians 13:28 (interpretation of tongues); 1 Corinthians 12:9–30, Mark 3:14–15, Mark 6:5, Matthew 8:16–17, Mark 6:13, Mark 16:18, Acts 5:12–15, Acts 9:17–18, Acts 28:8–9, James 5:14–15 (healing of the sick); Acts 2:17–18, Acts 21:8– 9, Romans 12:6, 1 Corinthians 12:10, 1 Corinthians 13:2, 1 Corinthians 14:3 (prophecy); Acts 9:10–12, Acts 11:4–10, Acts 16:9–10, Acts 18:9–10, Acts 22:17– 21, Acts 26:19, 2 Corinthians 12:1 (visions); Matthew 1:20, Matthew 2:12, 19, 22 (dreams); Luke 1:26–38, Acts 5:19–20, Acts 10:3–8, Acts 12:6–11, Acts 23:11, Acts 27:22–24 (ministering of angels); Acts 6:8, Acts 19:11, 1 Corinthians 12:10 (mira- cles); Matthew 8:23–27, Mark 4:35–41, Luke 8:22–25 (controlling the elements); Matthew 9:23–26, Mark 5:35–43, Luke 7:11–17, John 11:1–45, Matthew 10:5–8 (raising the dead); Matthew 17:14–21, Mark 1:34, Mark 9:17–29, Acts 19:11–12 (casting out evil spirits).

320. 1 Peter 5:2; Luke 20:21, 22:35–36; 1 Corinthians 9:18; 2 Thessalonians 3:8–9; 1 Timothy 3:3.

321. Hebrews 13:8.

322. Deuteronomy 30:1–6; Isaiah 11:11–13; Jeremiah 16:14–16, 3:18, 31:7–12; Ezekiel 20:33–36, 28:25–26, 37:21–27.

323. McConkie, *Doctrinal New Testament Commentary*, 1:644–45.

324. Luke 21:24; Revelation 11:3–14.

325. Revelation 13:5–8; Acts 9:13; Romans 1:7, 15:26–27; 1 Corinthians 14:33; Ephesians 4:11–14; Philippians 1:1–2, 4:21–23; Colossians 1:2–5; 2 Thessalonians 1:7–10; Jude 3; 1 Thessalonians 4:17.

326. Luke 6:1–11, 13:11–17; John 20:1, 20:19; Acts 20:7; 1 Corinthians 16:1–2.

327. Matthew 6:5–13, 26:41; Luke 11:1–13, 18:1–8; 1 Thessalonians 5:17; James 1:5–6, 5:14–18.

328. 1 Corinthians 15:19–23; John 5:28–29, 11:25–26.

329. Acts 2:44–47, 4:32–37, 6, 11:28–30; Romans 12:13, 15:25–26; 2 Corinthians 8:12–15, 9:12–13.

330. Revelation 4:6, 15:2.

331. See 1 Peter 1:18–20; Romans 11:2; Jeremiah 1:5; Ephesians 1:4.

332. Justin Martyr, The First Apology of Justin, ACW.

333. Ehrman, *Lost Christianities*, 99–103. See also Shelley, *Church History*, 50 ("The first position was held by a Jewish-Christian sect known as the Ebionites. They taught that Jesus was a mere man who by his scrupulous obedience to the Law was 'justi-fied' and became the Messiah.").
334. Ehrman, *Lost Christianities*, 99–103.

CHAPTER 3

THE GNOSTIC CHURCH

WHO WERE THE GNOSTIC CHRISTIANS?

Another popular branch of Christianity was headquartered in Egypt.[1] It is well known that for a few centuries there existed alongside the catholic Christian tradition various heretical groups categorized as "gnostic." This name comes from *gnosis*, the Greek word for "knowledge." Hans Jonas explains that gnostics believed they were saved by knowledge, specifically the knowledge of God, or that knowledge was the form of salvation itself. They believed in a radically transcendent God; however, this knowledge was not something innate, but something that had to be divinely bestowed on the gnostic.[2]

The beginning of Gnostic Christianity may have had its birth in the person of a man by the name of "Marcion." Marcion lived by the Black Sea in Asia Minor around AD 100–140. His followers appear to be off-shoots of the Greek or Hellenized Church. They were Gentiles who converted to Christianity and rejected everything that was Jewish, including the law of Moses. They took the opposite view from the Ebionites. That is they worshiped Paul and took his teachings to the Galatians, Ephesians, and Hebrews literally. Works meant nothing to them; faith and grace in

Christ meant everything. They looked at the Hebrew God Jehovah as a God who concentrated on obedience to the Law rather than looking at the individual. Jehovah was exacting, easily angered, wrathful, vengeful, and punished those who were disobedient. Hence, Jehovah was thought of by the Marcionites as an evil God. On the other hand, Jesus Christ was merciful, loving, and kind. This dichotomy led to the Marcionites disdaining the entire Old Testament on the basis that it was written by the followers of the evil Jewish God.[3]

> Once Marcion arrived at this understanding, everything else naturally fell into place. The God of the Old Testament was the God who created this world and everything in it, as described in Genesis. The God of Jesus, therefore, had never been involved with this world but came into it only when Jesus himself appeared from heaven. The God of the Old Testament was the God who called the Jews to be his people and gave them his Law. The God of Jesus did not consider the Jews to be his people (for him; they were the chosen of the other God), and he was not a God who gave laws. . . . The God of Jesus came into this world in order to save people from the vengeful God of the Jews.[4]

To the Marcionites, Jesus was not the Jewish Messiah as that would be contrary to their view of the Old Testament. This belief in Jesus as the Savior from the Jewish God, Jehovah, eventually became a core belief of the Gnostics.

Much of what we now know about Gnosticism comes from the discovery in 1945 of the Nag Hammadi library in upper Egypt. This discovery was a cache of Gnostic books from early Christianity. The books were buried in earthenware jars to preserve and save them from the Hellenized Christians who were out to destroy the Gnostic texts as heretical, probably in the last half of the fourth century after the Council of Nicaea. It probably would have been at the time of Athanasius, the bishop of Alexandria, in AD 367, when he began a campaign to destroy heretical books. Nag Hammadi is just three miles from a fourth century Gnostic monastery, so it would appear that these books came from that monastery. Did Gnostic monks hide them? No one knows for sure. What we do know is that there were forty-six books in the thirteen jars found.[5]

The Gospel of Thomas is the most controversial of the books. It is a list of 114 sayings of Jesus as recorded by his Apostle Thomas. Seventy-nine of the 114 sayings are nearly identical to sayings recorded in the New

Testament Gospels. It is the other thirty-five sayings that are the issue. Most of these sayings don't make sense. For example, saying number two, "Jesus said, Let him who seeks continue seeking until he finds. When he finds, he will become troubled. When he becomes troubled, he will be astonished, and he will rule over the all."[6] What is that supposed to mean? It is nonsensical. According to saying number one, if you can decipher the interpretation of the sayings, you will have found hidden knowledge and thus be saved. Hence, this Gospel of Thomas fits in perfectly with Gnosticism.

According to biblical scholar Bart Ehrman, the Gnostics did not have their own separate churches but were members within the existing Christian congregations. That is what made them so dangerous in early Christianity. They attended meetings with everyone else, but may have had separate study groups to discuss these Gnostic doctrines.[7]

One of the most famous Gnostics was bishop Valentinian (AD 100– 180), who was nearly appointed bishop of Rome. He taught that direct personal revelation was available to all men. This view struck fear into the hearts of some of the Apostolic Fathers because they feared it would lead to the corruption of pure doctrine. As a result, Irenaeus "taught his Christian community that no doctrine or knowledge existed beyond that which was revealed in apostolic writings."[8] This ultimately led to the Hellenistic view that revelation was no longer available.

WHAT DID THE GNOSTIC CHRISTIANS BELIEVE?

THE CREATION

There is a Supreme God, who is unknowable. He created the Universe. The Supreme God is described as omniscient, omnipotent, truly benevolent, immovable, invisible, intangible, and ineffable. He is married to Sophia.[9] Together they have produced many eternal beings, called "Aeons." A lessor God, the Creator God (Satan or Yahweh of the Old Testament), often represented by the figure of a lion and called "Demiurgos," made the earth from pre-existent matter.[10] His design was to imitate the Supreme God's creations. Demiurgos is the son of Sophia and the Supreme God. Demiurgos created seven "Archons" who preside over the earth—some would consider them equivalent to evil angels and the demons of the Old Testament. They do the bidding of Demiurgos.[11]

The earth is imperfect and flawed.[12] Human spirits were captured by Demiurgos and his Archons and placed here in this mortal existence. Hence, the human family and all spirits are captives to Demiurgos. The goal of humans is to escape the earth and ascend to a higher plane of reality to live again with the Supreme God. Earth is therefore viewed as evil; it is considered a prison for its inhabitants. This is actually similar to Buddhism, which seeks to free people from the suffering that exists in the world.[13]

The human family lived as spirits with the Supreme God before the earth was created.[14] However, due to the workings of Satan or Demiurgos, man "fell" into the material realm, and by so doing, fell into material bodies. Our spirits, according to Gnosticism, go through a process of awakening that leads them to seek to escape their material bodies (which are evil, as they were created by Satan) and ascend back to their divine nature with the other Aeons in heaven.

This awakening is called the "Gnosis," or knowledge that is a central factor in ascending back to the Supreme God. Christ, an Aeon, came to bring the gnosis and save man from the error or sin of the Creator God, Demiurgos. What's more, Gnostics adhere to the understanding that Christ and Demiurgos are brothers coming from the same mother Sophia; Christ being the eldest and Demiurgos being the younger.[15] Hence Christ representing the Supreme God came to earth to defeat his younger brother and gave this gnosis to the Apostles during his forty-day teachings after the Resurrection (which resurrection of Christ is denied by Gnostics).

Gnostics believed in polytheism or the worship of multiple gods, for each Aeon, like Christ, are gods unto themselves. The gnosis then is the knowledge of the divine origins of humanity.[16]

THE NATURE OF CHRIST

Gnostics adhere to the doctrine that God is not material because anything that is material is evil and God is not evil.

Christ then could not be mortal; he was a hologram. This belief in a non-physical Christ is often referred to as "Docetism."

The term derives from the Greek verb "dokeo", which means "to seem." Docetics maintained that Jesus had only seemed to live among men, to suffer, and to die. In reality, they said, the heavenly Christ did not come into contact with the world of matter, for that would have defiled his divine nature. . . . In fact, the doctrine of salvation was subverted into the idea that Christ was a special messenger who brought to earth secret knowledge that would allow the elect to escape this corrupt world and to make their way back to the presence of the Father.[17]

So how does this view of Christ fit into the gospel story of Jesus of Nazareth? According to most Gnostics, Christ was a spirit that temporarily entered into the body of Jesus. Through the man Jesus, Christ was able to teach the gnosis or hidden knowledge of how we can be freed from our mortal bodies, which imprisons our spirits. Gnostics believed that Jesus, being fully human, had a "soul body" instead of a "flesh body," which is what enabled him to be the host of Christ's spirit. It was at Jesus's baptism that Christ entered into the body of Jesus, which is symbolized in the Gospels by the "dove." At the crucifixion, Christ's spirit left Jesus to suffer alone and ultimately to die. Thereafter, according to Irenaeus, Christ re-entered the body of Jesus in the Garden tomb; thus culminating in the Resurrection of Jesus.[18]

In the Acts of John, a Gnostic gospel, Jesus is described as both material and spirit. Thus a docetic flavor. "One time, John indicates, he noticed that Jesus never left any footprints—literally a God striding on the earth."[19] Most important to Gnostics who do not believe in the Atonement, is Acts of John 101, where Jesus says after His Resurrection "You hear that I suffered, yet I suffered not; that I suffered not, yet I did suffer; that I was pierced, yet was I not wounded; hanged, and I was not hanged; that blood flowed from me, yet it did not flow; and in a word, those things that they say of me I did not endure, and the things that they do not say, those I suffered."[20] Consequently to Gnostics, Christ merely inhabited the body of a mortal Jesus and then when the suffering began, Christ simply vacated Jesus, leaving Jesus to suffer and die alone on the cross. The Gospel of Peter 19, another Gnostic Gospel, asserts that when Jesus was on the cross he did not say, "My God, My God, why hast thou forsaken me?" as in Mark 15:34, but instead said, "My power, O power, you have left me,"[21] meaning that Christ had left Jesus.[22]

DEIFICATION

One of the great heresies according to orthodox Christianity that was practiced by the Gnostics was actually very similar to a doctrine practiced by the Hebrew Christians; namely, that man is divine. According to a Gnostic teacher, Silvanus:

> The divine word is God, he who bears patiently with man always. He wished to produce humility in the exalted. He (Christ) [as an] exalted man became like God, not in order that he might bring God down to man, but that man might become like God.[23]

So Gnostics believed that God and Christ were an exalted form of man, and that we should try to become like them.[24]

ESOTERIC DOCTRINES

A belief in esoteric doctrines was a central tenant of the Gnostic faith.[25] They had ritual handclaps,[26] passwords,[27] prayer circles,[28] and baptisms for their dead ancestors.[29] As part of their secret knowledge, was the understanding that they could become one with Christ in substance (and thus become deified and fused with the Godhead).[30] Among their secret rites was that of eternal marriage—the philosophy that marriage would continue beyond this mortal life.[31] As will be seen, although Gnostics opposed begetting children in this life, they were assured that they would beget children after the Resurrection in this eternal marriage.[32]

Gnostics typically used John 16:12 to show that Christ had secret doctrines. In fact, "the oldest definition of the gnosis specifies that it was the knowledge imparted secretly by the Lord to the Apostles after the Resurrection."[33] During this post resurrection forty-day ministry, Christ takes the Apostles to a mountain top and gives them certain "signs and tokens" and then departs.[34]

WOMEN

Many Gnostics considered sex to be evil. In the Acts of Thecla 5–6, a life without sex is encouraged. Those who are celibate are told that they will be saved. Central to this theme is the discouragement of bearing children, which simply provides more captives to the Demuirgos.

As a result, The Acts of Thecla, have strong feministic overtones, holding that men are generally evil and women are always good. In the story, the Apostle Paul is constantly portrayed in a poor light—even allowing an important man of the city to attempt to rape Thecla. Thecla is allowed to preach and baptize herself.[35] The Apostolic Father, Tertullian, found the portrayal of Paul appalling.

An astonishing fact is that the writer of The Acts of Thecla confessed that the book was a forgery—he simply made it up.[36] Nevertheless, among the Gnostics it was an important book, for Gnostics celebrated the equality of men and women in an age where women were thought of as property, consorts, and servants to the men.

> That is why the tales of Thecla and other ascetic women were not an anomaly in the early Christian movement. They were a significant statement of an important stream of early Christianity. Here were women who refused to participate in the constraints of patriarchal society. They remained unmarried, not under the control of a husband. They were travelers, not staying at home under the authority of a paterfamilias, a father, a male head of household.[37]

This was the women's movement of the time, embodied in Gnosticism. The practice within Gnosticism prohibiting procreation continued in the Acts of Thomas 12, where the writer quotes Jesus as discouraging both marriage and child bearing. In fact, it cites Jesus as suggesting that children are sinners. This, of course, is completely at odds with the Gospels in the New Testament where Christ tells us that all should be innocent as little children.[38] Again, the writer of The Acts of Thomas also admits to it as a forgery—that Christ never actually said any of it.[39]

So why did the Gnostics believe in these forgeries?[40] It is because the Christian apocryphal texts are about a change in the traditional way of life, which is far different than the traditional family relationship. Consequently, these books were "disruptive to traditional society." The intent of the authors was to "tear apart the fabric of communal existence and split up the home." These were the new age cultists who looked forward to a life beyond this mortal sphere. They believed in denying themselves the pleasures and enjoyments of the here and now. Why? Because this mortal existence was concocted by the devil. To enjoy life is to accept the devil as your God.[41]

Why should Gnostic women avoid marriage and children?

Because Jesus taught that the world was at an end. "If this world is soon to disappear, why be attached to its pleasures? It is better to prepare for the coming Kingdom, living simply and humbly in expectation of that final day."[42] This Gnostic doctrine actually became known in later years as Pauline Christianity and formed the early basis for the doctrine of celibacy and the practice of the monks within the Hellenized Church.[43]

SALVATION

The Gnostic idea of salvation obviously has its roots in this gnosis—the knowledge that we are held here against our will and need to escape to heaven. However, suicide was not the answer for the Gnostics. That was the easy way out—cowardly. They were confronted with the "how" of the gnosis; what to do with it. One of the compelling reasons people converted to Gnosticism in the first place is that it explained not only war, oppression and injustice, but also natural disasters—floods, hurricanes, and so on. It was not the acts of the true God, but of the evil Jehovah. Yet they still needed a way to the Supreme God. For that, they used the five sacraments: baptism, anointing with oil, Eucharist, ransom, and the bridal chamber.[44] How each pertained to the escape of this world is not well understood. Two things are certain with respect to the sacraments: first, salvation is by faith alone (not works),[45] and second, the Eucharist embodied the Doctrine of Transubstantiation.[46]

NOTES

1. Ehrman, *Lost Christianities*, 174.
2. Bickmore, *Early Christianity and Mormonism: Gnostic Esoteric Rites* (Bickmore, 1997).
3. Ehrman, *Lost Christianities*, 105–109.
4. Ibid., 105.
5. Ibid., 47–55.
6. Ibid., 56.
7. Ibid., 126.
8. Petersen, *Where Have All the Prophets Gone?*, 130.
9. This belief in a Heavenly Mother, Sophia, has led many to suggest that the Gnostics worshiped the divine feminine. James Robinson, *The Gospel of Philip*, The Nag Hammadi Library in English (1978), 138; Barker, *The Great Angel*, 185. In fact, Gnostic books speak of a holy trinity consisting of Father, Mother, and Son. James Robinson, *Secret Book of John*, The Apocryphon of John, The Nag Hammadi Library in English (1978), 103.

10. Creation "Ex Nihilo" came from the Gnostic philosopher Basilides. Hatch, *The Influence of Greek Ideas and Usages upon the Christian Church*, 195–96.

11. See generally, Shelley, *Church History*, 47–55; Bently Layton, *The Gnostic Scriptures* (SCM Press, 1987), cited in http://en.wikipedia.org/wiki/Gnosticism.

12. An interesting side note is that Adam helps the Creator God in the Creation of the earth. Segal, *Two Powers in Heaven*, 253. This may explain the Gnostic belief in original sin; for Adam had allied himself with Demiurgos. Bickmore, *Restoring the Ancient Church*, chapter 4.

13. Buddhists, however, do not believe in God as the Gnostics did.

14. Doctrine of the premortal life of spirits was recognized by the Gnostics. Hans Jonas, *The Gnostic Religion*, 3rd ed. (Boston: Beacon Press, 2001), 44. In fact, Gnostics believed in a premortal council officiated by the Supreme God: "Then before the foundation of the world, when the whole multitude of the Assembly came together upon the places of the Ogdoad." Second Treatise of the Great Seth VII, 2 65.33–37 in Ehrman, *Lost Scriptures*, 82–86.

15. Bickmore, *Restoring the Ancient Church*, chapter 3 (this doctrine was regularly taught by the Bogomils).

16. Bentley Layton, *The Gnostic Scriptures* (SCM Press, 1987); James Robinson, *The Nag Hammadi Library in English* (1978); Plotinus, *The Enneads* translated by Stephen MacKenna & BS Page (Harvard University Press, 1989). See also Ehrman, *Lost Christianities*, 123–24 for an alternative Gnostic myth.

17. Brown, "Wither the Early Church," *Ensign*, Oct. 1988.

18. Ehrman, *Lost Christianities*, 125.

19. Ibid., 42

20. Ehrman, *Lost Scriptures*, 107, quoting Acts of John 101.

21. Ibid., 33 quoting Gospel of Peter 19.

22. "The gnostic liked the idea of the good God sending Christ so they thought that the Ultimate Deity sent one of his subordinate 'powers' called 'Christ' into the world to free men from the chains of matter. Christ, however, could have no real contact with matter so at the baptism of Jesus of Nazareth, or thereabouts, the Christ descended into him; then at the arrest of Jesus, or thereabouts, it withdrew. What was scourged and slain was not it." Shelley, *Church History*, 52.

23. The Teachings of Silvanus 111:5–13, in Robinson, *The Nag Hammadi Library in English*, 392.

24. Corpus Hermeicum (10.25) translated by G. R. S. Mead (2001 Blackmask Online) ("God in the heavens is an immortal man"); Apocryphon of John (14.14), Robinson, *The Nag Hammadi Library in English* (refers to God as a "Man"); Brown, *All Things Restored*, 105.

25. Jean Danielou, *The Theology of Jewish Christianity* (The Westminster Press, 1973), 365; Morton Smith, *The Secret Gospel* (Dawn Horse Press, 1981), 137.

26. Bickmore, *Restoring the Ancient Church*, chapter 6.

27. Ibid.

28. Ibid.

29. Gnostics performed baptisms for the dead of only their non-Hebrew ancestors. The Jews were a damned people. Theodoretus, *Heretical Tales*, 1:24, cited in Nibley, *Mormonism and Early Christianity*, 123, note 120.

30. Jean Doresse, *The Secret Books of the Egyptian Gnostics* (Hollis and Carter, 1960), 71; Max Pulver, *Jesus Round Dance and Crucifixion According to the Acts of St. John*, (New York, Pantheon, 1955), 173.

31. Irenaeus, Against Heresies 1:21:3, ANF, 1:346; The Gospel of Philip in Robinson, *The Nag Hammadi Library in English*, 139, 142; Danielou, *The Theology of Jewish Christianity*, 351.
32. The Gospel of Philip in Robinson, *The Nag Hammadi Library in English*, 139.
33. Nibley, *Mormonism and Early Christianity*, 15.
34. Gospel of Bartholomew 14b–15a, in E. A. Wallis Budge, Coptic Apocrypha (London: British Museum, 1913).
35. Acts of Thecla 34, 41, Ehrman, *Lost Scriptures*, 113–121.
36. Ehrman, *Lost Christianities*, 31–32.
37. Ibid., 46.
38. Matthew 18:3–4; 19:13–15.
39. Ehrman, *Lost Christianities*, 29–30.
40. Irenaeus asserts that the Gnostics forged new gospels to try to authenticate their version of the gospel. An example are the Infancy Gospels. Ibid., 205.
41. Ibid., 44.
42. Ibid., 45.
43. Ibid., 45–46.
44. Ibid., 126, 133.
45. David Bercot, *Will the Real Heretics Please Stand Up: A New Look at Today's Evangelical Church in the Light of Early Christianity* (Scroll Publishing, 1989), 73–74.
46. Hatch, *The Influence of Greek Ideas and Usages Upon the Christian Church*, 308.

CHAPTER 4

THE HELLENIZED OR PROTO-ORTHODOX CHURCH

WHO WERE THE HELLENIZED CHRISTIANS?

As the Apostle Paul proselyted to the Roman Empire, non-Jews were taught the gospel and joined the Church. They brought with them the traditions of their fathers. The strongest of these proselytes were the Greeks.

> In the realm of the mind, in letters, the arts, and in most of the sciences, it was the ancient Greeks, most educated people will concede, who walked off with nearly all the first prizes. If any people ever knew and lived life well and fully, it was the chosen spirits among the Greeks. They explored every avenue of human experience; they inquired into every possibility of broadening and improving the mind; they sought the truth as persistently and as honestly as men can ever be expected to seek; and, sounding the depths and skirting the outmost bounds of man's wisdom, came to the unanimous conclusion that the wisdom of man is as nothing.[1]

Greek philosophy was prolific and became the intellectual underpinnings of the Roman Empire.

> Although openly opposed by Jewish elements, early Christian missionaries generally found the empire a congenial place in which to

travel and preach. This was due in large measure to the Greek influence, or Hellenism, as it was called. The Greeks were anything but idle witnesses to Roman domination. Where the Romans built the roads, established the postal systems, and sought for law and order, the Greeks were a thinking, planning and philosophizing society. If the Romans were the doers, the builders, the politicians, the Greeks were the thinkers, the planners, the philosophers; if Rome conquered Greece with its armies, Greece conquered Rome with its ideas. . . . Greeks equated religion with man's efforts to understand all aspects of human existence. . . . The Greek influence had two immediate effects on Christianity, one beneficial and the other detrimental. It was beneficial in that it provided a medium through which the teachings of Jesus and his apostles could be spread rapidly: the Greek language. In addition, Christianity, as we have seen, was new, and the Greek attitude to see and to hear new things had influenced many. It was detrimental because men could not resist the temptation to embellish the Christian revelation with their own interpretations. The result was a new Christianity altogether. . . . The major problem presented to Christianity was how to keep the gospel message pure and free from the false philosophies so prevalent in the empire. In time, the Christian resistance to Greek philosophy broke down. Christianity became wedded to Greek thought, and the marriage proved to be disastrous for the once pure gospel of Jesus Christ. Christian converts educated in the philosophies of Socrates, Plato, Aristotle, and other current schools of thought found the temptation to mix their newfound faith with Greek learning too great to resist. Temples dedicated to Athena, Zeus, and Diana became, in time, centers of Christian worship.[2]

The basis for the mix of Christianity and Paganism has its center in the philosopher Plato, who lived between 424 BC and 348 BC. His mentor was Socrates and his leading student was Aristotle. He founded the Academy in Athens (the first university in the world). He composed a series of "dialogues" in which he discussed his philosophies. Plato denied the reality of the material world and his most famous philosophy is called the "Theory of Forms" in which Plato asserts that the material world as it seems to us is not the real world, but only a shadow of the real world. Physical objects and events are merely "shadows" of their ideal or perfect forms, and exist only to the extent that they imitate the perfect versions of themselves.[3] Hellenized Christians applied "Forms Theory" to their interpretation of God as a perfect being. Since

God was perfect, God could not be from the material world. God had to be from a spiritual world. Hence, Christ, the son of God, could not have been mortal either. This school of thought would eventually form the basis of what would become the Nicene Creed.

A good example of how Greek theory became Christian dogma is "Geocentrism"—the theory that the Earth is the center of the universe and thus the sun and planets revolve around the Earth. This was a Greek theory put forward by Ptolemy. The Hebrews did not believe this. However, the Geocentric theory was incorporated into the Catholic or Hellenized Church. Copernicus and Galileo were excommunicated from the Catholic Church for stating otherwise in the sixteenth and seventeenth centuries AD. Thus, Greek "Geocentrism" had been canonized by the Church.[4]

Conflict began early between Hebrew Christian and Hellenic philosophy. Paul records his debates with Greek philosophers in Acts, 1 Corinthians, and in Colossians. Notwithstanding Paul's defense of the pure faith, Christianity was ultimately Hellenized. Clement of Alexandria put it this way, "philosophy has been given to the Greeks as their own kind of Covenant, their foundation for the philosophy of Christ . . . The philosophy of the Greeks . . . contains the basic elements of that genuine and perfect knowledge which is higher than human . . . even upon those spiritual objects."[5] In sum, the Greeks melded their own philosophy with the doctrines of Christianity and declared that from such, Christianity had been made better than it had been during the meridian of time. Apparently, Jesus the Christ could only go so far in teaching the gospel without the assistance of the Greek philosophers, who improved it.

WHAT DID THE HELLENIZED CHRISTIANS BELIEVE?

NATURE OF GOD—THE HOLY TRINITY

God is "a most pure spirit, invisible, without body, parts or passions. "[6] As stated in the Nicene Creed of AD 325.

> We believe in one God, the Father Almighty, maker of all things visible and invisible; and in one Lord Jesus Christ, the Son of God, the only begotten of his Father, of the substance of the Father, God of God,

Light of Light, very God of very God, begotten, not made, being of one substance with the Father. By whom all things were made, both which be in heaven and in earth. Who for us men and for our salvation came down [from heaven] and was incarnate and was made man. He suffered and the third day he rose again, and ascended into heaven. And he shall come again to judge both the quick and the dead. And [we believe] in the Holy Ghost. And whosoever shall say that there was a time when the Son of God was not, or that before he was begotten he was not, or that he was made of things that were not, or that he is of a different substance or essence [from the Father] or that he is a creature, or subject to change or conversion—all that so say, the Catholic and Apostolic Church anathematizes them.[7]

This Creed became known to history as the doctrine of the Holy Trinity. The problem with this doctrine, however, was that "the New Testament itself is far from any doctrine of the Trinity or of a triune God who is three coequal Persons of One Nature."[8]

Christian scholars have agreed that "the formal doctrine of the Trinity as it was defined by the great church councils of the fourth and fifth centuries is not to be found in the New Testament."[9]

Christian scholar Emil Brunner commented,

When we turn to the problem of the doctrine of the Trinity, we are confronted by a peculiarly contradictory situation. On the one hand, the history of Christian theology and of dogma teaches us to regard the dogma of the Trinity as the distinctive element in the Christian idea of God, that which distinguishes it from the idea of God in Judaism and in Islam, and indeed, in all forms of rational Theism. Judaism, Islam, and rational Theism are Unitarian. On the other hand, we must honestly admit that the doctrine of the Trinity did not form part of the early Christian-New Testament message. Certainly, it cannot be denied that not only the word "Trinity," but even the explicit idea of the Trinity is absent from the apostolic witness of the faith. The doctrine of the Trinity itself, however, is not a biblical doctrine.[10]

Christian scholar Edwin Hatch further explains

It is impossible for anyone, whether he be a student of history or not, to fail to notice a difference of both form and content between the Sermon on the Mount and the Nicene Creed. The Sermon on the Mount is the promulgation of a new law of conduct; it assumes beliefs rather than formulates them; the theological conceptions which underlie it belong to the ethical rather than the speculative side of theology; metaphysics are wholly absent. The Nicene Creed is a statement partly of historical facts and partly of dogmatic inferences; the metaphysical terms which it contains would probably have been unintelligible to the first disciples; ethics have no place in it. The one belongs to a world of Syrian peasants, the other to a world of Greek philosophers. The contrast is patent. . . . The question why an ethical sermon stood in the forefront of the teaching of Jesus Christ, and a metaphysical creed in the forefront of Christianity of the fourth century, is a problem which claims investigation.[11]

So where did the doctrine of the Trinity come from in the Hellenistic Church?[12] Simply put, it came from the great Greek philosophers. Aristotle (347 BC) taught that God is

immobile, immaterial, self-existent substratum; [for] the most basic of all first principles is that nothing can be and not be at the same time. It cannot have parts, as these are limiting, and the infinite is not limited. Hence God is infinite and unlimited. The great primal body, moving on its own axis, is uncreated, indestructible and not subject to increase or diminution.[13]

Similarly, Philo, a Jewish Philosopher living in Egypt around AD 39, taught that "God is simple, absolutely one, and unmixed. He has no parts, no body, which would diminish him, therefore God is not compound. While he is older than the cosmos, he is the creator of the cosmos. He is a monad, One. Impossible to view God, all we can comprehend is His existence, everything else is beyond us."[14] It was Philo who combined Judaism with Greek philosophy at the time of Christ and helped introduce it to Christian Jews living at Alexandria, Egypt.[15]

Thus, the Nicene Creed is taken directly from Greek philosophers.[16] "Unlike Greek, Hebrew does not conceive of anything immaterial or unembodied, even in thought."[17] The Greeks believed in the contemplative and immaterial world of God. According to professor Faulconer, "I think it is not too much to say that, by itself, Greek thinking locks us out of an understanding of God as a living and acting being, handing us over to the theology of a static and immutable, in other words, dead, god."[18] Professor Faulconer continues, "I believe that most of what passes for talk about God, whether positive or negative, is talk about a god who is not the God of Israel."[19] This

Greek invasion of the Church began to make traction in the middle of the second century AD. Clement of Alexandria, Athenagoras, and Irenaeous all believed in the God of the philosophers. Hence God cannot have a body. As a result, there was a complete rejection of any notion of Hebrew anthropomorphism. The scriptures that talk of an anthropomorphic God were suppressed by the Hellenized Church as "allegorical interpretation."[20] Bishop Augustine went so far as to state "whatever there is in the word of God that cannot, when taken literally, be referred either to purity of life or soundness of doctrine, you may set down as figurative."[21] Augustine's reasoning, says Bickmore, was adopted from the Greek philosophers who viewed the Greek myths as allegories; hence by simple extrapolation, it was not a great jump to view Christian stories as mere allegories as well.

Indeed, Origen stated that not only "the Jews . . , but also some of our people, supposed that God should be understood as a man, that is, adorned with human members and human appearance. But the philosophers despise these stories as fabulous and formed in the likeness of poetic fictions."[22] Thus, even at the time of Origen, there were Christians who still believed, as the Hebrews did, in an anthropomorphic god. The fact that Hellenistic Christians did not believe in an anthropomorphic god gave rise to the total rejection of the idea of deification, which had been such a mainstay in the early Christian Church.[23] A corollary to this was the rejection of polytheism in the Hellenized Church at the Council of Constantinople in AD 381 adding to the view that subordinationism,[24] as practiced by the early Church, was heretical.[25]

As evidence of the strength of their position concerning the nature of God, orthodoxy points to John 10:30, where the Apostle John claims that Christ and His Father are one in person. Notwithstanding such an interpretation of John 10:30 by the orthodox Church, the common understanding by early Churchmen was completely different; namely, that John referred to Christ and the Father as being one in will and purpose only, not one in person.[26] This understanding is supported by scholarly research. The Greek word "one" in John 10:30 is not in the "masculine" tense, but instead it is referred to as "neuter." If it were masculine, "one" would mean oneness of person as orthodoxy claims. But it's neuter use implies a oneness of purpose, as was the historical interpretation.[27]

The Hellenized Church also uses 1 John 5:7–8 to suggest that the Father, Son, and Holy Ghost are one. However, according to Church historians, the Church changed the original wording of this scripture in the fourth century to make the language consistent with Trinitarianism. "Thus, the Trinitarian texts in the first Epistle of John, which make explicit what other texts merely hint at, originally read simply: 'There are three which bear witness, the spirit and the water and the blood, and the three are one'. . . [This] was altered in the fourth century to read: 'There are three which bear witness on earth, the spirit and the water and the blood, and these three are one in Christ Jesus; and there are three who bear witness in heaven, the Father, the Word, and the Spirit, and these three are one.'"[28] Most Bible translations omit 1 John 5:7 due to this clear lack of authenticity.[29]

> It has often been pointed out that with the Council of Nicaea Christianity had entered upon a new stage in its development. It was now officially linked with Hellenic [Greek] philosophy. Metaphysics had been brought into assist religious faith, and in an authoritative formula it had been found necessary to employ a terminology coined in paganism.[30]

According to Shirley Guthrie, "the Christian philosophers of the second century AD borrowed the ideas of Middle Platonic philosophers such as Plutarch. By doing so, they radically reshaped the Christian view of who and what, God was." Brown concludes, "The language of the doctrine is the language of the ancient church, taken not from the Bible but from classical Greek philosophy."[31]

The trouble with the Nicene Creed came not only from the Greek philosophers, but also from the peasants—the lay ministry who were confused by the creed. Said Shelley,

> Christians themselves are hard pressed to explain what they mean when they sing of the "blessed Trinity." Most are content to treat the doctrine as a piece of sublime mystery. It wasn't so in the early church. Fourth-century Christians felt a nagging restlessness about the doctrine, like scholars who have a piece of unfinished research. Three in One and One in Three, each identical and yet different? With such mysteries to disagree upon, it wasn't long before everyone was calling somebody else a heretic.[32]

THE PRIESTHOOD—THE FALLACY OF THE SUCCESSION OF THE APOSTLESHIP TO THE BISHOPS

The Hellenized Church had a strong belief in the succession of the priesthood following the martyrdom of the Apostles.[33]

> Certainly in very early sources the "successors" of the apostles are consistently depicted as the "presbyters" [priests]. In the agape [church], says the Apostolic Constitutions, the presbyters represent the apostles "as counselors of the bishop and the crown of the church, for they are the sanhedrin and council of the church."[34]

According to Ignatius, "the presbyters are the true successors of the apostles."[35] Notwithstanding Ignatius's assessment, Apostolic Father Anacletus reports that, "now the bishops occupy the place of the Lord's apostles, while the presbyters occupy that of the seventy-two disciples."[36] How do these two divergent points of view square with one another?

> It was long maintained by many that episcopus and presbyterus held one and the same office, and the theory was that the president of the college of presbyters gradually became the bishop of the entire local church. . . . When it came about that the highest office in all the church was that of bishop, it was an absolute necessity to make the office the equivalent of the apostolate in order to avoid facing the terrible alternative of admitting that the apostolic power—the whole stay and support of the Church of Christ—had been withdrawn.[37]

So it appears that bishops were local priests who had been elected by both their peers and congregations. They had never before been general authorities of the church. However, with the death of the apostles and the seventy-two elders, they became the general authorities by necessity. There was no other choice. Notwithstanding such, there continued to be a lot of consternation about this idea of successors to the Apostles. Ignatius, the bishop of Antioch, was so uncomfortable with this concept that he went so far as to admit that he was merely a bishop and not an Apostle and could not act with the authority of an Apostle.[38]

> It is impossible to dispute that the episcopate as represented in the Epistles of Ignatius is essentially a local function, the authority of which is

limited to the community in which it was exercised. Never does Ignatius appeal to his title of bishop of Antioch to give more authority to his instructions.[39]

Nibley notes, "no one viewed them [the bishops] as apostolic officers in the end of the first century."[40] Bishop Polycarp confesses he is not an Apostle either, "for neither I, nor any other such one, can come up to the wisdom of the blessed and glorious Paul. He, when among you, accurately and steadfastly taught the word of truth in the absence of those who were then alive. And when absent from you, he wrote you a letter . . . which will build you up in that faith which has been given you."[41] Even Clement distinguishes himself from the Apostles, for when discussing the office of bishop, he emphasized that "the apostles set up the bishops after the old Jewish pattern."[42] That pattern was not one of general authority as was the Apostles, but instead was the pattern of local authority.

> Consider here that all along the bishops and apostles existed side by side as contemporaries; we never hear of bishops traveling with apostles to be trained up as their successors, for the activities of the two were totally different. . . . The fact that the two offices existed as full-time functions side by side for many years without overlap shows that each was doing its own work.[43]

Notwithstanding the distinction between bishops and apostles in the early Church, the Hellenized Christians proclaimed that since the Apostles ordained bishops, these bishops had claim to apostolic authority by virtue of that ordination. This reasoning, however, wears thin in that the deacons were also ordained by the Apostles and the orthodox Church does not claim apostolic authority through them.[44]

A new ordination process was also instituted by the Hellenized Church in order to account for the fact that bishops could no longer be ordained by apostles (since all the Apostles were dead). Bishops were ordained by three other bishops. Presbyters or priests were ordained by one bishop. While bishops had the power of laying on of hands, the presbyters could baptize, but not ordain or lay on hands.[45] Mass was patterned after the order of the Jewish diaspora synagogue in that bishops preached in a manner similar to that of the elders of the Jews.[46]

The qualifications for ordination to the office of bishop were four-fold: one must be over the age of fifty, married to one wife, and have a good background in the doctrine. Being called of God as was Aaron was no longer to be a requirement of priesthood authority.[47]

The final requirement for ascension to the office of bishop was a vote of the congregation, the popular "acclamatio" from Roman tradition. Thus, there came to be rival candidates for bishop, each with their own backers who sometimes took to the streets to riot on behalf of their candidate. Clement of Rome noted on one occasion, 137 people were killed in such a riot between two rivals. The bishops became aristocrats in Roman society. And according to Duchesne, the population of each city was used to determine the prominence of the bishop's seat as compared to other bishops.[48] "Every bishop in Christendom has his office designated by the name of a city. No one doubts that the office of bishop is primarily a city office."[49] Of particular note, at a Synod in Antioch around AD 341, the Church adopted Canon 9, which officially designated the bishop of the capitol city of the province as having authority over all other bishops in the province. Thereafter, the selection of bishop changed again with the adoption of Canon 16, which provided that a vacant bishop's seat would be filled by the Synod and not simply by election of the congregation.[50]

"Rome, capital of the empire, seat of St. Peter, holy place of the apostles, became without dispute the metropolis—the mother city— of the church."[51] Hence the common practice was for the peeking order in the Church to be determined by the importance of the city where a bishop served. The more prominent the city, the more distinguished the bishop and the more influence he exercised over the other cities within his province. Hence the bishop of the capitol city of the province became a supervisor of sorts over the other bishops. Synods would be held in the capitol city and the bishop of such would naturally be the host and officiate at the meeting. It is thought that "the position Archbishop was established to distinguish the bishops in the capitol cities of provinces from the lower bishops in the province." At the "Council of Constantinople in 381, five cities were chosen as over all the provincial bishops—Rome, Antioch, Alexandria, Constantinople, and Jerusalem (for tradition only). However, it declared primacy for the bishop of Rome over all others." One of the factors generally noted for ranking the importance of a city was not only its hierarchy in the Empire, but also the exploits of the Apostles who visited the city. Hence, Rome stands supreme due to not only its position as the capitol of the Empire, but also because of the missionary journeys of Peter and Paul. Although it should be added that it was at Rome that both were murdered. "Tradition has it that Constantine (who was a pagan) founded Constantinople as the 'new Rome' and home to Christianity untouched by the paganism of Rome after having Christ appear to him in a dream. . . . How ironic that a pagan, and not the bishop of Rome, has Christ appear to him so as to found a new Christian capitol."[52]

The popularity of the Christian Church under Constantine was the result of not only the politics of Rome (being a member of the national religion was a requirement for advancement in Roman society and government), but also of the charisma of these influential city bishops. Consequently, when Rome ultimately fell, it was to these bishops that the citizenry turned for leadership and guidance. "Their courage, devotion, and enterprise are too well known to need a description or encomium at this point. But such men were not a new thing in the cities of the Mediterranean."[53] The City-state was a staple of old Rome and Greek traditions. "The world of late antiquity was a city-world; each city was an island universe, completely engrossed in its own affairs and wholly under the rule and sway of leading personalities."[54]

By the beginning of the twelfth century, Cardinals, instead of Archbishops, became the bishops of all major cities. The College of Cardinals thereafter replaced the Synods. It is this College who elects the Pope or bishop of Rome.[55]

However, there has always been a conundrum within the Church because bishops were all equal in rank. Therefore, who is to decide where there is a disagreement among equals?[56] In the end, according to bishop Eusebius, "when there were differences among the various provinces, acting as a common bishop appointed by God, he [the emperor who was not even a baptized Christian at the time] would summon synods."[57] Then at these synods, a majority rule was in order. "Number was everything—as it would not have been had the church enjoyed the leadership of a general authority."[58] So it appears that the only general authority over the church in the fourth century was a non-member, the Emperor. It is Constantine who commands. Naturally, this was after the pattern of Rome and the Roman Senate, with which the Emperor was familiar. In sum, procedurally, the synods exactly resembled the proceedings of the Senate almost down to the smallest matter.[59] Some suppose that it is these synods that truly replaced apostolic authority. However, the first synod of any kind was not held until AD 256 in Carthage. So if the Synod was to take the place of the Apostles, why did it not exist for over 150 years after the death of the Apostles?

Celibacy

The Hellenized Church considered celibacy to be a higher way of life.[60] Celibacy was part of the Monastic Ideal—the idea that there is a higher status that followers may aspire to. The church based the idea of a monastic life on the Pastor of Hermas.

The man who would be regarded as the first monk, Anthony of Koma, was born in the third century. In Luke 18:22, we read: "Now when Jesus heard these things, he said unto him, Yet lackest thou one thing: sell all that thou hast, and distribute unto the poor, and thou shalt have treasure in heaven: and come, follow me." This verse struck Anthony with great power and force. He followed the admonition of the Savior and sold his possessions and became a recluse, living in solitude in a tomb. Others followed Anthony's example. However, the monastic movement did not take off until the beginning of the fourth century when a former soldier, Pachomius, formed the first monastery.[61]

The Rule of Discipline came into existence around AD 379 and became the governing regulations of monks. In a monastic life was found a full commitment to Christ. All monks take a threefold vow of poverty, chastity, and obedience. "Thus, the true spiritual warriors tried to divest themselves of their possessions, their marital happiness, and their freedom to choose." Monasteries became centers of learning and scholarship. Most Church leaders became monks or closely aligned themselves to the monastic movement.[62]

This is not to say that the practice of the monastic life was not controversial. Martin Luther, who had been a monk, disagreed with the idea of the "two roads to God."[63]

THE GOSPEL AND GREEK PHILOSOPHY

The principles of the gospel within the Hellenized Church centered upon grace and baptism (but not by immersion),[64] although some within the Church believed that baptism was optional. No laying on of hands for the gift of the Holy Ghost was practiced.[65] This was a departure from the church of the Apostles. The shifting of doctrinal emphasis was the result of Greek philosophy pushing into the church and its culture.

> The voice of the apostles had scarcely fallen silent when the church faced the need to define the faith in terms that intelligent men could understand. A clear presentation of the gospel calls upon the powers of reason. God has made men to think so the truth advances, at times, as Christians defend the gospel against pagan arguments and the errors of professing disciples. Men can reason, however, only with the knowledge and concepts they have. In the ancient world this meant Hellenic (Greek) philosophy and pagan authors. So Christianity was forced by the needs of men and the mission of the church into the world of pagan thought.[66]

This move toward Greek philosophy was not without its dissenters. Tertullian opposed any type of reconciliation between Christian thought and Hellenistic philosophy. Shouted Tertullian,

> heresies . . . are prompted by philosophy. Valentinus was a Platonist! Marcion was a Stoic! What do Athens and Jerusalem have in common? Away with all attempts to produce a mottled Christianity of Stoic, Platonic, and dialectic composition! We have no need of curiosity reaching beyond Christ Jesus. When we believe, we need nothing further than to believe. Search that you may believe; then stop![67]

Clement of Alexandria and his student Origen are thought to be the foremost Christian scholars who attempted to blend into Christian thought the culture of the Hellenistic world. Clement's argument for using Greek philosophy was that just as the law of Moses was a schoolmaster for the Jews to lead them to Christ, so it would be that with Platonic philosophy, the Greeks would be led to Christ in a similar manner.[68] Consequently, Clement's life and ministry became yet another fork in the road of Christianity. One road stayed with the pure doctrine, while the other, the one taken by the Church through

Clement, led to a conglomeration of Greek and Christian philosophies. All of the ecumenical councils of the early Church were heavily influenced by Greek thought. In fact, none of the pronouncements of these councils would have been possible without it.[69]

> Origen's expansive mind and Clement's generous spirit have always made orthodox Christians uncomfortable. Did they go too far in the accommodation to the Hellenistic environment? Did the language and concepts of Greek philosophy invade Christian ranks and lead the original gospel into captivity? Sincere Christians raise these questions because they know that love of the world can compromise the revealed articles of faith.[70]

Greek philosophy was generally housed in various creeds. However, this is not the only reason that creeds were used in the early Hellenized Church. The battle for the soul of Christianity was being fought not just against the Hebrews, but also against the Gnostics. The idea of Apostolic succession in combating the Gnostics centered upon the argument that only churches founded by the Apostles could teach the gospel. All in all, these battles resulted in a set of creeds. Those creeds were known as "regula fidei" or "the rule of faith."[71]

According to Tertullian,

> typically included in the various formulations of the regula was belief in only one God, the creator of the world, who created everything out of nothing; belief in his Son, Jesus Christ, predicted by the prophets and born of the Virgin Mary; belief in his miraculous life, death, resurrection, and ascension; and belief in the Holy Spirit, who is present on earth until the end, when there will be a final judgment in which the righteous will be rewarded and the unrighteous condemned to eternal torment.[72]

These early creeds always had their basis in the godhead and the interpretation thereof. By the fourth century, these creeds coalesced into the now famous (or infamous depending upon one's viewpoint) Nicene Creed.

ORIGINAL SIN

The belief in original sin, that is the doctrine that little children enter into this world with the taint of Adam's sin marring their souls and prohibiting entrance into heaven, was a doctrine first espoused by Augustine, the bishop of Hippo in North Africa, in the early fifth century AD.[73] However, this doctrine was not received well in many parts of the Empire. Around AD 419, Pelagius, a British monk, was preaching in North Africa against the doctrine of original sin. He denied the concept of original sin, and instead taught that man has his own individual freedom to choose good or evil. He openly repudiated the doctrine of predestination. This drew the ire of Augustine and his belief that Adam's fall condemned all mankind and only the grace of Christ could save—man's works meant nothing to Augustine. Notwithstanding Augustine's views, the Catholic Church taught that the wicked, whose works were evil, go to hell and the faithful, whose works were righteous, go to heaven; however, those who are not perfect (which is everyone) must suffer for their sins in purgatory before passing to heaven. Christ's atoning sacrifice apparently does not shield one from the punishment for a sinful life. In AD 431, Pelagius and his followers were condemned by the General Council of the Church meeting at Ephesus and expelled from the Church.[74] It is from the origin of original sin that the doctrine of infant baptism became a necessity in the gospel.

The Resurrection

The Hellenized Church also took a dim view of a physical resurrection. Instead they believed in a spiritual resurrection only.[75] The basis of this change in doctrine from the Hebrews apparently came from an orthodox interpretation of the words of the Apostle Paul where he told the Corinthians that "flesh and blood cannot inherit the kingdom of God."[76]

The Confession: Saints and the Sale of Indulgences

According to Shelley, "when the churches granted to bishops the power to forgive sins, Catholic Christianity was complete."[77] Here was the birth of the confession in modern Christianity.

> The first to accept repentant sinners as a matter of policy was the bishop of Rome [circa 217–222]. . . . He argued that the church is like Noah's ark. In it unclean as well as clean beasts can be found. Then he

defended his actions by insisting that the church of Rome was the heir of Peter and the Lord had given keys to Peter to bind and to loose the sins of men. This marks the first time a bishop of Rome claimed this special authority.[78]

Other bishops followed suit after the disaster of AD 250. The Roman Emperor Decius was determined to rid the Empire of Christians, who he viewed as being unloyal because they would not swear allegiance to the traditional Roman Gods. He gave an imperial order at around AD 250 that all within Rome had to sacrifice to the Roman Gods. Those who refused were tortured or killed. Many Christians were tortured and denied Christ. The following year, Decius was killed in battle and the order was withdrawn. The question then arose within the Hellenized Church as to what to do with all of the Christians who had denied the faith under torture. For unlike normal sin, this was viewed as the "sin against the Holy Spirit," which according to Christ is not pardonable. The theory arose within the Church that there was a "Treasury of Merit" built up by those of unusual courage in the faith, and this Treasury could be drawn upon to save even those who had sinned against the Holy Spirit. The Treasury was filled by the acts of Saints. Thus the doctrine of Sainthood began within the Catholic Church as a way for those who confessed to be forgiven of sin.[79] The worship of Saints was officially instituted by the Catholic Church in AD 375.[80]

Shortly thereafter, in AD 431, the Church began to worship the Virgin Mary.[81] The reason for this is tied more to the battle with the Gnostics than it is to the result of the doctrine of the Treasury of Merit, although that played an important role too. To combat the Gnostics (who did not accept the virgin birth) and venerate the Virgin Mary (a sinless woman because she never had sex), Hellenized Christians forged the Proto-Gospel of James, which showed that Mary was conceived miraculously, was raised by high priests in the temple, and then given to an old widower, Joseph, in marriage to ensure that she remained a virgin and that she gave birth to Christ in a miraculous manner. It also showed that Jesus's brothers were his stepbrothers and that Mary remained a virgin throughout her life. Hence, if there was ever a Saint who had a Treasury of Merit, it was the Virgin Mary. Interestingly, this presented problems later because Church Father Jerome claimed that the brothers of Jesus in the Bible were really cousins, which is inconsistent with this forged gospel. Another forgery used to defend the Virgin Mary was the third letter to the Corinthians by Paul. There, the fake Apostle Paul responded to Gnostic charges that there was no virgin birth, that God did not create the world or humans, and that there was no resurrection of the flesh.[82]

Ultimately, this concept of the Saints and their Treasury of Merit gave rise to the Doctrine of Indulgences, which was practiced during the Middle Ages (AD 1190).[83] The Theologian Novatian (an Elder) opposed the ability of the bishops to forgive sins through this Treasury of Merit. He believed that only God could forgive sins and that the church was a society of saints. He lost his election for bishop of Rome to one Cornelius, who preached the doctrine of the Treasury of Merit and that the church was instead a society of sinners. "By a simple ceremony [sacrament of penance] the church administered forgiveness. Grace had come to terms with time," writes Shelley, "the bishop controlled the Spirit."[84] This doctrine, known as Supererogation (where the surplus good deeds of Saints can be dispensed by the Pope to others) was officially established in the thirteenth century AD.[85]

THE SACRAMENT OF THE LORD'S SUPPER AND TRANSUBSTANTIATION

Thomas Aquinas (AD 1224–1274) believed in the seven sacraments of the Catholic Church: baptism, confirmation, Lord's Supper, penance, extreme unction, marriage, and ordination.[86] However, the most important of these sacraments was the Lord's Supper. The Church taught that this sacrament was a continuation of Christ's suffering on the cross. Consequently, the bread and wine of the sacrament were believed to change miraculously into the actual flesh and blood of the Christ, a doctrine that came to be known as transubstantiation.[87]

This new doctrine of transubstantiation was officially sanctioned by the Catholic Church in AD 1215.[88]

THE DOCTRINE OF PREDESTINATION

Belief in predestination, although preached by Martin Luther, was not his original work, nor was it the original work of John Calvin, who adopted it later, but instead it was a tenant taught by the early Hellenized Church. Specifically, it was taught by Augustine, bishop of Hippo. "This dogma asserts that men do not have free will and that their fate is sealed before they ever come to earth, either to salvation or damnation, according to God's good pleasure."[89] This explains why we are born into our various circumstances in life (rich, poor, race, disabilities, and so forth). It also demonstrates God's perfect knowledge of the future.

Such a doctrine has long troubled many within the Hellenized Christian world. In comparing early Hebrew Christianity (which does not believe in predestination) and Catholicism/Protestantism (which do believe in predestination), Evangelical Christian scholar David Bercot revealed:

> From what I have observed, many—perhaps most—evangelical Christians say they believe in predestination. Yet their prayers and actions show they really don't. Others simply throw up their hands, admitting, "I don't know what I believe." On the one hand, the scriptures teach that God is patient with us, "not willing that any should perish, but that all should come to repentance" (2 Peter 3:9). But on the other hand, it says that God has "mercy on whom he will have mercy, and whom he will be hardeneth." (Romans 9:18). . . . I have wrestled with these seeming contradictory passages most of my adult life. So it was very comforting to discover that the early Christians had logical—and scripturally sound explanations for these seeming contradictions. In fact, their understandings about God's foreknowledge and man's free will are among the most reasonable I've ever heard.[90]

ESOTERIC DOCTRINES

The Hellenized Church abhorred the practice of secret doctrines, which were the mainstay of the Gnostics and looked upon with some favor by the Hebrews.

The basis of this unbelief is found in John 18:20:

> Jesus answered him, I spake openly to the world; I ever taught in the synagogue, and in the temple, whither the Jews always resort; and in secret have I said nothing.

Notwithstanding, it is somewhat unusual that prior to the fight with

Gnosticism, the Hellenized Christian Church did practice secret rites. It was the fight against the Gnostics and their belief in secret doctrines, which ultimately resulted in the Hellenized Church giving up these beliefs in secret rites to distinguish themselves. "Victory over Gnosticism thus meant the eradication of esotericism from Christian doctrine."[91] Consequently, to keep the doctrine pure, the Church denied that esoteric rites ever existed and used John 18:20 to support that.

Of course the problem with this position was made clear in the lack of information recorded about the forty days between the resurrection and ascension, in which Hebrews and Gnostics both take note of the mysteries taught. The Church needed to fill in this forty-day gap with something less mysterious than the secret rites. As a result, the Church used the forty days to explain the founding of Catholicism. "Catholic theologians especially favor it as a time for settling all doctrinal issues, establishing proper officials, and preparing the Apostles for a missionary activity which the world was to find irresistible."[92] Notwithstanding its official position against esoteric rites, such rites within the early Hellenized Church continued to exist, and in point of fact, continue to this very day.

TRADUCIANISM

The Hellenized Church believed in "traducianism," which taught that both the bodies and souls of all humans were contained in embryo within Adam, and new souls were created by the psychic copulation of the souls of the parents. Thus, when Adam's soul was tainted with sin, so were those of the entire human family—no human soul comes into the world pure.[93] This was used as one of the bases for the doctrine of original sin. Nevertheless, this secret doctrine pertaining to the premortal life of man was declared "anathema" by a council of bishops in AD 553 at Constantinople.[94] There would be other ways to support the doctrine of original sin, which did not present the dilemma of a premortal life.

DEIFICATION

The secret doctrine of deification preached by both Gnostics and Hebrews alike was repudiated early on by the Hellenized Church.

Augustine was the first to preach against deification.[95] Yet, notwith-standing the official position, the Church still preached a secret form of deification. Bishop Athanasius preached this different version—you can't be a god but you can participate in the "Divine Substance."[96]

VICARIOUS BAPTISM (BAPTISM FOR THE DEAD)

Vicarious baptism was a secret doctrine fraught with difficulties for the Church at Rome. They denied it existed of course.[97] They even condemned it at the Synod of Hippo in AD 393 and at the Third Council of Carthage in AD 397.[98] Augustine made fun of it.[99] This is what led Augustine to promote infant baptism, because without baptism in this life (or vicarious in the next life), you were damned. There was no hope. Yet the Apostle Paul definitely spoke of "baptism for the dead" to the Corinthians who were practicing it at the time. Even more problematic to the Church is that it was a doctrine that explains a nagging concern for many Hellenized Christians.

> It is cold comfort for any church to claim that the gates of hell do not prevail against its small minority, but only against those who do not belong to it; that is the very doctrine which, as we saw at the outset of this study, the Christians of an earlier day found simply unthinkable and immoral. Even the stern St. Bernard when faced with the cruel logic that would damn "good persons, who meant to be baptized but were prohibited by death," balks at it; "God forgive me!" he cries, but he cannot admit they are damned, though his church offers him no alternative.[100]

Neither does the Church have an answer for the teachings of the Apostle Peter in 1 Peter 4, when he speaks of Christ's mission to those in the afterlife. These are the very class of people whom the Church believes are damned.[101]

It is of note that while repudiating this esoteric doctrine regarding vicarious baptism, Hellenized Christians preached that the Eucharist (or Sacrament of the Lord's Supper) was given not only for the benefit of the living, but also for the benefit of the dead. According to Shelley, "it may benefit the dead as well as the living, the dead, that is, in purgatory not in hell. If offered for anyone in purgatory, it will hasten the time of his release."[102] In Pope Gregory's Dialogues, he writes about a monk who had died after being found guilty of hoarding money:

Thirty days later, I began to feel strong compassion for the deceased Justus. As I considered with deep anguish the penalty he was enduring, I thought of a way to relieve him of his suffering. With this in mind, I called Pretiosus, the Prior, and said to him sadly, "Justus has now been suffering the torments of fire for a long time and we must show him our charity by helping as much as we can to gain his release. Beginning today, offer the holy Sacrifice for his soul for thirty consecutive days. Not one of these days is to pass without a Mass being celebrated for his release." The Prior obediently accepted the instructions and left. Days passed, and being busy with other affairs, I lost count of them. Then, one night, Justus appeared to his brother Copiosus, who asked him at once why he came and how he was. "Up to this moment I was in misery," he said, "but now I am well, because this morning I was admitted to communion." Copiosus hurried to tell the monks the good news. Taking exact count of the days, they discovered that this was the thirtieth consecutive day on which Mass had been offered for him. . . . At the very moment, therefore, when they became mutually aware of what had taken place, they realized that the vision, and the completion of the thirty Masses occurred at one and the same time. They were now convinced that the brother who had died was freed from punishment through the Sacrifice of the Mass.[103]

So notwithstanding comments to the contrary, the early Hellenistic Church did believe in vicarious ordinances for the dead.

PRAYER CIRCLES

The Hellenized believers considered prayer circles as valid esoteric rites until the eighth century when their practice was outlawed as heresy at the Second Council of Nicaea in AD 787. According to Church officials at the time, prayer circles came to be regarded as "too Gnostic."[104]

THE HOLY TEMPLE

The temple had been an important feature of the Hellenized Christian world. Christ referred to the Jewish temple (Herod's temple) as his Father's House and so it was respected by the early Christian Fathers, as well as by many of the pagan faiths at Rome. It fit in well with pagan beliefs, which gave adoration to multiple deities, each of which had their own temple and worshipers. However, for the early

Christians, the Jewish temple was no more. It had been destroyed by Rome in AD 70. The Catholic Church needed a replacement and they got one in the Church of the Holy Sepulchre.[105] "The Christians of the fourth century looked upon the holy sepulchre [Constantine's New Jerusalem] in dead earnest as the legitimate successor of the temple."[106]

Soon the early bishops of the fourth century preached that salvation required a ritual pilgrimage to Jerusalem and the Holy Sepulchre once in a believer's lifetime. Ultimately, however, the Catholic Church changed its position, declaring that with the destruction of the Jewish temple, the idea of a physical temple was gone. Instead, the virtues of a temple became a symbol of the spiritual, not the physical. In order for this theory to hold, the Book of Revelation, which speaks of the restoration of the temple, had to be viewed as allegorical and not literal. Nevertheless, the pilgrimages continued to Jerusalem.[107] "The Crusades are a reminder that Christianity was never able to settle for a spiritual temple or forget the old one."[108] Look at the Knights Templar—named after the temple of Solomon, not the Holy Sepulchre. The secrets of the Knights Templar were said to be of the esoteric rituals of the Jewish temple ceremonies.

SCRIPTURES

The scriptures have and will always serve as the intellectual basis of Christianity. Since the Hellenized Church believed that the cannon of scripture was closed and the heavens with it, all knowledge and understanding about the gospel had to come through the written words of the Apostles. However, there were several problems that needed to be overcome. First, what to do with the Jewish Old Testament? The Apostles, with the exception of Paul, who was of the tribe of Benjamin, were all Jews. As such, all recognized the Torah and various other ecclesiastical scrolls as authoritative scripture. In fact, Matthew uses this scripture to show how Jesus is the Messiah. Consequently, the Old Testament, which was translated into Greek and called the Septuagint, was used as an authoritative source to prove the divinity of the man Jesus of Nazareth. What's more, this selfsame Jesus, quotes from these works as authoritative. The Son of Man did not bring a new religion to the early Jewish adherents to Christianity, he simply added new understandings to the existent Hebrew Bible. According to many Gospel scholars, the battle that ensued between orthodox Jews, who rejected Christ as the Messiah, and the Christian Jews, who accepted him as such, resulted in the need for a new set of scriptures that Christians could look upon in order to reinterpret the Hebrew Bible differently than their Jewish brothers.

> The movement toward establishing a distinctively Christian set of authorities can be seen already in the writings of the New Testament. Jesus himself, of course, presented his interpretations of Scripture as authoritative, meaning that they were to be accepted as normative for his followers, who thought of them not only as right and true but as divinely inspired. After Jesus's death, his teachings—not just his interpretations of Scripture per se, but everything he taught—were granted sacred authority by his followers.[109]

To combat this early Christian link to Jewish scripture, the Hellenized Church, beginning with Augustine, taught that many of the stories and wonders of the Old Testament were to be interpreted not as real events, but instead once again as allegories.[110]

The second scriptural problem the Hellenized Church had was the issue of the New Testament. There were many, many books of Christian scripture in the fourth century. Which would be the official cannon of the Christian world? Both the Hebrews and the Gnostics had books that supported their versions of Christianity. These books had to be destroyed. Unfortunately, many of these books were popular among the believers, to include the Hellenized believers. Of these books, the offending portions needed to be cut out. Consequently, once the Hellenized Christians won out, they changed some of the wording of the canonical books of the New Testament to rewrite history or rather, to trumpet the winning doctrine. In this way, the tale of Christian history would be told only from the point of view of the victors—the Greeks.[111]

How do we know of this battle for scriptural superiority between the Greeks, Hebrews, and Gnostics—there are no original copies of any of the New Testament books? In fact, the oldest copies, which are partial copies of some of the books, are from AD 200. More complete copies, but still partials, are available in the fourth and fifth centuries. By the Middle Ages, we have 5,400 Greek copies of all or parts of the New Testament that existed after the fourth century AD. None of the copies, however, are exactly the same. In fact, most scholars estimate that there were some two hundred thousand to as high as three hundred thousand changes to the original books of the New Testament—demonstrating the battle above referenced. Says Ehrman, "there are more differences among our manuscripts than there are words in the New Testament."[112] Couldn't all of these differences be caused by negligent scribes who made mistakes as they continually copied manuscripts (there were no photocopiers during the Dark Ages)? Some of the differences can most assuredly be allotted to honest errors and mistakes. However, not all of them can be so accounted.

An example of this is found in the Gospel of John, chapter 1, verse 18, which in the original reads, "No one has seen God at any time; but only the Son, who is in the bosom of the Father, that one has made him known." In order to amplify the view of Christ's divine character, a scribe changed the wording to reflect, "No one has seen God at any time; but the only God, who is in the bosom of the father, that one has made him known."[113]

To the winner go the spoils, and part of the spoils is to alter the scriptures to re-enforce your doctrine over any competing doctrines, in this example, re-enforcement over the Ebionites (who some would categorize as right wing Hebrew Christians).

Further demonstration of this is seen with the Acts of Peter, where Hellenized scribes show Peter battling the founder of the Gnostics, Simon Magus. "The doctrinal function of these confrontations is clear: The representative of proto-orthodoxy, Peter, eventually bishop of the Church of Rome, is shown to be superior in every way to Simon, father of the Gnostics."[114]

It was in Alexandria, Egypt, on Easter Sunday in AD 367, that bishop Athanasius named the first complete list of books, as we have them today, in the New Testament. Shortly thereafter councils in North Africa at Hippo (AD 393) and at Carthage (AD 397) published the same list.[115] The battle of scripture had ended.

What is not well known, however, is the chronology in this battle, which led to its conclusion at the end of the fourth century.

In AD 100, the only accepted cannon of scripture (a clear majority of Hebrews, Greeks, and Gnostics) were the four Gospels (Matthew, Mark,[116] Luke, and John), as well as the letters of Paul. However, by the end of the second century, the cannon had expanded to include the Book of James, 1 and 2 John, Jude, the Revelation of John, the Revelation of Peter, the Wisdom of Solomon, and the Pastor of Hermas. Excluded by the Hellenized Christians at this time was one of Paul's letters that was a favorite among the Hebrew Christians, the Book of Hebrews. Fifty years later, 1 Peter and 1 John were accepted, but the Book of James, 2 Peter, 2 and 3 John, Jude, the Pastor of Hermas, Letter of Barnabas, Teaching of Twelve Apostles, and the Gospel of the Hebrews were rejected for inclusion, along with the Book of Hebrews. At the close of the third century, the authorship of the Revelation of John became hotly disputed. Nevertheless, with the pronouncement by bishop Athanasius in the fourth century, the current cannon was complete. The Books of Hebrews, James, 2 Peter, 2 and 3 John, and Jude were ultimately accepted.[117]

LOST BOOKS[118]

However, as a result of the Hellenized list that was accepted as cannon, many of the other books of early Christianity were lost to history—they were deemed heretical and thus shunned. These books would have included 1 Clement, written in AD 95 to the Corinthians who had rebelled against their leaders and installed new ones in their place. The author does not name himself, but it is generally understood that it is Clement writing as the bishop of Rome. He chastises the Corinthians and tells them to reinstate their former leaders. This letter was used by the Church at Corinth and may be indicative of the influence of Roman bishops over the other Christian congregations in the early days of the Church following the death of the Apostles.

The Gnostics had a complete library of their gospels, many of which were unearthed in 1948 in Nag Hammadi, Egypt. These would include the Gospel of Mary Magdalene written in the late second century, the Gospel of Thomas written in the early second century, and the Gospel of Philip written in the third century. Most scholars believe that these books were hidden by Christian monks following the pronouncement of bishop Athanasius to destroy all heretical texts.

One of the Hebrew texts lost to history was entitled the Epistle of the Apostles. This text detailed the post resurrection "dialogue" between Christ and the Apostles during the forty days. Written about

AD 150, the Epistle talks about secret teachings to the Apostles that were not shared with the church at large. Gnostics used this to show that secret teachings were shared with the Apostles. However, the text is not Gnostic in nature. The Epistle testifies to the mortal Christ and his actual physical resurrection, doctrines contrary to Gnostics and supported by the Hebrews.

Clement, the bishop of Alexandria, spoke of a Secret Gospel of Mark. He proclaims that Mark wrote two gospels, one for church members and the second for the spiritual elites. This gospel was entrusted to the Christians in Alexandria, but now is lost to Christian historicity.

The Gnostic Acts of Thomas was written in the third century and provides accounts of the Apostle Thomas traveling as a missionary to India. This text has the Apostle discouraging the bearing of children, as it is a distraction to the work, a philosophy shared by the Gnostic Christians.

As noted earlier, the Hellenized Acts of Peter was written around the end of the second century and describes the "miracle contests" between Peter and Simon Magus, the founder of the Gnostics. It, however, also describes Peter's martyrdom at Rome.

The second Book of Clement was written around AD 150 and is thought of as a Hebrew text. It is not written by Clement of Rome. That is a misnomer. It is, however, a powerful sermon where the benefits of the resurrection are extolled. The Homilies of Clement are another Hebrew Christian text thought to be written in the third century. It contains twenty sermons that Clement of Rome had delivered to James the Just at Jerusalem. The text speaks of Clement's travels with Peter the Apostle. It was written from a Jewish Christian perspective and touts Peter as being superior to Paul and connects the Christian church to Jewish traditions. This is a text that adds to the claim by some that Peter and Paul were battling for supremacy in the early church, almost a parallel battle between the Hebrews and the Greeks that would continue well into the Fourth Century.

Another Gnostic text was the Treatise on the Resurrection written about AD 200. There was also a Hebrew text known as the Didache, "The Teaching." This was regarded as the first "church manual." Written between AD 110–120, it was discovered in a monastery library in Constantinople in AD 1873. It describes the "Two Paths of Life and Death" and tracts with the Sermon on the Mount. It also describes how to do ordinances, such as baptism, fasting, prayer, and the sacrament.

The Letter of Barnabas, written around AD 130, shows that the Old Testament is really a Christian text, a foreshadowing of Christ's appearance. It is very anti-Jewish, portraying Judaism as a false religion for violating God's covenant from the beginning. This text was originally included in early editions of the New Testament in the Fourth century.

One of the most controversial books of the Gnostics was that of the Secret Book of John. Written prior to AD 180, it speaks of the mother God, Sophia. If there is one book that came the closest to being chosen for the official cannon, but was not, it would be the Pastor of Hermas. Written around AD 150, it recounts the appearance of angelic beings to Hermas and provides divine revelations to him about living righteously and the process of repentance.

These lost books show that the battle for scriptural superiority was real. Many of these books are acknowledged forgeries, but all the same indicate that Gnostics, Hebrews, and Greeks had no qualms about promoting their versions of Christianity to the exclusion of the others.

THE ECUMENICAL COUNCILS OF THE HELLENIZED CHURCH

The Ecumenical Councils provide a good overview of the doctrinal progression of the Hellenized Church and will be repeated here. I have already discussed the first two Ecumenical Councils. The Third Ecumenical Council (First Council of Ephesus) was held in AD 431, wherein the Virgin Mary was canonized. The Fourth Ecumenical Council (Second Council of Ephesus), held in AD 449, officially rejected Nestorianism (Gnosticism). The Fifth Ecumenical Council (Council of Chalcedon) in AD 451 was a council, like Nicaea's, that would forever change the Church. It rejected monophysitism (Christ was both divine and human) and adopted the Chalcedonian Creed (Christ has two natures, one is human and the other is divine). However, what this council is most famous for (or infamous depending upon the sect you speak with) is the split of the Eastern Orthodox Church from the Catholic Church. It was here that the bishop of Alexandria (Pope of the Eastern Church) was excommunicated and the Roman Catholic

Church pronounced the primacy of the bishop of Rome, as the one and only Pope of Christendom. It had been the Eastern Orthodox Church belief that the Roman Catholic Pope was not superior to other bishops, but merely acted like an older brother to the other bishops. The Eastern Orthodoxy adhered to the principle that the Christian Church should be governed by a collegiality of bishops, not by the Pope. By AD 500, the Church had instituted the practice of convents and the nunnery.[119]

The Sixth Ecumenical Council (Second Council of Constantinople) held in AD 553 condemned Arianism, monophysitism, and nestorianism again, while the Seventh Ecumenical Council (Third Council of Constantinople) in AD 680–81, re-emphasized that Christ has dual natures: both human and divine. It was around this same time period in Emerita (around AD 666) that Canon 16 of the Catholic Church was adopted, which allowed bishops to keep one-third of all contributions in their congregations for their own personal wealth.[120] The Eighth Ecumenical Council (Second Council of Nicaea) in AD 787, restored the veneration of icons, which was as important to the Eastern Orthodox Church as the Virgin Mary was to the Roman Catholic Church. The Fourth Council of Constantinople (AD 869–70) continued the on-going battle between the Catholic and Eastern Orthodox Churches. At this council, the Eastern Orthodox Patriarch Photios I of Constantinople was deposed. This council is accepted by Roman Catholics, but not by Eastern Orthodox who view the Fourth Council of Constantinople to be in AD 879–80 and restored Photios I and condemned any who did not support the Nicene Creed. By AD 1090, the Church had established the use of the Rosary.[121]

The First Lateran Council (AD 1123) redefined how bishops would thereafter ordain, taking that power away from the Holy Roman Emperor (as it had been previously vested in the Byzantine Emperor and before that in the Roman Emperor) and gave that power to the Church and the Pope. The Second Council of the Lateran (AD 1139) was the Church's response to attacks on its clerics and made the punishment of such excommunication. The Third Council of the Lateran (AD 1179) was an historic change in Church government. Previously, all bishops elected the Pope. However, after this council, only Cardinals would elect the Pope.[122]

The Fourth Council of the Lateran (AD 1215) gave official credence to the Doctrine of Transubstantiation, which holds that the Eucharist is the actual blood and flesh of Jesus Christ. This council also re-emphasized again that the Pope was the leader of Christianity and had primacy over all bishops and cardinals. Speaking of the cardinals, at the First Council of Lyon (AD 1245), the cardinals were first authorized to wear red hats. Then in AD 1274 at the Second Council of Lyon, tithing was mandated in order to fund the high costs of the crusades. Additionally, the Conclave procedures to elect Popes were officially adopted. It was at the Council of Vienne (AD 1311–12) that the Knights Templar were disbanded and the Council of Constance (AD 1414–18) resolved the dispute between the French and Italians over the papacy. The Church provided for the Seven Sacraments at the Council of Basel, Ferrara and Florence in AD 1431–45. Bending to the criticisms of the Church during the Reformation, the Church first initiated reforms in AD 1512–1517 at the Fifth Council of the Lateran. This was followed by the Council of Trent (AD 1545–63) in direct response to Calvinism and Lutheranism.[123]

At the First Vatican Council (AD 1870), for the first time, the Pope was declared to be infallible. Also that Council empowered the Pope to make decisions on dogma and matters of faith unilaterally and without the consent of the Church or church councils.[124] It had been shortly prior to this (around AD 1854) that the Church had adopted the Doctrine of the Immaculate Conception.[125]

The most recent council was that of the Second Vatican Council (AD 1962–65). That council emphasized the importance of reconciliation with other Christian churches. This was part of a plan toward modernization of the Church. The council also altered Mass so as to be less mystical and read in languages other than Latin. Mass was for the common man and needed to be more understandable. This council took a step back from the infallibility of the Pope and gave bishops more authority to consult with the Pope. These changes gave rise to the belief among Catholics that they could now disagree with the Pope and they did so on issues from contraception to divorce.[126]

NOTES

1. Hugh Nibley, *The World and the Prophets* (Salt Lake City, Deseret Book: 1974), 1.
2. *The Life and Teachings of Jesus and His Apostles*, 2d. Ed. (The Church of Jesus Christ of Latter-day Saints: Salt Lake City, UT, 1978), 232–233.
3. http://en.wikipedia.org/wiki/Plato.
4. Daniel W. Graham & James L. Siebach, "Philosophy and Early Christianity" (FARMS, vol. 11, Issue 2, 1999), 210–220, cited in http://en.wikipedia.org/wiki/Hellenic_philosophy_and_Christianity.
5. Clement, Stromata, 6.8, ANF, 2:494–96.
6. Westminster Confession of Faith, *Creeds of the Churches—A Reader in Christian Doctrine from the Bible to the Present* (John Knox Press, 1982), 197.
7. Nicene Creed (AD 325), NPNF, 2:14:3.
8. William J. Hill, *The Three-Personed God* (Washington, D.C.: The Catholic University of America Press, 1982), 27.
9. P. Achtemeier, Editor, *Harper's Bible Dictionary* (San Francisco: Harper and Row, 1985), 1099; *New Testament Theology* (Grand Rapids, MI: Zondervan, 1967), 1:84. See also R. L. Richard, "Trinity, Holy," in *New Catholic Encyclopedia*, 15 vols. (New York: McGraw-Hill, 1967), 14:295 (The New Catholic Encyclopedia purports that Trinitarianism is an invention of the fourth century AD).
10. Emil Brunner, *The Christian Doctrine of God* (Philadelphia: Westminster Press, 1949), 205, 236. See also Father Charles Curran, "Creative Fidelity: Keeping the Religion a Living Tradition," *Sunstone* (July 1987) ("We went through the problem of appropriating the word in the fourth, fifth, and sixth centuries with the great trinitarian and Christalogical councils where we finally came to the conclusion of three persons in God and two natures in Jesus. Many people at the time said, 'Well, you can't say that because those words aren't in the scriptures." That's right, they aren't in the scriptures, they are borrowed from Greek philosophy.')
11. Petersen, "What has Athens to do with Jerusalem?: Apostasy and Restoration in the Big Picture"(FAIR Conference, 1999), quoting Edwin Hatch, *The Influence of Greek Ideas on Christianity* (Smith, 1970), 1.
12. "My friend and colleague Stephen D. Ricks likes to imagine an updated version of Matthew 16:13–17 in which Jesus, questioning his disciples, encounters a theologically more savvy Peter than the one depicted in scripture:

    He saith unto them, But whom say ye that I am?

    And Simon Peter answered and said, "Thou art the ground of all being, of whom no positive attribute may be predicated. Thou art the focus of our ultimate concern, transcending both existence and non-existence, ontologically one with the Father and the Holy Spirit in a manner that neither confuses the persons nor divides the substance.

    And Jesus answered and said unto him, "What?"

    Petersen, "What has Athens to do with Jerusalem?: Apostasy and Restoration in the Big Picture," (FAIR Conference, 1999).
13. Barry Bickmore, "The God of the Philosophers" (BYU, October 23, 2009).
14. Ibid.
15. Ibid.
16. Bickmore, *Restoring the Ancient Church*, chapter 3; Petersen, "What has Athens to do with Jerusalem?: Apostasy and Restoration in the Big Picture."
17. Bickmore, *Restoring the Ancient Church*, chapter 3, quoting Faulconer, Scripture

Study: Tools and Suggestions (FARMS 1999), 137.

18. Ibid., 150–151, quoting Faulconer.

19. Ibid., 136–37, quoting Faulconer.

20. "The mainstream Christian doctrine of God is nowhere attested in the Bible, and appears in Christian writings by the mid-second century. The definition of God as an indivisible, simple, immaterial, unique, and eternally unchangeable spirit essence appears to derive from the Greek philosophical schools popular during the period. Some Christian writers frankly admitted this correspondence, and in fact promoted the doctrine as a ready defense against the attacks of pagan critics. Around the turn of the third century, Tertullian wrote, 'whatever attributes therefore you require as worthy of God, must be found in the Father, who is invisible and unapproachable, and placid, and (so to speak) the God of the philosophers.'" Bickmore, "Doctrinal Trends in Early Christianity and the Strength of the Mormon Position" (FARMS 2001).

21. Augustine, On Christian Doctrine, 3:10, NPNF, 1:2:560.

22. Origen, Homilies on Genesis and Exodus, Genesis 3:1, Ronald E. Heine, *The Fathers of the Church*, vol. 71 (Washington, DC: The Catholic University of America Press, 1982).

23. Basil of Caesarea, On the Holy Spirit, 45, NPNF, 2:08.

24. "The notion that in the Trinity one Person may be the font or source of being or Godhead for another lingered on to be a cause of friction and controversy between the East and the West, and still persists today. The main thesis of these lectures, I have said, is that the act of faith required for acceptance of the doctrine of the Trinity is faith that the Divine unity is a dynamic unity actively unifying in the one divine life the lives of the three divine persons. I now wish to add that in this unity there is no room for any trace of subordinationism, and that the thought of the Father as the source or fount of God-head is a relic of pre-Christian theology which has not fully assimilated the Christian revelation." Leonard Hodgson, *Doctrine of the Trinity* (London: Nisbet, 1944), 102.

25. Bickmore, *Restoring Ancient Church*, chapter 3.

26. Raymond E. Brown, *The Gospel According to John I–XII* (Garden City, New York: Doubleday, 1966), 403, 407.

27. Ibid.

28. Paul Johnson, *A History of Christianity* (New York: Touchstone, 1976), 26–27.

29. Confraternity of Christian Doctrine, *The New American Bible* (World Bible Publishers, Iowa Falls, 1991), 1363; *New American Standard Bible* (La Habra, CA: The Lockman Foundation); New Revised Standard Version (Division of Christian Education of the National Council of the Churches of Christ in the United States of America, 1995).

30. JWC Wand, *A History of the Early Church to AD 500* (Routledge 1994), 159–160. See also Hatch, *The Influence of Greek Ideas and Usages upon the Christian Church*, 350 ("A large part of what are sometimes called Christian doctrines, and many usages which have prevailed and continue to prevail in the Christian Church, are in reality Greek theories and Greek usages changed in form and colour by the influence of primitive Christianity, but in their essence Greek still").

31. Brown, *All Things Restored*, 14, quoting Shirley Guthrie, *Christian Doctrine: Teachings of the Christian Church* (CLC Press 1968), 92.

32. Shelley, *Church History*, 99.

33. Tertullian, *Prescription Against Heretics* 32, ANF, 3:258.

34. Nibley, *Apostles and Bishops in Early Christianity*, 14.

35. Ibid., 17, quoting Ignatius.

36. Anacletus, Epistola, 3.1, cited in Nibley, *Apostles and Bishops in Early Christianity*, 18.

37. Nibley, *Apostles and Bishops in Early Christianity*, 18–19, 23.

38. Ignatius, Epistola, and Philadelphenses, 4, ANF, 1:81.

39. Jean Reville, "Etudes sur les Origines de l'Episcopat: La Valeur du Temoignage d'Ignace d'Antioche," *Revue de l'Histoire des Religions* 21 (1890), 284, cited in Nibley, *Apostles and Bishops in Early Christianity*, 26.

40. Nibley, *Apostles and Bishops in Early Christianity*, 27.

41. Ibid., 28 quoting Polycarp, Epistola ad Philippenses 3.2.

42. Nibley, *Apostles and Bishops in Early Christianity*, 29.

43. Ibid., 29.

44. Ibid., chapter 1.

45. Ibid., 68.

46. Ibid., chapter 1.

47. Ibid.

48. Ibid., chapter 1.

49. Ibid., 83.

50. Nibley, *Apostles and Bishops in Early Christianity*, 124–132, citing to Hefele, Histoire des Conciles d'Apres les Documents Originaux.

51. Duchesne, Origines, 14–15, cited in Nibley, *Apostles and Bishops in Early Christianity*, 84.

52. Nibley, *Apostles and Bishops in Early Christianity*, at 85, 89, 90, 96, 97.

53. Ibid., 74.

54. Ibid., 75.

55. Nibley, *Apostles and Bishops in Early Christianity*, 173–75, citing Constitutio de Sede Apostolica Vacante.

56. Nibley, *Apostles and Bishops in Early Christianity*, 104.

57. Eusebius, Vita Constantini, 1.44, cited in Nibley, *Apostles and Bishops in Early Christianity*, 204.

58. Nibley, *Apostles and Bishops in Early Christianity*, 104.

59. Ibid., 135–36.

60. David Hunter, *Marriage in the Early Church* (Fortress Press, 1992), 16.

61. Shelley, *Church History*, 118–20, 123.

62. Ibid.

63. Ibid., 117.

64. Didache 7, in Ehrman, *Lost Scriptures,* 211–18; Everett Ferguson, *Encyclopedia of Early Christianity* (Garland Publishing, 1990), 133.

65. Bickmore, *Restoring the Ancient Church*, chapter 4.

66. Shelley, *Church History*, 78.

67. Ibid., 79, quoting Tertullian.

68. Ibid., 80, 82.

69. Ibid., 82.

70. Ibid., 86–87.

71. Ehrman, *Lost Christianities*, 193–94.

72. Ibid., 194, quoting Tertullian.

73. Bickmore, *Restoring the Ancient Church*, chapter 4. Robert O'Connell, *The Origin of the Soul in St. Augustine's Later Works*, (Fordham University Press, 1987), 233.

See also Origen, *Commentary on Romans* cited in Bammel CP, *Adam in Origen* (Cambridge: CUP 1989).

74. Shelley, *Church History*, 129–30, 203.
75. Leo Rosten, *Religions of America* (Simon & Schuster, 1975), 205.
76. 1 Corinthians 15:44, 15:50.
77. Shelley, *Church History*, 69
78. Ibid., 74.
79. Ibid., 75–76.
80. Thomas Keith Marston, *Missionary Pal* (Salt Lake City, UT: Publishers Press, 1987), 96.
81. Ibid.
82. Ehrman, *Lost Christianities*, 207–211.
83. Ibid., 207–210.
84. Ibid., 77.
85. Marston, *Missionary Pal*, 97.
86. Shelley, *Church History*, 202.
87. Ibid.
88. Marston, *Missionary Pal*, 97.
89. Petersen, *Where Have All the Prophets Gone?*, 161.
90. Petersen, *Where Have all the Prophets Gone?*, 163–64, quoting Bercot, *Will the Real Heretics Please Stand Up: A New Look at Today's Evangelical Church in the Light of Early Christianity*, 100.
91. Stroumsa, *Hidden Wisdom*, 6, 39, 157.
92. Nibley, *Mormonism and Early Christianity*, 20.
93. Bickmore, *Restoring the Ancient Church*, chapter 4, quoting Wagner, *After the Apostles*, 194.
94. Brown, *All Things Restored*, 118.
95. Bickmore, *Restoring the Ancient Church*, chapter 3.
96. Davies, *The Early Christian Church*, 192.
97. Halley, *Halley's Bible Handbook* (Zondervan Publishing House, 1961), 600.
98. Brown, *All Things Restored*, 94.
99. Augustine, *Against Julian the Pelagian,* 57, cited in Nibley, *Mormonism and Early Christianity*, 142.
100. Nibley, *Mormonism and Early Christianity*, 144–45.
101. Ibid., 145.
102. Shelley, *Church History*, 171.
103. Ibid., quoting Pope Gregory's Dialogues.
104. Johannes D. Mansi, Sacrorum Conciliorum Nova et Amplissima Collectio, 54 vols. (Graz:Akademischer Verlag, 1960), 13:169–75.
105. Nibley, *Mormonism and Early Christianity*, 356, citing Jerome.
106. Ibid.
107. Ibid., chapter 9.
108. Ibid., 408.
109. Ehrman, *Lost Christianities*, 232–233.
110. Shelley, *Church History*, 126.
111. Ehrman, *Lost Christianities*, 217–223.
112. Ibid., 217–221.
113. Ibid.
114. Ibid., 212.

115. Shelley, *Church History*, 66.
116. The Gospel of Mark was written by John Mark, the son of a prominent family in the Church at Jerusalem. He was a missionary companion of Paul and Barnabas on their first missionary journey. He was at Rome with Peter where is he reported to have written his Gospel with the help of Peter.
117. Shelley, *Church History*, 67.
118. Ehrman, *Lost Scriptures* (Ehrman provides a complete explanation of the lost books of Christianity).
119. Marsden, *Missionary Pal*.
120. Nibley, *Apostles and Bishops in Early Christianity*, 124–132, citing to Hefele, Histoire des Conciles d'Apres les Documents Originaux.
121. Marsden, *Missionary Pal*.
122. Ibid.
123. Catholic Encyclopedia: The 21 Ecumenical Councils; Marsden, *Missionary Pal*.
124. Shelley, *Church History*, 362.
125. Marsden, *Missionary Pal*.
126. Shelley, *Church History*, 457–459, 454.

CHAPTER 5

THE BATTLE FOR ORTHODOXY

According to Shelley,

> Under the leadership of the apostles the fledgling movement maintained its unity by two special ceremonies [covenants] that kept the reality of Jesus's death and resurrection at the center of the fellowship. The first, baptism, was familiar to them because most of the early disciples had followed the ministry of John the Baptist. . . . The second ceremony, the Lord's Supper, as it was soon called, looked back to Jesus's betrayal and death and found in the events of Calvary and the empty tomb evidence of the "new covenant" promised by the prophet Jeremiah. Jesus's death and the new life in the Spirit were symbolized and sealed to the congregation of disciples in their drinking from the cup and eating the consecrated bread. This simple meal renewed their covenant with God and with one another.[1]

Hence, a new disciple of Christ took upon himself the covenant of baptism, committing himself to a life based upon the teachings of Christ. This new covenant was renewed thereafter during the sacrament of the Lord's Supper. This emphasis on covenants by the early Church is not new. In fact, the reliance upon covenants is very old. So what is a covenant? A covenant is a two-way promise between God and man. If man does X, God will do Y. One of the most important covenants of the Old Testament was between Jehovah and the

THE HEBREW ROOTS OF MORMONISM

patriarch Abraham. Abraham passed on this covenant to his descendants, the children of Israel, who in turn passed it on to their descendants. Hence, Judah passed the covenant to the Jews. This covenant formed the basis for much of the Old Testament books that tell the story of Abraham's descendants and their ancient worship of Jehovah. An important component of the Abrahamic covenant was the promise that the Savior or Messiah would come through Abraham's lineage. Consequently, "Christians believed that Jesus of Nazareth was God's promised Messiah, who established a new covenant with his new people, the church. So the New Testament stands for the books telling the story of Jesus Christ and the birth of [His] church." The Bible, therefore, is compromised of "two portions: the Old Testament, which the early Christians claimed—along with the Jews—and the New Testament, which the early Christians produced—in spite of the Jews. [What] the Old Testament promised [the old covenant]; the New Testament fulfilled [the new covenant]."[2] The battle for orthodoxy within the Church has its underpinnings in these covenants.

After the murder of James the Just in AD 62 and the finishing of the Jewish temple in AD 66, the Jews revolted against Rome, resulting in the destruction of the temple in AD 70. Shelley states that this marked the end of the Apostolic Church—as all of the Apostles were dead or presumed dead, as in the case of the Apostle John.[3]

Around AD 70, approximately 7 percent of the Roman Empire was of Hebrew descent. Therefore, there were synagogues in most cities within the Empire. Christian missionaries, who many thought to be spreading a sect of Judaism, would be invited to these synagogues to speak. It is there that they were able to spread the gospel first to the Jews, and then to the Gentiles in the area.[4] States Shelley,

> after the fall of Jerusalem in AD 70, the center of the Christian movement moved north and eventually west. The second home of the church was Antioch of Syria [Antioch was the third largest city in the Empire] . . . Moving west from Antioch, the next city of note would be Ephesus.[5]

The Governor of the province of Ephesus noted in a contemporaneous letter to the Emperor Trajan in AD 112 of the spread of Christianity in the area. According to one scholar, Adolf Harnack, by

AD 250, Rome had a population of thirty thousand Christians. The churches in the metropolitan areas soon assumed the leadership of the church, with Rome being the foremost. Alexandria, the second largest city in the Empire, also had a sizeable Christian population, due in many respects to its sizeable Jewish population in the second century. However, Alexandria was still heavily influenced by Greek philosophy.[6]

> Throughout the first three centuries the majority of believers were simple, humble people—slaves, women, traders, and soldiers. Perhaps this is due to the fact that most in the population were in this class. . . . By the end of the second century the new faith was on its way to becoming the most forceful and compelling movement within the empire. Many people with the keenest minds of the day were becoming followers of Christ.[7]

As has been discussed, the Church appeared to begin breaking up into various factions early on after the death of the Apostles; the main factions being the Hebrews, Greeks, and Gnostics. Much of the differences between these factions had to do with how they viewed the new covenant that Jesus had made with His followers. The Hebrews believed that the covenant relationship would lead to godhood, deification. The Greeks believed that the covenant relationship would lead to a place called "Heaven," where man could rest from all his labors. The Gnostics believed that the covenant relationship would lead to the "gnosis" and an escape from this mortal world. Simultaneously, pagan ideas were intermingling with the pure doctrines of Christ as new adherents brought with them their cultural traditions. Said Shelley,

> in the second half of the second century a change was coming over the church. The days of enthusiasm were passing and the days of ecclesiasticism were arriving. The church was no longer a place where the Spirit of prophecy could be heard. More and more people were joining the church, but the distinction between church and [the] world was fading. The church was becoming secularized; it was coming to terms with heathen thought and culture and philosophy. The way of the cross was no longer rough and steep.[8]

This is not to say that there were only three factions. In fact, there were many more than three. As the Christian Church expanded, so did the number of offshoots.

Marcion

We have already briefly discussed Marcion and his connection to the Gnostics. However, his movement was unique and is worth repeating in much more detail here. If you will remember, Marcion was born in AD 100 around the Black Sea. He loved the writings of Paul and interpreted those to mean that the law of Moses was evil. Thus the God of the Hebrews, Jehovah, was evil, while the God of Jesus was good. Christ came into the world to save the people from the vengeful God, Jehovah. Notwithstanding his devotion to Christianity, Marcion rejected that Jesus was the Messiah. This was only natural since Marcion had to admit that Jesus would have to have been born into a world created by Jehovah, and this would be inconsistent with his theory—evil cannot create good. Consequently, Marcion believed, as did the Gnostics, that Jesus was a hologram. He wasn't really human, but just appeared to be such.[9]

This would make Marcion a doestist.[10] "The word [diest] comes from a Greek verb, 'to seem.' Some bright theologian has suggested we call it Seemism. The title comes from their teaching that Christ was not really a man, he was a spectral appearance. He only 'seemed' to suffer for man's sins since we all know divine phantoms are incapable of dying."[11]

> The God of the deists has sometimes been called the watchmaker God. God created the world as a watchmaker makes a watch, and then wound it up and let it run. Since God was a perfect "watchmaker," there was no need of his interfering with the world later. Hence the deists rejected anything that seemed to be an interference of God with the world, such as miracles or a special revelation through the Bible. The deists believed that their religion was the original religion of man. From it had come, by distortion, all other religions. These distortions were the work of priests who concocted the theologies, myths, and doctrines of the various religions to enhance their own power. The most influential propagandist for deism was Voltaire (1694–1778), who personified the skepticism of the French Enlightenment. Voltaire once said, "if a God did not exist, it would be necessary to invent one."[12]

Marcion's book entitled *The Antitheses* is a commentary on the Bible where Marcion demonstrates that Jehovah is a different God than the God of the New Testament, the God of Jesus. Marcion portrayed

Jehovah as a wrathful God who punished people, while Jesus's God is one of love and forgiveness. Notice that to Marcion, Jesus is not God. Marcion points out that the Apostles, who were Jewish, did not fully comprehend Jesus. That is why Jesus appeared to Paul and converted him to teach the true gospel, because the other Apostles could not be trusted. It was Marcion who put together one of the first Bibles—his included the letters from Paul (in which any references to the Old Testament were edited out) and the Gospel of Luke (which was a literary gospel written to the world at large).[13]

Marcion lived at Rome and tried to convert people to his brand of Christianity. However, he was unsuccessful and relocated to Asia Minor. It is there that Marcionism spread like wildfire and became a very popular Christian sect in Asia with its headquarters at Edessa in Syria.[14]

> As the North African lawyer Tertullian put it, Paul had become the apostle of the heretics! Of course, Marcion had to misinterpret Paul to make the apostle fit his beliefs, but that didn't make the churches' problem any less real: how could they accept Paul's letters as God's word without endorsing Marcionite teaching? In the end Paul meant too much to the church to dismiss him because of Marcion's extreme views. The Apostle's letters were too well known and too widely used to discard. The Church chose, instead, to restore the Pastorals and the letters of the other Apostles and to link all the letters to the four Gospels by using the Book of Acts as the bridge. While the church treasured the grace of God preached by Paul, it realized that jettisoning the Old Testament was suicidal. Does the New Covenant make sense without the Old? . . . If Marcion, a heretic, nudged the churches into thinking about forming a New Testament, another troublemaker, Montanus, forced the churches into thinking about closing it.[15]

MONTANUS

Another offshoot of Hellenized Christianity was Montanus. He preached a re-interpretation of the doctrines through modern revelation. Montanus appeared in Asia Minor about AD 156 to 172. His doctrine was one of the first to emphasize the separation of church and state. He enlisted the help of two prophetesses, Prisca and Maximilla. Through these prophetesses, Montanus preached a new gospel message, different from the original doctrines taught by the Apostles. Since these new doctrines came through direct revelation from God, they superseded the old doctrines. According to Montanus, the gospel should no longer center on Christ. It should move beyond that. Obviously, this was of great concern to the Hellenized Christians. Montanus, however, went even further in insisting that disobedience to these new doctrines was tantamount to blasphemy against the Holy Ghost.

> In the face of this challenge how could the church keep the gospel central? It had to make all later Christian worship, teaching, and life center in Christ and the apostolic witness. Free utterances of the Spirit would not guarantee that; Montanism was making this clear. The best way to make the original apostolic gospel basic was to set apart the apostolic writings as uniquely authoritative. This would require all later faith and action to be judged in the light of that central message. It was not that the church had ceased to believe in the power of the Holy Spirit. The difference was that in the first days the Holy Spirit had enabled men to write the sacred books of the Christian faith; in the later days the Holy Spirit enabled men to understand, to interpret, and to apply what had been written.[16]

However, now out of fear of these newfound revelations taught by Montanus, the Church flinched and closed the canon of scripture. To the bishops, this was thought to be their only logical choice. The gospel message needed to be fixed in stone and unchangeable. The idea of modern revelation would jeopardize all of that by suggesting that God could simply change His mind and His doctrines. Additionally, the hierarchy of the Church would be jeopardized if an outsider could usurp the local bishop and ascend higher by declaring a new revelation from God. The downside, however, was that revelation, which Christ built His church upon as a foundation, was dead. How would the Church survive without one of its building blocks?

THE RISE OF ARIANISM

Arius of Alexandria, Egypt, was a presbyter (elder) who lived from approximately AD 250 to AD 336. Arius had been a student of the canonized Catholic theologian Lucian of Antioch. Arius taught that God the Father, who was un-begotten and eternal, is the creator of the world. Further, he taught that the Father is a separate and distinct being from Jesus Christ, who was begotten by the Father and is a lesser being than the Father. Thus, Arius taught the Hebrew doctrine of "subordinationism"—that is that Christ and His Father are both divine, but that there is a hierarchy to that divinity. Christ was begotten or created by the Father. Thus Christ had a beginning and is subordinate to the Father.[17]

As the basis for this teaching, Arius quoted 1 Corinthians 8:5–6.[18]

> For though there be many that are called gods, whether in heaven or in earth, (as there be gods many, and lords many,) But to us there is but one God, the Father, of whom are all things, and we in him; and one Lord Jesus Christ, by whom are all things, and we by him.

In a letter from Arius to Eusebius of Nicomedia, Arius confides:

> Some of them say that the Son is an eructation, others that he is a production, others that he is also un-begotten. These are impieties to which we cannot listen, even though the heretics threaten us with a thousand deaths. But we say and believe and have taught, and do teach, that the Son is not un-begotten, nor in any way part of the un-begotten; and that he does not derive his subsistence from any matter; but that by his own will and counsel he has subsisted before time and before ages as perfect God, only begotten and unchangeable, and that before he was begotten, or created, or purposed, or established, he was not. For he was not un-begotten. We are persecuted, because we say that the Son has a beginning, but that God is without beginning.[19]

At one point, Arius wrote to Constantine the Great, the Emperor of Rome, and in many respects, the head of the Church:

> We believe in one God, the Father, all-sovereign; and in the Lord Jesus Christ his only-begotten Son, who came into existence from him before all ages, God the Word, through whom all things in the heavens and on earth came into existence, who came down and assumed flesh and suffered, rose and went up into the heavens and comes again to judge the living and dead. And in the Holy Spirit and in the resurrection of the flesh and in the life of the future age and in the kingdom of heaven.[20]

Arius also preached that both the Father and Christ together created the Holy Spirit or Holy Ghost, who is lesser than the Christ in the same manner as Christ is lesser than the Father. Hence, to Arius there is "only one true God," who is God the Father.

Arius's teachings were very influential in the major educational centers throughout Alexandria in Egypt. He published his teachings in a book entitled the "Thalia." In AD 321, Horius of Cordoba convened a synod (group of bishops) in Alexandria to investigate Arianism.[21] The results of this synod, which declared Arianism a heresy, provided the spark that led Emperor Constantine I to convene the first ecumenical council at Nicaea in present day Turkey.[22]

CONSTANTINE THE GREAT

Constantine the Great was an evil man. "He had his eldest son Crispus executed . . . and his wife Fausta locked in an overheated steam room and poached to death!"[23]

In AD 312 Constantine accepted the Christian faith (although he was never baptized until his death) and called an end to its persecution in AD 313 with the "Edict of Milan." Constantine saw in Christianity a religion that could bind his empire together.

> It was Constantine who ordered a large body of Christian leaders to meet at Nicaea in order to take a vote upon what would come to be the officially accepted doctrine of the nature of God (now known as the Nicene Creed). It was Constantine who oversaw the contentious debate and the taking of a vote to settle a religious controversy regarding the Godhead. It was Constantine who issued an edict that branded the losers of the vote with an extremely bad reputation. It was Constantine who decreed that books written by the losers of the vote were to be burned, and anyone found possessing them put to death. It was Constantine who pronounced banishment upon those Christian leaders who would not subscribe themselves to the dogmas of the Nicene Creed.[24]

Thus, Constantine was the de facto leader of the Christian Church. Notwithstanding the fact that he was not a baptized Christian (at least not until his death), Constantine ultimately decided what should or should not be the doctrine. Says Shelley,

> Constantine ruled Christian bishops as he did his civil servants and demanded unconditional obedience to official pronouncements, even when they interfered with purely church matters. There were also the masses who now streamed into the officially favored church. Prior to Constantine's conversion, the church consisted of convinced believers. Now many came who were politically ambitious, religiously disinterested, and still half-rooted in paganism. This threatened to produce not

only shallowness and permeation by pagan superstitions but also the secularization and misuse of religion for political purposes.[25]

THE COUNCIL OF NICAEA

The debate over Arianism gave rise to the first ecumenical council of the Church, the Council of Nicaea. The question to be answered was of great import. Although Arius was not a Hebrew Christian, his plight became the plight of the Hebrews. The answer to the question that Arius posed was the fork in the road between the Hebrews and the Greeks. The differences between Hebrew and Hellenized Christianity had been simmering for centuries, and now it was to be reconciled. One faction would become the orthodox; the other, a heresy. Although the Catholic Church of today denies any real debate over the nature of Christ, "there is evidence that very widely differing views of the nature of Christ were held by Christian believers in the Early Church. . . . There is some irony in that the Roman Catholic Church canonized Lucian of Antioch as a brilliant and talented early Christian leader and martyr, although Lucian taught a very similar form of what would later be called Arianism. Arius was a student of Lucian's private academy in Antioch."[26]

According to most scholars, the Council of Nicaea was the first church-wide leadership council since the Jerusalem Council in AD 44 when Peter proclaimed that the gospel would be preached to the Gentiles.[27] This council was presided over by Alexander of Alexandria, Egypt, and Horius of Cordova, who had convened the original Synod that had convicted Arius.[28]

Constantine invited all eighteen hundred bishops in the Church to attend from all over the Roman Empire. However, only 250–318 actually attended. Of those bishops present, the majority were from the Eastern part of the Roman Empire. The overall mix of bishops at the conference represented both the then majority view of Hebrew Christianity, as well as the minority view of the Greeks. The Gnostics were not represented.[29]

The Hebrew Christians were led by Eustathius of Antioch, and Macarius of Jerusalem.[30] Alexander of Alexandria led the Eastern contingent of Hellenized Christians. Eusebius of Caesarea,[31] the famed

Christian historian and bishop, was also present and was a strong supporter of Arius.[32] As were at least twenty-two other Eastern bishops who were of a Hebrew Christian persuasion.[33] It should be noted that Eusebius, a Hebrew Christian originally from Palestine, had previously proposed a creed that was consistent with Arius's beliefs in the Father and Son as two distinct persons and that was acceptable to the Council of Antioch in AD 264–268, although not without argument. Thus, strictly speaking, Arius was not the heretic; rather, he was preaching the orthodox doctrine of subordination, a doctrine, however, of considerable debate between the Greeks and the Hebrews in the third and fourth centuries.[34]

The Western contingent of the Hellenized Christians of the Roman Empire were represented by Horius of Cordoba (Spain), Marcus of Clabria from Italia (Italy), Cecilian of Carthage from Africa, Nicasius of Dijon from Gaul (France) and Domnus of Stridon from the Danube.[35] These bishops were entirely from the Greek persuasion.

Accompanying the Hellenized bishop Alexander was a young Deacon, Athanasius of Alexandria. Surprisingly, the Pope or bishop of Rome, Silvester I, did not attend. Constantine made an appearance at the Council as an observer, but did not vote, although he exercised enormous power over the bishops. The Council lasted for an entire month. In the end, Arianism was almost unanimously condemned as a heresy.[36]

The results of the Council became known to history as the "Nicene Creed," which was probably authored by Horius of Cordoba. What is surprising is that most bishops throughout the Empire agreed more with Arius, than with Horius. So why did Horius's position hold sway at Nicaea? Two reasons: First, Arius's teachings were branded erroneously by Horius as Gnostic. Although Gnostics did believe in a form of subordinationism, that was not the subordinationism taught by Arius. Suspicions are that Horius intentionally misrepresented Arius's teachings as Gnostic in order to trick the Hebrews into a corner; for once the issue became one of Gnosticism versus orthodoxy, the Hebrews were trapped. Both Hebrew and Greek bishops alike viewed Gnosticism as heretical and wanted to distance themselves from that sect of Christianity. The Hebrews were in a catch twenty-two; on one hand, they couldn't support Arius without supporting Gnosticism, and on the other hand, they couldn't support Horius without surrendering one of their principal doctrines. Second, they did not want to fall out of favor with the Emperor, whose closest "confidant" was Horius, the defacto leader of the Roman Christian world.[37] Although Horius and Alexander were the official presiding officers over the Council, Alexander's place was more of a formality. It was Horius who was the real leader of the council. Ultimately, the Hebrew bishops negotiated with Horius. They agreed upon language in the Nicene Creed. Eusebius opposed the settlement, as the agreed upon language amounted to legalese that provided enough wiggle room for the Hebrews to avoid a conflict with their doctrines. But, as will be discussed, the Hebrews were double-crossed by Horius.[38]

So how did it all happen? According to Petersen, at the Council of Nicaea, the bishops divided into three camps: those in support of Arius, those in support of Athanasius (the deacon turned voice of the Hellenized Christian bishops), and the Homoeousianists (who embraced the Hebrew Christian position of three divine persons united in will). The Homoeousianists were the majority view but were poorly organized. Athanasius was supported by Constantine and his advisor, bishop Horius of Cordova. Petersen asserts that in order to win the support of the Homoeousianists, bishop Horius agreed to a compromise in language within the Creed. In describing Christ's nature, the Creed would allow for Christ to be of a "similar substance," instead of the "same substance" as God the Father. By allowing this wordsmithing, both the Hellenized and Hebrew Christians could claim victory. Ultimately, this became the reason why so many of the eastern Hebrew Christian bishops went along with the Creed. However, once they realized that the Creed was being interpreted to mean that Christ and God the Father were *homoousios* (one substance) and not *homoiousios* (like or similar substance), they became concerned. So much so that Athanasius and Horius agreed to modify the language in the Creed to ensure that everyone understood that the majority viewpoint of the Hebrews was still valid. However, "due to the negligence of a scribe" the modifications were never placed in the Creed. Many scholars now believe that the scribe was instructed by Horius not to make the modification. As a result, the Hebrew Christian bishop's majority view, the one espoused by Eusebius, became heretical.[39]

The minority view had prevailed. Immediately following the Council, and believed to be on the recommendation of the winning side (bishop Horius), Emperor Constantine exiled and excommunicated all who refused to endorse the Nicene Creed. Constantine's edict did more than simply exile; he ordered the confiscation of all property and the killing of all heretics in the Church.[40] Arius's book, the *Thalia*, was to be confiscated and burned.[41] Those bishops who would not accept the Nicene Creed had their lives spared but were excommunicated and exiled.[42]

H. A. Drake, professor of history at the University of California, calls the Hellenized Christians, "militant Christians" and asks: "Why did the militant wing prevail?" He answers that the "militant wing of the once broad Church of Christianity prevailed because . . . it was the first to acquire access to the coercive apparatus of the state"—Constantine.[43] Horius had successfully used his relationship with Constantine to foist on all Christianity his own personal views of God. The Council of Nicaea was a *fait compli*—neither Arius, nor the Hebrew bishops had a chance. Horius had already made the decision before the Council had begun, and he used the young Athanasius to do his bidding and the power of the State to ensure compliance by the other bishops.

There were at least twenty other cannons adopted at the Council. Among these were ordination of a bishop by three other bishops and confirmation by the congregation; bishops of Alexandria and Rome were given authority over the other bishops; and the bishop of Jerusalem became more of an honorary position than one with any authority in the Church.[44]

Surprisingly, Emperor Constantine, a non-member, not only called the Council, but used the power of Rome (the State) to enforce the creed. Arius was exiled. Arianism, however, continued to spread and was not completely extinguished until the eighth century AD.[45]

Athanasius of Alexandria, who succeeded Alexander as bishop of Alexandria, soon became the most vocal opponent of the exiled Arius. However, allies of Arius quickly gained favor with Constantine and convinced him to have Athanasius deposed and banished in AD 335 at the First Synod of Tyre. Athanasius became the convenient scapegoat; his usefulness to Horius was at an end. The following year, Arius's banishment was ended by Constantine, but Arius died before he could return to Alexandria. It is reported that by his life's end, Constantine had become sympathetic to Arianism.[46]

Not surprisingly, after the Council of Nicaea and Constantine's change of heart, many Eastern (Hebrew) bishops openly began to oppose the Nicene Creed. By AD 337, Eusebius who was on the side of Arius at the Council of Nicaea, became a close friend to Constantine and his son, Constantius II. Thereafter, he was made bishop of Constantinople and led the fight to reverse the Nicene Creed. When Constantine died, his son, Constantius II became Emperor of Rome that same year. Due to the influence of Eusebius, Constantius became increasingly sympathetic to some of the Arians and, as a result, overturned the Nicene Creed during his reign. It was Constantius who removed Pope Liberius in AD 355 because Liberius refused to distance himself from the Nicene Creed. Constantius then installed a pro-Arian Antipope Felix II. However, Constantius's support of Arianism was not to true Arianism, but rather it was to a philosophy called "semi-Arian," in that he opposed the Nicene Creed but did not fully accept the idea that the Son was subordinate to the Father. Hence, even he continued to persecute the true Arians. During this time period (AD 340–360), there were fourteen synods held to discuss the issue, leading one "pagan observer, Ammianus Marcellinus, to comment sarcastically, 'The highways were covered with galloping bishops.'"[47]

The dispute over Arianism and Hebrew Christianity would end temporarily in AD 361 when the next Roman Emperor, Julian, got out of the business of directing Church activities. Julian was a devout pagan, not a Christian at all.[48] The next Emperor, Valens, reinstituted the policies of Constantius II and backed the Arians.[49]

In AD 378 Emperor Valens died in the Battle of Adrianople and by February AD 381, an edict was published by the new Caesar, Theodosius I, requiring anew adherence to the Nicene Creed at the Second Ecumenical Counsel in Constantinople in AD 381. That ended the issue in the Empire—Theodosius I had the Eastern bishops swear fealty to the Nicene Creed.[50] As noted earlier, the modification or *iota* was never made, to the chagrin of the Hebrew Christians and to the delight of the Hellenized Christians.[51] Catholic theologians insist that the scribe was inspired by the Holy Spirit not to insert the modification.[52]

In sum,

> after Nicaea . . . first Constantine and then his successors stepped in again and again to banish this churchman or exile that one. Control of church offices too often depended on control of the emperor's favor. . . . As a result, the imperial power was forever ordering bishops into banishment and almost as often bringing them back again when some new group of ecclesiastical advisers got the upper hand in the palace.[53]

By AD 390, the battle for supremacy within the Christian Church was at an end. Hellenized Christianity prevailed over the Hebrews, who now and in the future would be the heretics.[54]

> The outcome of these internecine Christian battles was significant. The group that emerged as victorious and declared itself orthodox determined the shape of Christianity for posterity—determining its internal structure, writing its creeds, and compiling its revered texts into a sacred canon of Scripture. Had things turned out otherwise, not just the Christian Church but all of history would have been quite different.[55]

German scholar Walter Bauer has asserted that the Greek Christians won out because the battle was not just over ideology, but power to control the Church. The Greeks, who principally became what would be known to modern history as the Roman Catholic Christians, were numerous and effluent. They were at the center of the Empire, its heart, and knew how to wield influence to gain power and predominance. The writings of 1 Clement clearly demonstrate the influence even early on of the Roman congregation. According to those writings, Clement, the bishop of Rome, sought to intervene in a dispute at the Church in Corinth. Seventy years after the end of that dispute, Clement and his book had become authoritative scripture at Corinth according to the Corinthian bishop Dionysius. What's more, according to this same bishop Dionysius, the Church at Rome had been sending financial aid to Christian communities throughout the Empire. Hence, Rome was intervening both ecclesiastically and financially. In sum, Rome was buying loyalty.[56]

According to Nibley,

the letters in Patrologiae Latinae 13:583–88 show that in the West and in the East the Arian controversy was merely an aspect of the great struggle for episcopal priority. It is not a contest between theologians but between bishops, and the issue is not doctrine but power. It is only proper that in every case it is the emperor alone who is responsible for the final decision and solution, and that bishop is strongest who has the emperor's ear.[57]

While scholars stress the importance of what occurred at Nicaea, Orthodox writers suggest that the Council of Nicaea was not a big deal at all. They say that Arius was merely a popular priest in Alexandria who was disciplined by the bishop of Alexandria for preaching heresy. They assert that Arius did not believe that Jesus was God because God cannot have a beginning and therefore Arius's assertion that the Father created the Son would deem Jesus as no more than a messenger from the Father. A great messenger, but not God. However, this orthodox position appears completely at odds with what Arius actually taught and some would suggest it is merely an attempt by Orthodox writers to smear Arius and whitewash history.

In short, Arius was a Christian priest in Egypt. He preached the doctrine of subordination; namely, that Christ was subordinate to the Father. That was a basic doctrine of the Hebrew Christians and was the orthodoxy from at least the AD 264 Council of Antioch. Arius's focus on this doctrine drew the ire of the bishop of Alexandria who deemed Arius a Gnostic. The Gnostics were a major problem to both the Hebrew and Hellenistic Christians. Horius of Cordova (present day Spain) called a synod to condemn Arius. The sympathy among Hebrew Christian bishops was as a result of Arius being falsely painted as a Gnostic. However, no one wanted to side with the Gnostics and that, together with no one wanting to be on the opposite side of the Emperor, sealed Arius's fate. What is interesting is that the Gnostics did not even believe in Arius' form of subordinationism. Instead, they believed in a plurality of Gods, similar to the pagan Greek and Roman myths. Nevertheless, since the Hebrews also believed in some form of plurality, it was easy to target Arius by confusing the two within the Hellenistic Church. The Arius question was then used as an excuse for the Emperor Constantine, under the influence of Horius, to call the Council of Nicaea and use it as a forum to get rid of the Gnostics and build a foundation for the downfall of the Hebrews. None of the Hebrews would defend Arius at the Council.[58] Hence, by not standing up for their beliefs, which were being improperly targeted, the Hebrews sowed the seeds to their own destruction. Once Arius's teachings were deemed a heresy, then a major tenant of the Hebrew variant of Christianity was equally viewed as heresy.

One would think that after the Council of Nicaea, the issue would be settled. However, there were continued murmurings about the doctrine of the trinity; for even "trinitarian scholars recognize[d] that 'no doctrine of the Trinity in the Nicene sense is present in the New Testament.' Likewise, 'there is no doctrine of the Trinity in the strict sense in the Apostolic Fathers,' meaning that no one, before AD 150, attempted to define more than what was already provided in the text of the Old Testament, the Gospels, and the apostolic writings."[59]

ERASING HISTORY

Complicating matters for the Hellenized Church was the absence of a consensus set of scriptures. It was not until the Council of Carthage in AD 397 that the books of the New Testament would be published. Before that, each congregation had their own set of books and epistles that they used. The standardized set that we have today came as a result of this Council at Carthage. The list of books in the present Bible are, therefore, the books and epistles that were agreed to by consensus at the Council. As has been discussed previously, there are many other books, both Hebrew, Greek, and Gnostic, that were used extensively by many congregations, but were ultimately not included in the Bible.

> It may be worth reflecting on what was both lost and gained when these books [those not included in the Bible], and the Christian perspectives they represented, disappeared from sight. One thing that was lost, of course, was the great diversity of the early centuries of Christianity. . . . Virtually all forms of modern Christianity, whether they acknowledge it or not, go back to one form of Christianity that emerged as victorious from the conflicts of the second and third centuries. This one form of Christianity decided what was the "correct" Christian perspective; it determined who could exercise authority over Christian belief and practice; and it determined what forms of Christianity would be marginalized, set aside, destroyed.[60]

Scholar Bart Ehrman, quoting German scholar Walter Bauer (AD 1877–1960) and his work *Orthodoxy and Heresy in Earliest Christianity* (1934), asserts that "in some regions of ancient Christendom, what later came to be labeled 'heresy' was in fact the earliest and principal form of Christianity." There were "views later deemed heretical [which] coexisted with views that came to be embraced by the church as a whole, with most believers not drawing hard and fast lines of demarcation between them." There was no "orthodoxy" in the "second and third centuries. . . . Beliefs that later came to be accepted as orthodox or heretical were competing interpretations of Christianity, and the groups that held them were scattered throughout the empire."[61] To the victor go the spoils, and in this case, the victors knew that any controversies over doctrine needed to be quashed quickly and forgotten. The same strategy took place with the Spanish Conquistadors and the Dominican monks who accompanied them to the new world. There they found the great Mayan Empire and culture. The monks were vigilant in converting the Maya to Christianity and then to make it difficult for the Maya to return to their historic religious traditions, the monks destroyed the ancient codices—the history of the Maya was gone. There would be nothing for the Maya to return to if their experiment with Christianity failed.

> The wide diversity of early Christianity may be seen in the theological beliefs embraced by people who understood themselves to be followers of Jesus. In the second and third centuries there were, of course, Christians who believed in one God. But there were others who insisted that there were two. Some said there were thirty. Others claimed there were 365. . . . In the second and third centuries there were Christians who believed that the Jewish Scripture (the Christian "Old Testament") was inspired by the one true God. Others believed it was inspired by the God of the Jews, who was not the one true God. Others believed it was inspired by an evil deity. Others believed it was not inspired. . . . How could some of these views even be considered Christian? Or to put the question differently, how could people who considered themselves Christian hold such views?[62]

If instead of the Hellenized Christians, a differing Christian sect with its alternative views of Christianity, had won out, the current orthodoxy would never have come to fruition. There would never have been the need for a Nicene Creed because the doctrine of the Trinity would never have been developed. Christology, which purports to define Christ in terms of two natures, being both divine and human (the "God-man"), and the controversial creeds it spawned starting at the Council of Chalcedon in AD 451, would never have happened. In sum, the significance of the victory of one form of Christianity over another cannot be marginalized. It would have transformed all western civilization. In short, it was the most significant event in Christianity outside of the Resurrection itself.[63]

> As with political and broad cultural conflicts, the winners in battles for religious supremacy rarely publicize their opponent's true views. What if they were found to be persuasive? It is far better to put a spin on things oneself, to show how absurd the opposition's ideas are, how problematic, how dangerous. All is fair in love and war, and religious domination is nothing if not love and war. And so, in early Christianity, . . . most of the writings of the losing sides in the battles for dominance were destroyed, forgotten, or simply not reproduced for posterity—in one way or another lost.[64]

ROME AND THE PAPACY

The First Vatican Council (AD 1870) established that Jesus Christ was the founder and architect of the papacy. He began it with the Apostle Peter. Thereafter, the bishop of Rome, as Peter's successor, became the supreme authority of the Hellenized or Catholic Church.[65] There are many reasons behind this. First, Rome was the capitol of the Empire. Second, the Christians worshipping at Rome were the wealthiest and most politically connected of the Christian congregations. Third, the congregation at Rome was the largest in size. By the third century AD, it had 30,000 adherents and 150 priests. Fourth, the belief that Peter and Paul organized the church at Rome and thereafter designated the bishop at Rome as the successor to the Apostles drew much in terms of persuasive power. Tradition in the church has long held that churches established by the Apostles possessed spiritual superiority over those that were not. Consequently, although all bishops were equal in power, those from cities where the Apostles established the church held sway over those that did not.

The organization of the early Church further developed by following the organizational structure of the Empire. The hierarchy of authority became based upon location, size, and the ecclesiastical history of the area. So pastors in small communities reported to those in larger communities that reported to one of the four major seats of Christian power and then ultimately to Rome itself. When disagreements in doctrine occurred, the Emperor would convene church councils of bishops or Synods to resolve the issue, with the edicts of those councils becoming church dogma.[66]

At a synod in Rome in AD 382, the first mention was made that the Roman Church took primacy over all other Christian churches.[67] Pope Leo came to the papacy around AD 440, making him the "Supreme Head of all Christendom." It was Leo who laid out the theological foundation for papal authority. Leo reasoned that since (1) Christ in Matthew 16:18–19 pronounced that the foundation of His church would rest upon Peter, the "Rock," (2) Peter was the leader over the Church, he being the Apostle that Christ left in charge of the Church, and (3) Peter was the first bishop of Rome, all subsequent bishops of Rome would naturally be successors to Peter's authority over the entire Church.[68] Historically, Pope Leo also became the defacto leader of the Roman Empire when it was subsequently attacked by Attila the Hun (AD 452) and then the Vandals (AD 455). It was Leo who negotiated the settlements. He then took on the "old heathen title, *Pontifex Maximus*, the high priest of religion throughout the empire."[69] This is why the Pope is called the Pontiff.

THE WORSHIP OF ICONS AND SAINTS

In the sixth century, following in the footsteps of the pagans, the Church began the development of a system of icons, as well as the worship of monastic holy men or saints. Unfortunately, the Church did not realize that by empowering these icons and saints, they narrowed the focus of worship by the general masses from more spiritual matters to local shrines and figures.[70]

The results paralleled idolatry. The icon of the Roman Emperor was as revered as the Emperor himself. There was no distinguishing between the icon and the subject for which it stood. Imperial icons appeared in army camps, courthouses, and prominent places in the major cities, as well as on coins.[71] The Christian shrines and saints did likewise.

The rationale behind religious icons was not truly ferreted out until the eighth century when John Mansour (AKA "John of Damascus"), the last of the Apostolic Fathers, taught that an icon or image was not of the same substance of the original. Rather, it was a mere copy of the original. It was an imitation whose only real purpose was to act as a reminder to the original. If this appears close to Plato's forms theory of Greek philosophy, it is.[72]

Soon, Saints (icons) appeared to help those converted to Christianity with many of their daily tasks. According to Shelley "many tales circulated about the miraculous powers of the Saints. The story was told of two beggars, one lame, the other blind. They happened to be caught in a procession carrying the relics of St. Martin and were fearful lest they be cured and so deprived of their alms. The one who could see but not walk mounted the shoulders of the one who could walk but not see, and they hurried to get beyond the range of the Saint's miraculous powers, but poor fellows, they failed to make it."[73]

THE COLLEGE OF CARDINALS

For the first thousand years of the Church, a bishop or abbot was given two investitures of power, one spiritual and the other feudal or civil. The former was bestowed by the Church, while the latter was given by the king or head of the government. Notwithstanding such, the Church came to be dominated by civil government who controlled the appointment of church officials much in the same way that Constantine had in the fourth century. A movement arose (Cluniac reformers) to free the church from such secular interference. The result was the creation in AD 1059 of the College of Cardinals who, instead of the Roman Emperor, would elect the Pope.[74] With the College of Cardinals in place, the battle for supremacy was complete; just as the Hellenized Church had beaten the Hebrews in the fourth century, they had finally beaten Rome by the eleventh century.

NOTES

1. Shelley, *Church History*, 17.
2. Ibid., 58.
3. Ibid., 22–23.
4. Ibid., 29.
5. Ibid., 29–30.

156

6. Ibid., 30–32.
7. Ibid., 33.
8. Ibid., 64–65.
9. Ehrman, *Lost Christianities*, 103–109.
10. Ibid., 105.
11. Shelley, *Church History*, 50.
12. Ibid., 316–317.
13. Ehrman, *Lost Christianities*, 103–109.
14. Ibid., 103–109, 174.
15. Shelley, *Church History*, 63–64.
16. Ibid., 65–66.
17. Letter of Auxentius at http://ccat.sas.upenn.edu/jod/texts/auxentius.trans.html cited in http://en.wikipedia.org/wiki/Arianism.
18. Ibid.
19. Edward Peters, *Heresy and Authority in Medieval Europe*, (University of Pennsylvania Press, 1980), 41, cited in Arianism, Wikipedia.
20. Petersen, *Where Have all the Prophets Gone?*, 157 quoting Arius and Euzoius, Letter of the Presbyter Arius and Euzoius to the Emperor Constantine, in William Rusch, *Trinitarian Controversy* (Philadelphia: Fortress Press, 1980),61.
21. Warren H. Carroll, *The Building of Christendom* vol. 2 (2004), 10.
22. Ibid.
23. Brown, *All Things Restored*.
24. Ibid., 16.
25. Shelley, *Church History*, 96.
26. http://en.wikipedia.org/wiki/Arianism.
27. Carroll, *The Building of Christendom*, 11.
28. http://en.wikipedia.org/wiki/First_Council_of_Nicaea.
29. Ibid.
30. Aziz S. Atiya, *The Coptic Encyclopedia* (New York: Macmillan Publishing 1991).
31. Eusebius of Caesarea believed in three divine persons "separate in rank and glory but united in harmony of will." Bickmore, *Restoring the Ancient Church*, chapter 3.
32. Ibid.
33. Carroll, *The Building of Christendom*, 11.
34. In the third Century, a splinter Christian sect known as the Theodotians maintained that "Jesus was a mere man, born of the sexual union of Joseph and Mary, but chosen by God at his baptism to be the savior of the world." Ehrman, *The Lost Christiantities*, 152–53. They began to have a substantial following at Rome, appealing to the intellectuals of the Church. Ibid., 153. "But if Christ is God, and God is God—how can there be only one God? This caused huge problems for the proto-orthodox in Rome and elsewhere, bringing considerable dissension in their ranks." Ibid., 153. This led to a split within church leadership circles and gave rise to the first Anti-Pope, Hippolytus. Hippolytus claimed that the Roman bishops Zephyrinus (AD 198–217) and Callistus (AD 217–22) looked upon Christ as too divine, giving rise to the allegation that they were polytheists. These bishops of Rome dealt with the problem by suggesting that Christ was God the Father who had come into the world that he had created. Ibid., 153. Thus asserting their monotheism. However, this didn't sit well with many Hebrew Christians, including Apostolic Father Tertullian. He "raised a number of biblical and logical objections: Why does the Scripture say that God sent his son, rather than that he sent himself?

How can anyone be his own father? To whom is Jesus speaking when he prays? How can Jesus talk about going to his Father in John 20:17 if he is the Father? And is it really conceivable that God the Father was killed?" Ibid., 153. On the other side of the debate, the bishops of Rome and their followers asserted that to believe otherwise would make one a polytheist, not a monotheist. There can be only one God. Ibid., 154. Thus, the battle raged in the third century.

Origen (AD 185–254) attempted to quell the controversy. He theorized that God the Father created all things, including Christ. Hence, Christ was subordinate to the Father. Yet Origen also asserted that Christ was the creation closest to the Father and was of one mind with the Father. Thusly, Christ was a distinct person from the Father, but one in unity or substance with the Father. "Christ is God's Word made flesh." Ehrman, *Lost Christianities*, 155.

35. Ibid.
36. See Ehrman, *Lost Christianities*, 135–157; Shelley, *Church History*, 100–107; First Council of Nicaea, Wikipedia.
37. Nibley, *Apostles and Bishops in Early Christianity*, 143.
38. Ibid.
39. Petersen, *Where Have all the Prophets Gone?*, 157–59.
40. Brown, *All Things Restored*, 27, note 43.
41. Socrates Church History, chapter IX in NPNF.
42. http://en.wikipedia.org/wiki/First_Council_of_Nicaea. This use of political power to punish dissidents, heretics, and other opponents of the Church became common place. At the Synod of Toledo in AD 638, the Church published Canon 3 banishing all Jews from living in Spain. Shortly thereafter, in AD 694, the Church held another Synod at Toledo, this time enacting Canon 8, which forbid Jews from practicing their religion. In fact, the practice began that Jewish children were taken from their parents at seven years of age and re-educated as Christians. Nibley, *Apostles and Bishops in Early Christianity*, 124–132 citing to Hefele, Histoire des Conciles d'Apres les Documents Originaux.
43. Shelley, *Church History*, 103, quoting H. A. Drake.
44. Nicene and Post-Nicene Fathers, Series II, vol. XIV, The Canons of the 318 Holy Fathers Assembled in the City of Nice, in Bithynia.
45. http://en.wikipedia.org/wiki/Arianism.
46. Ibid.
47. http://en.wikipedia.org/wiki/Arianism.
48. According to Shelley, the fight over Arianism continued for fifty years. A group calling themselves Semi-Arians attempted to reconcile to the Church by asserting that Christ was not God, but was "like God." Hence, not fully subordinate. Shelley comments that this would have made two Gods and would be in his mind a form of paganism. The Semi-Arians did not succeed. Shelley, *Church History*, 103–04.
49. http://en.wikipedia.org/wiki/Arianism.
50. Athanasius of Alexandria, *History of the Arians*; Mark Belletini, *Arius in the Mirror: The Alexandrian Dissent and How it is Reflected in Modern Unitarian Universalist Practice and Discourse*; Rusch, *The Trinitarian Controversy*; John Henry Newman, *Arians of the Fourth Century* (London: Longmans, Green, 1908); Rowan Williams, *Arius: Heresy and Tradition*, rev. ed. (Grand Rapids, Michigan: Eerdmans, 2001).
51. Although the Nicene Creed has been orthodoxy since AD 325, the Hebrew concept of the nature of God was so well entrenched in Christian tradition that to this very day, the vast majority of mainstream Christians do not believe or practice the

tenants of the Creed, but rather still hold to the Hebrew Christian idea of a God who can best be described as a caring and wise grandfather.

52. Petersen, *Where Have all the Prophets Gone?*, 159.

53. Shelley, *Church History*, 103.

54. For an alternative history of the Council of Nicaea, see Shelley, *Church History*, 101–102.

55. Ehrman, *Lost Christianities,* 159.

56. Ibid., 175.

57. Nibley, *Mormonism and Early Christianity,* 109 citing to Sozomen, Historia Ecclesiastica 1.17.

58. "The victory over Arianism achieved at the Council was really a victory snatched by the superior energy and decision of a small minority with the aid of half-hearted allies. The majority did not like the business at all, and strongly disapproved of the introduction into the Creed . . . of new and untraditional and unscriptural terms." James Bethune-Baker, *An Introduction to the Early History of Christian Doctrine*, 8th ed. (London: Methuen, 1949), 171.

59. Petersen, *Where Have all the Prophets Gone?*, 154.

60. Ehrman, *Lost Christianities*, 4

61. Ibid., 173, quoting Walter Bauer, *Orthodoxy and Heresy in Early Christianity*.

62. Ehrman, *Lost Christianities*, 2–3.

63. Ehrman, *Lost Christianities* 6; Shelley, *Church History*, 108, 114–15.

64. Ehrman, *Lost Christianities* 47.

65. Shelley, *Church History*, 133.

66. Ibid., 133–35.

67. Ibid., 136.

68. Ibid., 137.

69. Ibid., 140.

70. Shelley, *Church History*, 147

71. Ibid.

72. Ibid., 148–49.

73. Ibid., 158.

74. Ibid., 180–181.

CHAPTER 6

THE SURVIVAL OF
THE GNOSTICS

Following the Council of Nicaea, "almost immediately after
coming into imperial favour the formerly persecuted Church
Fathers [Hellenized Church] themselves turned persecu-
tors. They sought to impose their control on Christians throughout
the Roman Empire, to suppress schisms and to distill a universally
agreed doctrine out of the great variety of teachings that the faith
had previously encompassed. Those with different variations of belief
were 'systematically hunted down and obliterated over the next three
centuries.'"[1]

The Hellenized Church sought to destroy all gnostic books.
Notwithstanding such, a group in upper Egypt hid away some of their
scriptures in large earthen-ware jars. These were found in December
1945 near the town of Nag Hammadi.[2] It is from the study of these
texts that most of our knowledge of the Gnostic doctrines come.

THE MESSALIANS

The Messalians (literally, the "Praying People") were "Christian
Gnostics whose origins can be traced back to the city of Edessa in the
mid-fourth century AD and who survived in coherent form until late
enough in the seventh century to overlap with . . . the first Paulicians."

According to heterodox Gnostic legends, they were said to have been the keepers of a secret tradition and of secret books.[3] The Bogomils, as we shall discuss, may have had access to these secret books. Messalians preached that there was but one God, who had two sons, Satan (the elder) and Jesus (the younger). Satan rebelled and he created the world, which is an evil place.[4] As Gnostics, they sought release from the evil prison of physical bodies.[5] Ultimately, the Messalians were targeted for extinction by the Catholic Church in AD 390.[6]

The Paulicians

Although branded as heresy, the Gnostics did not fade away into history. Instead, they kept resurfacing—as a harbinger of the past and a thorn in the side of the Roman Catholic Church. In AD 650 the Paulicians restored what they believed to be the pure Christianity of Paul. They lived in Arabia on the frontier of the Byzantine Empire. Their teachings were based upon the Epistles of Paul. They believed that Christ was a spiritual emanation of the God of Good. As traditional Gnostics, they rejected material things as being from the Evil God. They claimed that theirs was the only true Church, descended directly from the first Christian communities, and that the Roman Catholic and Orthodox Churches were imposters.[7] They were led by someone they referred to as "the apostle of Christ."[8]

This was a popular sect, as seen by the intensity of the persecution in the ninth century, resulting in the deaths of some one-hundred thousand members.[9] Paulicianism spread rapidly and had over one hundred thousand converts in Armenia alone. By AD 1204, some remnants were still living at Constantinople when the Crusaders invaded the city.[10]

The Paulicians accepted most of the New Testament, but rejected the Old Testament. As with the other Gnostic sects they adhered to the traditional Gnostic creation theory and thus viewed the symbol of the cross as idolatry; neither did they believe in literal baptism. However, unlike many Gnostics, the Paulicians did believe in marriage.[11] Ultimately, the Paulicians died out before the end of the ninth Century.[12] Whether the Catholic Church had any hand in that is unknown.

THE BOGOMILS

The next Gnostic sect originated in Bulgaria in AD 927 and lasted for nearly five centuries. It resulted from the forced Christianization of the Slavs in AD 863[13] and the belief that the Catholic Church was corrupt. They were heavily influenced by Paulicianism and denied the divine birth of Christ, the Trinity, any veneration to the Virgin Mary, and the miracles of Jesus. However, unlike the Paulicians, they believed in baptism of grown men and women, but not by water. They rejected the Catholic view of infant baptism. The Bogomils believed that all of its adherents could become perfect and "Christs" in their own right. Similar to other Gnostics, marriage was discouraged, and the symbol of the cross, as well as the veneration of Saints was regarded as idolatry. Surprisingly however, the Bogomils accepted most of the New Testament and had twelve Apostles in each of its communities as the governing body. Since the twelve governed, they refused to grant allegiance to any nation or kingdom, nor did they pay taxes. As it's tenants spread, the Bogomils soon became a serious threat to the Eastern Orthodox church at Constantinople.[14]

To the Bogomils, God the Father had two sons, Satan and Michael. Satan rebelled against the Father and was thrown out of heaven, where he created this world. Michael is identified with both Christ and the Holy Ghost. Michael came to redeem man through his perfect example. Satan was thought to be the originator of the Roman Catholic Church.[15]

The Bogomils were unusually good missionaries spreading east to Russia and west to Serbia. They were persecuted, however, by the king of Serbia. Many escaped to Bosnia. There they were hunted by the Hungarians, who tried to eradicate the heresy on behalf of the Roman Church. However, when the Turks captured Bosnia, it is alleged that most Bogomils converted to Islam, probably by force.[16]

The Catholic Church had just successfully put down the Bogomil heresy when a new Gnostic heresy suddenly resurfaced in the twelfth century in the form of Catharism in areas at the very heart of Western culture.[17] "Moreover, it proved to be no transitory movement linked to the lives of a few charismatic leaders but the most deadly threat ever to confront the Catholic faith since the days of the Hebrew Christians. Appearing as though from nowhere, it was a well-organized "anti-Church" that claimed an antiquity even greater than that of Catholicism itself."[18]

THE CATHARS

After the Council of Nicaea, the gnostics were forced into hiding—"it was such purges between the fourth and sixth centuries, said the Cathars and the Bogomils, that had forced their true Church underground. Only now, after the sleep of years, was it emerging once more from the shadows."[19]

In around AD 1012, the Cathars first appeared and quickly spread throughout the Provence and Languedoc regions of southern France, as well as in eastern Spain and northern Italy, and scattered in smaller communities throughout the rest of Europe as far afield as Belgium, northern France, and Germany. One of the reasons for the Cathars' success was their support by William, Duke of Aquitaine, as well as the Count of Toulouse and many other nobles in southern France. Some suggest it was the Templar Knights who protected the Cathars, but that is only legend. In any event, the Cathars successfully displaced the Roman Catholic Church in southern France. Although the Cathars referred to themselves as "Good Christians," the Catholic Church labeled them heretics.[20] The name *Cathar* is derived from the Greek meaning "The Pure;" they believed they were the true and original followers of Christ.[21] "Here was a heresy that could fight back, that would not easily be crushed by the use of secular force and that might conceivably, if allowed to grow further, push the Catholic religion out of Europe altogether."[22] Catharism became known to history books as the Great Heresy of the Middle Ages.[23]

Graham Hancock, a journalist who has studied the Cathars in depth, relates the following about their culture and customs:

> The missionaries were all Cathar Perfecti, and, as O'Shea rightly observes, it was their custom—like modern Mormons or Jehovah's Witnesses—to travel and evangelize in pairs. Their black robes would have given them something of the look of Christian monks or priests. . . . As even their most bitter opponents were willing to admit, the distinguishing characteristic of the Perfect was that they lived exemplary lives of chastity, humility, great poverty, and simplicity throughout the whole period of Catharism's rise and fall.[24]

Wherever Catharism was established, we know that its Believer class lived ordinary lives of no great self-denial. They married, produced children, owned property, ate well and generally enjoyed the world. They certainly attended the simple services and gatherings led by Perfecti that were part of the Cathar calendar.[25]

Cathars also referred to themselves as "Good Men and Good Women." Although most of their books were destroyed by the Catholic Church, who thought them to be a threat to the Church, a few survived. One of those books to survive was "The Book of Two Principles," which spelled out the Cathar's dualistic theology. Cathars claimed, as did the Bogomils, that they were the rightful heirs to the Apostles, and that the Catholic Church was corrupt. To Cathars, Christ was neither crucified, nor did he die for the sins of mankind. Rather, Christ's role in bringing salvation was through knowledge—the Greek "gnosis." They were duelists who believed in two deities—a "God of good and a God of Evil." The domain of the God of Good was entirely spiritual. That of the God of Evil was the material world.[26] Christ was the God of Good, while the Jewish God, Jehovah, was regarded as the God of Evil because, according to the Bible, it was Jehovah who made the material world and lured one-third of the angels of heaven to the earth with him to tempt mankind.[27] As a result, Cathars rejected the Old Testament (Jehovah) and embraced the New Testament (Christ).[28] Jehovah was considered to be "Satan."[29]

Christ, who was spirit, had a three-fold mission: first, to preach the gnosis, or secret knowledge about death, the true character of existence, and the fate of the soul.[30] Second, instill values into the populace so that they could have the ability to escape their physical bodies (and conquer the reincarnation of the soul in a new physical body), having attained the gnosis. Last, to impart the Holy Ghost on mankind (gift of the Holy Ghost), as was done on the Day of Pentecost.[31]

Cathars further believed that Christ and Jehovah (Satan) were brothers in the premortal existence with Jehovah being the eldest. Apparently at a great council in heaven Jehovah rebelled against the Father God and war broke out between the forces of Good led by Christ and the forces of Evil led by Jehovah. Ultimately, Jehovah was expelled from heaven with his angels. Jehovah then created the earth, as well as physical bodies of mud and water. He was able to persuade the Father God to place souls in these bodies only to have the Father God realize that he had been deceived and the souls were trapped on the physical plane, thus requiring a Savior in the form of Jesus Christ.[32]

Cathars accepted the concept of reincarnation as a way to progress in the on-going pursuit for perfection in this life, which perfection ultimately frees one to go to heaven. If you do not succeed, you are reincarnated to try again. Sometimes Cathars have been referred to as "Western Buddhists" because of their belief in reincarnation. As Gnostics, they believed in the gift of the Holy Ghost by the laying on of hands, which they termed the "consolamentum,"[33] but they did not believe in the physical resurrection of the body.[34] Rather, "they pictured the soul as a time traveler on an immense journey toward perfection."[35]

They further divided themselves into two classes: Perfects and Believers. The Perfects were the "heart" of the true Christian church. Although they rejected the idea of priesthood, Perfects acted in that capacity as teachers of the Believers. One became a Perfect through an ordinance called the "consolamentum" (as mentioned earlier), which meant "baptism of the Holy Ghost." These Perfects lived an austere life, having given up all worldly possessions, wearing a simple black robe, and living a life of chastity, prayer, charity, and preaching. The Believers, as already mentioned, did not live such lives but had to refrain from eating meat, dairy products, swearing oaths, and killing. The Cathars were docetists, meaning that they believed Jesus to be merely a manifestation of the spirit, who had no physical body. They revered the Gospel of John. They also believed that Jesus was a lesser God and that there was a higher God, the "True God," a Father God. Hence, the Cathars rejected the ideas of a Holy Trinity or the Eucharist in favor of a form of subordinationism similar to the Arians.[36]

To Cathars there is this world, which is hell, and there is heaven, where the True God resides. One concern to the king of France regarding the Cathars, however, was their refusal to give oaths. Since in medieval Europe, all business transactions were done by oath, as most people were not literate, those not willing to give an oath impeded commerce. Another cultural problem was the distaste Believers had for marriage. Hence, instead of a marriage contract, Cathar Believers favored informal relationships—in layman's terms, shacking up with no commitment to a long term familial relationship. Procreating children was discouraged, as this life was thought of as slavery and allowing more children to come into it was an abomination. Hence, although Believers or Credentes were allowed to engage in sexual relations, they were not encouraged to have children. When coupled with their beliefs about marriage, this led to a 1960s type free love cultural arrangement.[37]

Notwithstanding these progressive beliefs, most repugnant to the French king was their opposition to all manner of killing. As a consequence, they opposed all war, capital punishment, and the slaughtering of animals for food. In short, they refused to fight on behalf of their king.[38]

The appeal of the Cathar movement to Frenchman and others was its powerful theology, which directly contested the authority of Rome. In sum, it appealed to those disaffected by Rome.

> Equally potent, and apparently extremely convincing, was the heretics' insistence that theirs was Christ's original Church—the Primitive Church itself, reawakened after being forced to lie low "in Greece and certain other lands . . . from the time of the martyrs." Though Evil powers had made every effort to destroy the Church of the Good God, "we, and our fathers of apostolic descent, have continued in the grace of Christ and shall so remain until the end of time."[39]

From AD 1147 to AD 1198, the Catholic Church tried to convince the Cathars to give up their heretical views, but were unsuccessful. Pope Innocent III decided that something had to be done. In AD 1204 he suspended the bishops in southern France who were sympathetic to the Cathars. In AD 1206 Saint Dominic was sent to convince the Cathars of the error of their ways and he engaged in a series of debates with the Perfects. One legend has both throwing their sacred books in a fire as a contest of spiritual power—St. Dominic's didn't burn. He founded his Dominican Order in AD 1216. However, he was unsuccessful in converting the Cathars.[40] By January AD 1208 a papal legate had excommunicated Count Raymond VI of Toulouse, who was seen as a protector of the Cathars. Count Raymond responded by killing the legate. This was said to be just the thing that the Pope needed to order a Crusade against the Cathars, which lasted twenty years. It pitted the northern French nobles against the southern French nobles;

the northern nobles being persuaded by the Pope that for their assistance, they would be given the lands and possessions of the southern French nobles who had helped the Cathars.[41]

According to Hancock, "the Cathar heresy was crushed by a series of violent and genocidal 'Crusades,'" unleashed by the Catholic Church in the first half of the thirteenth century. The last of the resistance was then slowly and methodically finished off by the Papal Inquisition, which was officially established in AD 1233 specifically for the repression and extermination of Catharism.[42] Had it not been for the destruction and dislocation wrought by these so-called "'Albigensian Crusades,' some believe that the culture of the Languedoc could have anticipated the Renaissance in Italy by more than two centuries."[43] Astonishingly, Jewish communities (who worshiped Jehovah) flourished among the Cathars, while the Jews were being persecuted by Catholics.[44] Perhaps it was the notion that your enemy's enemy becomes your friend, or at least brothers in arms against a common foe, that contributed to this odd friendship.

> The tremendous success of the Cathar heresy in Occitania and other parts of Europe during the twelfth century had for many years been watched with envy and growing alarm by the Catholic hierarchy in Rome. By the early thirteenth century it is estimated that more than half the Occitanian population had abandoned the Church and that growing numbers were looking exclusively to Catharism to meet their spiritual needs. Worse still . . . the local nobility gave tacit and sometimes even overt support to the Cathars, frequently had relatives among them, sided with them in disputes with the bishops, and were closely linked to some of the leading perfecti. Once it had become clear that the Cathar religion was not a flash in the pan, but quite possibly formed part of a great coordinated plot against the Church, it was obvious that sooner or later one Pope or another was going to have to do something about it. The only question was what exactly, and when?[45]

Pope Innocent[46] declared a crusade against the Cathars on March 10, 1208. He considered the Cathars to be more dangerous than the Saracens of the Ottoman Empire. The original Crusader army was around twenty thousand soldiers and they massacred the Cathars wherever they were found.[47]

One example cites a Crusader army, which besieged the town

of Beziers on July 22, 1209. Astonishingly, the Catholics of the city refused to leave and fought along side the Cathars. When the Crusader army asked how to distinguish the Cathars from the Catholics, they were told "kill them all, the Lord will recognize His own." Some twenty thousand men, women, and children were slaughtered and the city was burned. The Crusade lasted until around AD 1229 and ended with the Treaty of Paris, but the Crusade was not successful in killing all the Cathars.[48]

It was at the Synod of Lateran IV that the Church officially declared that all heretics, and specifically the Cathars, were to have their property confiscated and anyone found to be helping a heretic would also be excommunicated.[49] Next came the Inquisition to convert or kill the remaining Cathars.[50] It took another hundred years. The last known Cathar Perfecti was executed in AD 1321.[51]

> Although the scale of the Church's response was new—indeed unprecedented—the Catholic authorities clearly recognized Catharism as an old and deadly enemy. It was for this reason that they so often referred to the Cathars as "Manichees" [gnostics], a heresy over which Rome had supposedly triumphed centuries before. For their part, though they would never have identified themselves as "Manichees," the Cathars claimed that their religion had come down to them from antiquity, "passed from Good Man to Good Man." It was, they said, the true faith that the Church had usurped in the early days of Christianity.[52]

Hancock summarizes:

> All wars are terrible—no matter in what epoch they are fought, or with what weapons. Medieval wars were particularly ghastly. But the wars of the Catholic Church against the heresy of Catharism in the thirteenth century, the so-called Albigensian Crusades, must rank high on that list of the most repulsive, brutal and merciless conflicts that human beings have ever had the misfortune to be involved in.[53]

The end of the Cathars, however, was not the end of the Gnostic Christian movement. The modern Gnostic church began in Edessa, Syria, and is called the "Thomasine Church." It is based on the Gospel of Thomas, and reports to have bishops, priests, and deacons still leading the Church to this day.[54]

NOTES

1. Graham Hancock & Robert Bauval, *Talisman* (Element, 2004), 28.
2. Ibid., 88–89.
3. Ibid., 74.
4. Ibid., 75.
5. Ibid., 76.
6. Ibid.
7. Ibid., 71–72.
8. Ibid., 72 citing Hamilton and Hamilton, *Christian Dualist Heresies in the Byzantine World* (Manchester University Press, 1998), 9.
9. Ibid., 73.
10. http://en.wikipedia.org/wiki/Paulicianism.
11. Johann Herzog, "Paulicians" *A Religious Encyclopedia or Dictionary of Biblical, Historical, Doctrinal, and Practical Theology*, 3rd ed., vol. 2 (New York, Funk & Wagnalls: 1894), 1776–77; Fred C. Conybeare, *The Key of Truth, A Manual of the Paulician Church of Armenia* (Oxford, Clarendon Press: 1898); Nina G. Garsoian, *The Paulician Heresy* (The Hague, Columbia University: 1967), 296.
12. http://en.wikipedia.org/wiki/Paulicianism.
13. One of the reasons that by the Middle Ages Church members did not have the same conviction in belief as existed previously was due to the use of mass conversion techniques. For example, the king or other authoritative leader within a community would convert to Christianity. As a natural consequence, all of the king's subjects or citizens would then convert as well. Consequently, the new members of the Christian Church were not devout, but brought with them their own culture and superstitions. Shelley, *Church History*, 158. Hence, the church was altered through this process, which is how most of Europe was converted to Christianity.
14. Hancock, *Talisman*, 47–67. See also http://en.wikipedia.org/wiki/Bogomilism.
15. Ibid.
16. JC Wolf, *Historia Bogomiorum* (Wittenberg, 1712); V. Sharenkoff, *A Study of Manicheism in Bulgaria* (New York: 1927); D. Obolensky, *The Bogomils: A Study in Balkan Neo-Manichaeism* (Cambridge: 1948); M. Loos, *Dualist heresy in the Middle Ages* (Dordrecht: 1974).
17. Christian scholars Hans Soderberg and Sir Steven Runcipman argue that "'an uninterrupted traditional chain connects Cathars and the Bogomils to the religion known as Christian Gnosticism that flourished in Egypt and the Middle East a thousand years earlier." Hancock, *Talisman*, 70.
18. Hancock, *Talisman*, 29.
19. Ibid., 67.
20. Ibid., 26.
21. Ibid., 27.
22. Ibid., 29.
23. Ibid., 33.
24. Ibid., 33.
25. Ibid., 35.
26. Ibid., 26–27. See also http://en.wikipedia.org/wiki/Catharism.
27. Ibid., 57–59.
28. Ibid., 58.
29. http://en.wikipedia.org/wiki/Catharism.

30. Hancock, *Talisman*, 60.
31. Ibid., 61.
32. Ibid., 62.
33. Ibid., 55.
34. Ibid., 56.
35. Ibid.
36. http://en.wikipedia.org/wiki/Catharism.
37. Ibid.
38. Ibid.
39. Hancock, *Talisman*, 56 quoting Everwin, cited in Lambert, *The Cathars* (Oxford: 1998), 22.
40. Popes tried sending in the Dominicans to preach to the Cathars. To try to win them over, in AD 1206 the Dominicans went to them "as a poor man, barefoot and begging." Shelley, *Church History*, 210. This was consistent with the vows of poverty that Cathar preachers took. They failed after two years, but their order later gained papal approval. Ibid., 211. Pope Innocent used a crusade and an inquisition to finally destroy the Cathars by AD 1300. Ibid., 212.
41. Shelley, *Church History*, 209–212; "Catharism," Wikipedia.
42. "We know that the Church did not identify it as a new rival, but as an old and dangerous one seemingly returned from the dead. Perhaps this sense on the Church's part, of being drawn back into an ancient conflict, one that struck at the very heart of all its shaky claims to legitimacy and authenticity as the true faith, explains the terrible events that followed." Hancock, *Talisman*, 114.
43. Hancock, *Talisman*, 39.
44. Ibid., 40–41.
45. Ibid., 116.
46. According to Shelley, "three weapons were at the Catholic church's disposal: preaching to return them to the truth, a crusade to crush all hardened resistance, and the Inquisition to uproot heresy completely." Shelley, *Church History*, 210.
47. Shelley, *Church History*, 119.
48. Shelley, *Church History*, 128.
49. Nibley, *Apostles and Bishops in Early Christianity*, 124–132 citing to Hefele, Histoire des Conciles d'Apres les Documents Originaux.
50. Hancock writes, "When we began this research we did not know ourselves that the famed (but misnamed) "Spanish Inquisition" . . . had first been established in April 1233 by Pope Gregory IX. Nor did we know that the original and explicit purpose of the Inquisition was to root out and destroy the Cathar heresy. Building on the repressive structures that had already been firmly laid down in Occitania, the Dominican Inquisitors were empowered after 1233 to use virtually any measure they wished to extract confessions and to crush the Cathar faith. They began at once to institute a reign of terror—true and awful terror from which no one was safe." Hancock, *Talisman*, 133. By the 1250s all but a few Cathar perfecti were dead. Although some Cathars survived for nearly another century, the movement was at an end. Ibid., 141. In AD 1321 the last of the Cathar perfecti was captured and burned at the stake. It took the Catholic Church roughly 112 years to fully eradicate the Cathar heresy. Ibid.
51. Zoe Oldenbourg, *Massacre at Montsegur: A History of the Albigensian Crusade* (Phoenix Giant, 1998); Sean Martin, *The Cathars* (Pocket Essentials: 2005), 105–121; Rene J. A. Weis, *The Yellow Cross: The Story of the Last Cathars* (Penguin

Books 2000); Walter Waskefield and Austin Evans, *Heresies of the High Middle Ages* (Columbia University Press: 1991); N. A. Weber, "Albigenses", *The Catholic Encyclopedia* (1908); Emmanuel Le Roy Ladurie, *Histories of the Cathars* (Vintage Books: 1979).
52. Hancock, *Talisman*, 46.
53. Ibid., 114.
54. "Thomasine Church (Gnostic)," Wikipedia (September 2007).

CHAPTER 7

THE APOSTASY

One of the most controversial doctrines in the Christian world settles upon the coming of the Apostasy. Christ prophesied that "many shall come in my name, saying, I am Christ; and shall deceive many."[1] In fact, Christ preached in private to his Apostles:

> For there shall arise false Christs, and false prophets, and shall shew great signs and wonders; insomuch that, if it were possible, they shall deceive the very elect.[2]

Paul taught, "be not soon shaken in mind, or troubled, neither by spirit, nor by word, not by letter as from us, as that the day of Christ is at hand. Let no man deceive you by any means: for that day shall not come, *except there come a falling away first*."[3]

The consensus among the original Apostles spoke in favor of this foretold future apostasy coming before the advent of the Second Coming of Christ.[4] In Matthew 24, Christ, himself, spoke to His Apostles of the signs of the times—those events that would transpire before the Second Coming. The only real question to the early Christians with regard to the return of Christ was one of timing; namely, when would this falling away and subsequent Second Coming occur? Christ spoke of this when he told His Apostles,

Now learn a parable of the fig tree; When his branch is yet tender, and putteth forth leaves, ye know that summer is nigh: So likewise ye, when ye shall see all these things, know that it is near, even at the doors.[5]

Hence, Christ counseled His Apostles to look for the signs—wars, famines, pestilences, earthquakes, false prophets, the teaching of the gospel to the entire world, Daniel's prophesied Abomination of Desolation, great tribulation and iniquity, the sun and moon to be darkened, stars falling from the sky, as well as the sign of the Son of Man, among other signs.[6] These signs began to appear shortly after Christ's crucifixion and resurrection. False prophets sprung up overnight. Paul warned against Greek philosophy infiltrating the Church, as an early act of apostasy.[7] Ultimately, the apostasy began in earnest at the close of the Apostolic era when the Church was left without its general authorities.

But all agree that the apostles did spend their time preaching to the nations and then passed away, almost all at once and suddenly, leaving no apostles in their place. The apostles must have been special officers of some sort, it is assumed. Their work was closely centralized in Jerusalem—the main office to which we may assume they would repair for yearly conferences to make reports on their missions in the presence of the whole church and to which at other times they would steadily send written reports on their work.[8]

According to Louis Duchesne, "when the first age of the church passed away, this itinerant, ubiquitous personnel disappeared entirely, and nothing was left but the local ecclesiastical organizations."[9] However, make no mistake, the sudden disappearance of the Apostles was not by accident. The Apostles did not die of old age, rather they were murdered: Phillip was scourged, thrown into prison, and, afterwards, crucified at Heliopolis in Phrygia around AD 54; Matthew was either slain with a Halberd (battle axe) at Nadabah Ethiopia around AD 60 or was cruelly beaten and then crucified by pagans in India; James was beaten and stoned by the Jews and had his brains dashed out with a fuller's club; Matthias was stoned at Jerusalem, then beheaded; Andrew was crucified at Edessa; Mark was dragged to pieces in the streets of Alexandria; Peter was crucified at Rome around AD 64 or 65; Paul was beheaded at Rome by order of Nero in AD 65; Thaddeus was crucified at Edessa around AD 72; Thomas preached in Parthia and India, where exciting the rage of the pagan priests, he was thrust through with a spear; Luke was hanged on an Olive Tree by pagan priests of Greece; Simon Zelotes was crucified in Britain around AD 74; and Barnabas was killed around AD 73. The only Apostle to survive was John the Beloved, who inexplicably disappeared around AD 110 and was never seen again.[10]

In 2 Thessalonians 2:3, Paul compares the advent of Christ at the meridian of time, which was preceded by a period of apostasy, with the Second Coming—which he preached would likewise not occur until a similar apostasy had taken place. "The use of the term *apostasy* here in 2 Thessalonians 2:3 without an accompanying adjective points to the fact that, by and large, the visible Church will forsake the true faith."[11]

Notwithstanding these biblical evidences, the Hellenized Church resisted the idea of an apostasy. In truth, the Catholic Church, as well as the Protestant Churches, assert that there was no apostasy. Their argument is based upon a curious reading of Matthew 16:18.

> He saith unto them, But whom say ye that I am?
>
> And Simon Peter answered and said, Thou art the Christ, the Son of the living God.
>
> And Jesus answered and said unto him, Blessed art thou, Simon Bar-jona: *for flesh and blood hath not revealed it unto thee, but my Father which is in heaven* [i.e.; revelation].
>
> And I say also unto thee, That thou art Peter, *and upon this rock* [i.e.; revelation] *I will build my church;* and the gates of hell shall not prevail against it.
>
> And I will give unto thee the keys of the kingdom of heaven: and whatsoever thou shalt bind on earth shall be bound in heaven: and whatsoever thou shalt loose on earth shall be loosed in heaven.[12]

According to Catholic theologians, Peter is the "rock" and the Lord's Church will be built upon Peter and the "gates of hell" shall never prevail against her. A modern reading of this scripture would appear to confirm that interpretation. However, this scripture was written at the meridian of time, not 2013. "Two of the most distinguished theologians of the fourth century, Hilary and Basil, both say the rock was revelation."[13] The original Aramaic translates "rock" in this passage as Christ's Messianic calling, which is the foundation of the church.[14] It is against this revelation, and more specifically the revelation that Jesus is the Christ, the Son of the living God, which is the foundation of the church and upon which "the gates of hell shall not prevail." In sum, according to early Christian scholars through the first three centuries, Matthew 16:18 was never used to conclude that there would be no apostasy.

Notwithstanding their position on Matthew 16:18 as to the absence of an apostasy, the Catholic Church was still left with the problem of apostolic succession. The Apostles died without leaving successor apostles in their place. Without apostolic leadership, how could the Church continue? Isn't this further evidence of an apostasy? Catholic scholars answer this by suggesting that Peter conferred the leadership of the Church on Clement, the bishop of Rome, in AD 90, through a letter that Peter instructed Clement to write to James the Just in Jerusalem. This course of events, however, is completely illogical. Clement was not an ordained apostle. James the Just, however, was an Apostle. If Peter had wanted to pass leadership of the Church to someone, it would have logically been to James, not Clement.[15]

This is but one of many flaws to Clement's claim to Apostolic succession. Another example of the flaws in Clement's claim has to do with the chronology of events. Peter died before AD 90 so he could not have ordained Clement bishop of Rome as the head of the Church. Additionally, the *Epitome de Gestis Sancti Petri of Clement*, where Clement purportedly lays out his claim to succession, is widely considered a fourth century forgery.[16]

The fact that a system of choosing new apostles had been set up following the suicide of Judas Iscariot indicates that apostolic succession and therefore, continued apostolic leadership of the Church had been contemplated. If Clement was to be the new head of the Church, he would have to submit to the same process as Matthias and Barnabas when they became apostles. That would have required a gathering of all of the Apostles. Such a gathering never occurred after the First Jerusalem Council. Hence, Clement could not have succeeded to the apostleship and leadership of the Church.

With the death of the Apostles, the general leadership of the Church was gone and soon the Church became a tangle of bishops competing with each other for supremacy and doctrinal orthodoxy as has previously been discussed. This is what ultimately led to the Council at Nicaea in AD 321.

There is, however, one mystery that remains to this day—what happened to the Apostle John? Some say that Christ granted the Apostle whom the Lord loved the desire of his heart; namely to remain on the earth until Christ's Second Coming.

> Then Peter, turning about, seeth the disciple whom Jesus loved following; which also leaned on his breast at supper, and said, Lord, which is he that betrayeth thee? Peter seeing him said to Jesus, Lord, and what shall this man do? Jesus saith unto him, If I will that he tarry till I come, what is that to thee? follow thou me. Then went this saying abroad among the brethren, that that disciple should not die: yet Jesus said not unto him, He shall not die; but, If I will that he tarry till I come, what is that to thee?[17]

Notwithstanding the disposition of John, after AD 110, he no longer took a leadership role in the Church. The Apostolic era was at an end.

NOTES

1. Matthew 24:5.
2. Matthew 24:24.
3. 2 Thessalonians 2:2–3 (emphasis added). The original Greek word for "a falling way" is "apostasia." Hickenbotham, *Biblical Evidences of an Apostasy* (Bountiful, UT: Horizon Publishers, 1995).
4. Matthew 24:4, 9–13, 24; John 16:2–3; Acts 20:29–30; 1 Corinthians 1:10–13; Galatians 1:6–8; 2 Thessalonians 2:1–12; 1 Timothy 4:1–3; 2 Timothy 3:1–9, 12–13; 2 Timothy 4:3–4; Titus 1:10–16; 2 Peter 2:1–3, 2 Peter 3:3; 1 John 2:18–19; Jude 3–4; Revelation 13:4–8.
5. Matthew 24:32–33.
6. Matthew 24.
7. Colossians 2:8.
8. Nibley, *Apostles and Bishops in Early Christianity*, 7–8.
9. Duchesne, Origines du Culte Chretien: Etude sur las Liturgie Latine avant Charlemagne, 14, cited in Nibley, *Apostles and Bishops in Early Christianity*, 12.
10. Fox, *Book of the Martyrs* cited in Keith Marston, *Missionary Pal* (Salt Lake City: Publishers Press, 1987), 10–11.
11. Brown, *All Things Restored*, 5, quoting Hendriksen and Kistemaker, *New Testament Commentary: Exposition of Thessalonians, the Pastorals, and Hebrews* (Baker Books 1995), 169–70.
12. Matthew 16:15–19. Emphasis added.
13. Nibley, *Apostles and Bishops in Early Christianity*, 225.
14. Herman L. Strack and Paul Billerbeck, *Kommentar zum neuen Testament aus*

Talmud und Midrash (Munich: Beck, 1922), 1:732.

15. Nibley, *Apostles and Bishops in Early Christianity*, 152–57.
16. Ibid., 152–163.
17. John 21:20–23.

CHAPTER 8

THE
REFORMATION

Courageous men such as Wycliffe, Hus, Luther, Tyndale, Zwingli, Knox, and Calvin all declared that since the Mother Church had become abusive and corrupt, it desperately needed to be reformed. Some of these protestors were excommunicated for their views, some were banished from society, and some were burned at the stake.[1]

T he seeds of reformation began in earnest with the sale of indulgences by the Catholic Church, a practice that was introduced during the Crusades. Indulgences soon became an important source of papal income. The idea behind indulgences involved a *quid pro quo* of sorts. A sinner contributed money to a worthy cause or made a pilgrimage to a shrine. In exchange, the "church offered the sinner exemption from his acts of penance by drawing upon its 'treasury of merits.' This consisted of the grace accumulated by Christ's sacrifice on the cross and the meritorious deeds of the saints."[2]

MARTIN LUTHER

The sale of indulgences was an established practice by the time of Martin Luther. He was a Catholic priest and monk living in Wittenberg, Germany. He fundamentally disagreed with the Catholic orthodoxy that "works," and therefore the need for physical acts to obtain grace, played any role in salvation.[3] Consequently he was offended by the practice of indulgences and began to criticize the theology in his Sunday sermons, instead preaching that "faith" alone unlocked the grace of Christ. A turning point came in AD 1517, "when the Dominican John Tetzel was preaching throughout much of Germany on behalf of a papal fund raising campaign to complete the construction of St. Peter's basilica in Rome. In exchange for a contribution, Tetzel boasted, he would provide donors with an indulgence that would even apply beyond the grave and free souls from purgatory. As soon as the coin in the coffer rings, went his jingle, the soul from purgatory springs."[4] This prompted Luther to pen his 95 theses for theological debate and "on 31 October 1517, following university custom, he posted them on the Castle Church door at Wittenberg." In the theses he argued that "indulgences cannot remove guilt, do not apply to purgatory, and are harmful because they induce a false sense of security in the donor."[5]

The Reformation had begun. Luther went on to assert a second principle (outside of the justification by faith), the standard for Christian belief should be the scriptures and not ecumenical councils or the Pope. Next Luther suggested that only Baptism and the Lord's Supper had foundation in the scriptures, so he deemed the other five Catholic sacraments to be invalid. He also noted that priesthood authority, which was so essential to the Catholic orthodoxy and dominance, was unnecessary, and that a "community of believers" could perform the sacraments. In June 1520, Luther was condemned by Pope Leo X and in January 1521 he was declared a heretic and expelled from the Church. Luther went into hiding at Wartburg Castle in Saxony (Germany), as the princes and dukes of Germany sided with Luther, their homegrown priest, not with the Pope and Rome. By 1522, Luther was out of hiding and leading a religious revolution in Germany. However, there was a political backlash to Luther's teachings because peasants demanded freedom from serfdom because such slavery was not found in the scriptures. The Germanic princes and dukes crushed the peasant revolt in AD 1525—killing one hundred thousand peasants in the process. Thereafter, the peasants considered Luther a false prophet and returned to Catholicism. Yet the aristocracy continued to back him and Lutheranism, as it came to be known, continued to grow in Germany among the upper class. Charles V (Holy Roman Emperor) made it clear to the Lutheran princes that he would destroy their heresy in AD 1530. But the Lutheran princes banded together the following year and raged a religious war between 1546 and 1555. The Peace Treaty of Augsburg (AD 1555) was a major victory for the Lutheran princes—Rome allowed Lutheranism in Germany. With that concession, Lutheranism soon became the state religion in much of Germany.[6]

THE ANABAPTISTS

Luther had broken a twelve hundred year strangle hold on Christianity by the Catholic church.

Other reformers arose. The Anabaptists (Baptists, Quakers, and Congregationalists) rose to reject Catholic infant baptism and all other practices that they believed were inconsistent with apostolic Christianity. Their rejection of oath taking, an important concept in the Middle Ages, raised concerns throughout Europe (just as had been the case with the Cathar heresy). The first Anabaptists were formed in Zurich, Switzerland in 1525 where Felix Manz was its first martyr in 1527. By 1529, Anabaptism was declared to be a heresy and between four and five thousand Anabaptists were executed. Apparently, even the Lutherans were concerned about this new heresy. The Anabaptists met in 1527 at their first Synod and adopted the Schleitheim Confession. The Confession stated that Anabaptists would (1) be disciples of Christ, (2) be pacifists, (3) be congregationalists as to church authority—the church would be governed by majority vote of its membership, and (4) be insistent upon the separation of church and state—no state religion.[7] Consequently, all members were considered to be priests to the other members of the congregation and missionaries to the unbelievers.[8]

JOHN CALVIN

The next reformer was John Calvin (1509–1564). The Reformed Church or Calvinistic Christianity, included the Presbyterians and many other Baptists and congregationalist churches. He preached that God had a plan for all of humanity. "He called it God's sovereign will. Just as Luther's central doctrine was justification by faith, so Calvin's was the sovereignty of God."[9] Calvin had been a lawyer and he formed his movement in Geneva, Switerzerland, in 1531. Interestingly, he was first thrown out of Geneva for his preaching, but returned in 1541. Calvin preached that there were four offices in the priesthood: pastors, teachers, elders, and deacons.[10] His main thesis was the doctrine of predestination. God divinely elected those who would be saved. "While Calvin did not profess to know absolutely who were God's chosen— the elect—he believed that three tests constituted a good yardstick by which to judge who might be saved: participation in the two sacraments, Baptism and the Lord's Supper; an upright moral life; and a public profession of the faith."[11] This gave rise to Calvin's social activism—personal character was fundamental to show who was chosen by God to be saved and who was not.

EPISCOPALIANS

The Anglican Church came as a result of king Henry VIII (1509–1547) and his belief that England was independent of Rome.[12] Historians assert that Henry did not intend to break with the Catholic faith; rather, he viewed himself as "a guardian of Catholic dogma." It was Henry who, in 1521, came to the defense of the Church by penning a "Defense of the Seven Sacraments" wherein he attacked Martin Luther as a "poisonous serpent" and a "wolf of hell." "In gratitude, the pope bestowed on Henry the title "Defender of the Faith"—a title still carried by English monarchs" to this day.[13] But the Church of England began to change, furthering its doctrines and policies from Rome. First, monasteries were abolished. Then the Bible was translated into English for the masses. This second change led to the Puritan movement. Puritans believed that they were saved through a covenant relationship with God, just as the Hebrews had believed. The Puritans through Oliver Cromwell (1599–1658) temporarily dethroned the English monarch and remodeled the Church of England.[14]

EVANGELICALS

Pietism arose in the seventeenth century—it emphasized the importance of personal faith and emotion as playing an essential part of salvation. These Christian reformers began the practice of Bible study. This was the beginning of the Evangelical movement. "The Age of Reason saw a dramatic spiritual renewal in Western Christianity called the Evangelical Awakening."[15] The main Evangelical denomination that arose from this was the Methodists in England.

John Wesley (1703–1791) was their leader. Wesley began to preach in the "open air" in New England. Thus was born the Methodist Revival. At first, the Methodists were simply a society within the Church of England, but by 1773 they held their first conference in Philadelphia. When the Church of England refused to ordain ministers to the conference, Wesley ordained his own and by 1784 the split into a new denomination was complete. Of interest is that the "Great Awakening," as it is known in evangelic circles, was the result of a friend of Wesley's, George Whitefield. In 1739, Whitefield began preaching in the evangelical style throughout the east coast of the United States gaining many converts to the Methodist religion.[16]

Evangelicals eventually split in the United States between the North and South following the Civil War. The Northern Evangelicals adopted "pre-millennialism"—preaching Christ's imminent return around 1878 (New York) and 1886 (Chicago).[17] They were disappointed when Christ did not arrive at these predetermined times and locations. As a result, they began to take on a more liberal view of the Bible and the teachings of the gospel.

The Bible was no longer an infallible authority. For the most part, it was viewed as allegory, similar to St. Augustine's views. In the past, Christians had a hard time explaining a God who ordered the genocide of an entire people, as was done with the Canaanites at the time of Israel's entrance into the promised land in the days of Joshua or where God had sent bears to eat little children who had pulled a prank on a prophet. Hence, it was a welcome change to begin to interpret the Bible anew for modern man.[18]

They eventually became the new Gnostics and began their search for the "historical Jesus."[19] They accepted science and Darwinism. According to these modern Christian liberals, science and religion are merely different sides of the same coin. While science is about facts, religion is about the interpretation of those facts. Hence, these Unitarians can accept that man has evolved from apes, but can differentiate that man is superior to the ape due to his "sense of values."[20] As a result, they concluded that Jesus was just a man, a brilliant teacher of values. There were no miracles and no virgin birth. The attempt was to fold religion with science much the same way that the early Christians merged Christianity with the God of the Philosophers. These modern Christian liberals are known today as the Calvinist and Congregationalist of New England.[21]

To combat Modernism, a new movement of Fundamentalist arose in 1910 (the remnants of the Southern Evangelicals). William Jennings Bryan was the symbol of that movement. Although he won the scopes monkey trial in 1925, as depicted in *Inherit the Wind*, the media crucified him in the press, as well as his fundamentalist beliefs.[22]

Pentecostalism was part of this fundamentalist movement, which arose within Evangelical Christianity in 1906 in Los Angeles. The largest of these sects were the Assemblies of God.[23]

SUMMARY

In sum, the Reformation gave rise to many offshoots of the Catholic Church, such as the Lutheran (AD 1526), Church of England (AD 1534), Episcopalian (AD 1534), Calvinists (AD 1536), Presbyterian (AD 1560), Baptists (AD 1609), and Methodists (AD 1739).[24] Yet Shelley is troubled by the modern Christian churches.

> Any Christian reading his New Testament senses the difference between the faith of the apostles and the Christianity of our day. . . . How did denominations come to be the primary expression of Christianity in modern times? The simple fact is Christians are divided today, in part at least, because they have the freedom to differ. In earlier centuries they did not.[25]

It is, however, Brown who states it best.

> The Reformation, for all of its good, had several crippling limitations. First, it did not restore any legitimate priesthood authority. Instead, it necessitated the creation of the non-scriptural belief in a "priesthood of all believers." Neither did the Reformation restore a unified system of doctrine and ordinances, as evidenced by the widely divergent beliefs and practices that it helped to flourish. And finally, the Reformation did not open the heavens and provide divine guidance in ecclesiastical affairs. The Reformers believed that the heavens were forever sealed and that the final, and complete, word of God was to be found in the Bible.[26]

NOTES

1. Brown, *All Things Restored*, 18.
2. Shelley, *Church History*, 240–41.
3. Martin Spalding, *The History of the Protestant Reformation* (General Books, LLC, 2010); Edith Simon, *Great Ages of Man: The Reformation* (Time-Life Books, 1966), 120–21; Herbert J. A. Bouman, "The Doctrine of Justification in the Lutheran Confessions," *Concordia Theological Monthly* (26 November, 1955), no. 11:801.
4. Shelley, *Church History*, 241. See also Henry Clay Vedder, *The Reformation in Germany* (MacMillan, 1914), 405.
5. Shelley, *Church History*, 241. See also Simon, *Great Ages of Man: The Reformation*, 120–21.
6. Michael Hughes, *Early Modern Germany: 1477–1806* (London: MacMillan, 1992), 45–47; Shelley, *Church History*, 241–245.
7. Shelley, *Church History*, 248–54.
8. Ibid., 254. See also Walter Klaassen, *Anabaptism: Neither Catholic nor Protestant* (Waterloo, Ontario: Conrad Press, 1973).
9. Shelley, *Church History*, 257.
10. Ibid., 258–260.
11. Ibid., 261. See also THL Parker, *Calvin: An Introduction to His Thought* (London: Geoffrey Chapman, 1995), 97–103, 114, 147–57.
12. Shelley, *Church History*, 264.
13. Ibid., 267.
14. See William Lamont, *Godly Rule: Politics and Religion 1603–60* (London: MacMillan, 1969); Shelley, *Church History*, 267, 294, 298–99.
15. Shelley, *Church History*, 331.
16. Ibid., 340, 346. See also John Wesley, Wikipedia (January 2012).
17. Ibid., 432.
18. Ibid., 399.
19. David Miano, *An Explanation of Unitarian Christianity* (American Unitarian Conference, 2003, 2007), 15.
20. Shelley, *Church History*, 402.
21. Miano, *An Explanation of Unitarian Christianity*, 15; Shelley, *Church History*, 402–403; J. Gordon Melton, *Encyclopedia of American Religions* 8th ed, 3 vols, (Triumph Books, 1991).
22. Robert Ernest Sandeen, *The Roots of Fundamentalism: British and American Millenarianism 1800–1930* (Chicago: University of Chicago Press, 1970), chapter 1; Shelley, *Church History*, 433, 435; Mark Edwards, "Rethinking the Failure of Fundamentalist Political Antievolution after 1925" (Fides Et Historia, 2000).
23. http://en.wikipedia.org/wiki/Assemblies_of_God.
24. Marston, *Missionary Pal*, 100.
25. Shelley, *Church History*, 301.
26. Brown, *All Things Restored*, 18.

CHAPTER 9

THE RISE OF MORMONISM

THE DISPENSATION OF THE FULNESS OF TIMES

Between dispensations there occurs an apostasy or a falling away from the pure gospel. An apostasy has four main characteristics: (1) rejection of living prophets, (2) loss of divine authority, (3) loss of pure doctrines, and (4) loss of specific authority to perform sacraments and rites.[1] "Religious history as recorded in the Old Testament (which includes the Torah), Pseudepigrapha, and Quran indicates that five significant dispensations have occurred, beginning with Adam, and followed by Enoch, Noah, Abraham, and Moses."[2] Each new dispensation always begins after an apostasy with direct contact between God and man, generally through the calling of a new prophet who restores the ancient religion; namely, the gospel of Jesus Christ. Hence, as discussed earlier in chapter 1, the restoration of the gospel has not just happened once, but in fact has happened many times throughout history.

Early Christianity understood the various dispensations and recognized that the gospel itself was not new. The Apostolic Father Ignatius, bishop of Antioch, testified in approximately AD 108, "for the divine prophets [referring to the ancient Patriarchs and prophets of old] lived according to Jesus Christ. Therefore they were also persecuted, being inspired by his grace, to convince the disobedient that there is one God, who manifested himself through Jesus Christ his son."[3]

Unlike a reformation, which seeks to take what is already present and change it, a restoration is a complete replacement of the old (corrupt) with the new (a return to the original). The Prophet Joseph Smith taught, "It is in the order of heavenly things that God should always send a new dispensation into the world when men have apostatized from the truth and lost the priesthood."[4] Continued Smith,

> It is necessary in the ushering in of the dispensation of the fulness of times, which dispensation is now beginning to usher in, that a whole and complete and perfect union, and welding together of dispensations, and keys, and powers, and glories should take place, and be revealed from the days of Adam even to the present time. And not only this, but those things which never have been revealed from the foundation of the world, but have been kept hid from the wise and prudent, shall be revealed unto babes and sucklings in this, the dispensation of the fulness of times.[5]

Consequently, the dispensation of the fulness of times requires not only the restoration of past doctrines and ordinances, but also a bringing forth of new doctrines and ordinances that have never before been revealed.[6] Concluding, Joseph testified that "all the ordinances and duties that *ever have been required by the priesthood*, under the directions and commandments of the Almighty in *any of the dispensations, shall all be had in the last dispensation*, therefore all things had under the authority of the priesthood at any former period, shall be had again, bringing to pass the restoration spoken of by the mouth of all the Holy Prophets."[7]

Such was not a surprise to the Apostles some two millennia earlier, for they foretold of this restoration and referred to it as "the times of restitution of all things."[8] According to the Apostle Paul, he wrote "that in the *dispensation of the fulness of times,* He [meaning God the Father or Elohim] might gather together all things in Christ, both which are in heaven, and which are on earth."[9] This would be the final dispensation to commence immediately prior to the Second Advent of Christ. According to the Apostle John, before the great and dreadful day of the Lord, an Angel "having the everlasting gospel to preach unto them that dwell on the earth, and to every nation, and kindred, and tongue, and people" must come.[10] Scholar Matthew Brown summed it up this way.

> Just as the Apostle Paul testified that the Second Coming of Jesus Christ would not occur until after "the apostasy" had taken place (2 Thessalonians 2:1–5), so too did the apostle Peter testify that Christ would remain in the heavenly realms "until the times of restitution of all things." This restitution, Peter explained, had been foretold by "all of God's holy prophets since the world began" and would be coupled with fixed or definite periods of revival that would come "from the presence of the Lord" (Acts 3:19–21). The Greek word translated in this passage as "restitution" [*apokatastaseos*] is translated as "restored" in Matthew 12:10–13 and is used to describe something that had once deteriorated but was then returned to its proper function.[11]

Just as new dispensations had been ushered in by Enoch, Noah, Abraham, Moses, and Christ, so too a new dispensation was set to come upon the stage.

THE DREAM OF NEBUCHADNEZZAR

A clue concerning the timing of this last dispensation was given to the Israelite Prophet Daniel in the sixth century BC. Following the downfall of the Southern Kingdom of Judah, many were carried off to Babylon as servants to the empire. Daniel found himself in the court of Nebuchadnezzar, king of Babylon. Daniel's wisdom and knowledge captivated the King. In Daniel 2:31–45, a peculiar set of events transpired that would shape the future of the world.

The king had a dream, which troubled him, but upon waking he could not recall it. He summoned his magicians, astrologers, and sorcerers and demanded they tell him his dream and then interpret it. The wise men told the king that such power was beyond their abilities. Angry, the king sent out a decree that all wise men in the kingdom should be slain. When Daniel discovered that the king's men were on the move to slay he and his Jewish companions, he approached the king and offered his services to both tell the king his dream and then interpret it for him.

The dream was of a great and terrible figure whose head was made of gold, his breast and arms of silver, his belly and thighs of brass, his legs of iron, and his feet part clay and part iron. The dream showed a "stone [which] was cut without hands" and rolled forth destroying the figure. Subsequently, the stone becomes a mountain and fills the entire earth.

Daniel's interpretation to the king indicated that the dream was a time line showing the era when the final restoration of the gospel would unfold—a calendar for plotting the final dispensation; that of the fulness of times. Daniel recounted to the king how the time line plays out. Each body part of the great and terrible figure is a kingdom, which shall fall to the next kingdom until finally, the stone, which is the gospel, shall destroy all earthly kingdoms and fill the entire world.

Babylon is the gold head.[12] Babylon fell to Cyrus the Great, king of Persia, in 539 BC. The Medes and Persians are the silver breast and arms.[13] Persia, under Darius III, fell to Alexander the Great at the Battle of Gaugamela in 331 BC. Greece is thus the belly and thighs of brass.[14] After Alexander's death, his Empire broke into four separate kingdoms with Macedonia encompassing Greece proper. It fell to Rome at the Battle of Cynoscephalae in 197 BC during the Second Macedonian War. The Roman Empire headquartered in Rome are the legs of iron.[15] However, the Empire split into two parts—the Western Empire continued to be headquartered in Rome, but the Eastern Empire had a new capitol at Constantinople, in modern day Turkey. The Western Empire fell in AD 476 to Germanic mercenaries (barbarians) under the leadership of Chieftain Odoacer, thus leaving the Byzantine Empire (the Eastern Roman Empire) at Constantinople remaining. Hence it is these two parts of the Roman Empire that are the feet of iron and clay; at times strong, and at other times weak. The Byzantine Empire existed for many centuries as one of the great Empires, eventually falling in AD 1453 to the Ottoman Empire when the City of Constantinople fell. However, this was not the end of the Roman Empire, for the Western Empire was reconstituted as The Holy Roman Empire in AD 800 at Rome. After Pope Leo III crowned Charlemagne king of the Romans, the feet of clay and iron continued for nearly four hundred years past the end of the Byzantine Empire. The Holy Roman Empire fell to Napoleon and his French Armies on August 6, 1806 when Francis II, the last of the Roman Emperors, abdicated his throne.[16] According to Daniel's interpretation of the dream, which has been accurate down to the last detail, the restoration of the gospel (the stone made by divine powers without hands) would now begin in earnest, rolling forth to consume the earth.

Joseph Smith, the boy prophet, was born December 22, 1805. The New England area was a hotbed for the Great Awakening, with many Christian sects competing for adherents. It was on a spring day in 1820, when the fourteen-year-old Joseph Smith went to a grove of trees to pray in order to know which Christian sect he should join. To his surprise and astonishment, God the Father (Elohim) and the resurrected Jesus Christ (Jehovah) visited him, directing that he should be the prophet of the restoration spoken of by the mouths of the holy Apostles and that he would usher in the final dispensation, that of the fulness of times. To Mormons, this is referred to as the "First Vision." Three years later, the prophet Joseph was visited by an angel, who identified himself as Moroni, a prophet who lived around AD 421 in the Americas. From Moroni, Joseph learned of an ancient Christian people who lived on the American continent in the meridian of time.

THE NEPHITES AND THE LAMANITES

According to the history books, Jerusalem fell to the Babylonians in around 600 BC. This was during the ministry of the prophet Jeremiah, who warned the Jews of the unwiseness of their decision to ally themselves with the Egyptians instead of the Babylonians. There were apparently many prophets during this tumultuous period wandering the streets of the capitol giving these same telltale warnings of what was to come. One of these prophets was a merchant by the name of Lehi, who was of the tribe of Manasseh. Jehovah (the premortal Christ) warned Lehi in a dream that he should take his family and flee into the desert before the Babylonians captured the city. Lehi took with him another merchant friend, Ishmael of the tribe of Ephraim and his family. Together, Lehi and Ishmael, representatives of the seed of Joseph, who was sold into Egypt by his brothers, began a journey across the desert, ultimately culminating in a sea voyage to the American continent, there to raise up a new civilization.

Shortly after their arrival in America, the descendants of Lehi and Ishmael split into warring nations, the Lamanites and the Nephites. The Lamanites were the most numerous,[17] but the Nephites were the most technologically advanced. It was the Nephites who carried on the traditions of their fathers and the gospel of Jesus Christ. The Nephites were distinguished from the Lamanites by their white skin, a remarkable trait that will be discussed later.[18] The Nephites had prophets, many of whom prophesied of the coming of Jesus Christ, the Savior of the world. In fact, there is an account of the Savior actually coming to the Americas after His Resurrection in Jerusalem at around AD 33.

Ultimately, the Lamanite nation, who acquired darker skin through intermarriage outside of their race, destroyed the Nephite nation in a great battle in what is now upstate New York at a hill called Cumorah around AD 400. The Nephites were erased from history. However, in the tradition of their fathers, the Nephites had kept a record of their nation describing Lehi's exodus from Jerusalem, Christ's appearance to them in the meridian of time, and of their final destruction at the hands of their brothers. Moroni was the last of the Nephite Prophets and buried the record in the hill Cumorah. The histories were written on golden plates and contained the fulness of the gospel of Jesus Christ. The record lay buried for centuries until the Prophet Joseph was instructed by the Angel Moroni to uncover the hidden record and use it to restore the gospel that had been taken away from the earth through the great apostasy, which apostasy had transpired following the death of the Apostles. This record is referred to as the "Book of Mormon."[19]

Many have speculated as to where the Prophet Lehi landed in the Americas or where a civilization totaling over one million inhabitants could have lived. Some suggest that the ancient Mayans in the Yucatan peninsula, who lived from 600 BC to AD 400, comprised these nations, while others deny even the existence of the Nephite and Lamanite nations in their entirety. But there may be a more logical answer to the mystery.[20]

> An ancient and unknown people left remains of settled life, and of a certain degree of civilization, in the valleys of the Mississippi and its tributaries. We have no authentic name for them either as a nation or a race; therefore they are called "Mound-Builders," this name having been suggested by an important class of their works.[21]

According to historian Robert Silverburg, the early American settlers were at first oblivious to the artifacts of the Mound-Builders (1,000 BC–AD 500),[22] finding them in their fields as they tried to cultivate the land for farming.

> The mounds lacked beauty and elegance, perhaps. They were heaps of earth. Some were colossal, like the Cahokia Mound in Illinois, 100 feet high and covering 16 acres; others were mere blisters rising from the earth. Some stood in solitary grandeur above broad plains, while others sprouted in thick colonies. All were overgrown with trees and shrubbery, so that their outlines could barely be distinguished, although, once cleared, the mounds revealed their artificial nature by their regularity and symmetry of shape. Within many of them were human bones, weapons, tools, jewelry.[23]

Astonishingly, there is substantial evidence of metallurgy among the Mound-Builders, including the forging of copper, gold, and silver.[24] Over ten thousand mounds ranging from Western New York to Ohio have been discovered. According to at least three American archaeologist, the Mound-Builder nation at its peak is estimated at between 7–18 million inhabitants.[25] The Mound-Builders were a race far advanced from the American Indian found by Columbus.

In 1796, Francis Baily accompanied a party of settlers down the Ohio River and discovered numerous earthen monuments. So impressive were they that Baily wrote,

> The mounds must have been built by a race of people more enlightened than the present Indians, and at some period of time very far distant; for the present Indians know nothing about their use, nor have they any tradition concerning them.[26]

So who are these Mound-Builders and where did they go? Such has been an archeological mystery for hundreds of years.

According to Phyllis Olive,

> Early explorers were so convinced the mounds could not have been built by local savages that they attributed them to Vikings, Romans, Phoenicians or any number of other ancient mariners; anyone other than the Native American Indians, for surely they were far too primitive to have erected such wonderful works. Others, on the other hand, were just as convinced the forerunners of the Native Americans did build the mounds and suggested they were simply a more enlightened race at some earlier period in time.[27]

During the eighteenth and nineteenth centuries the most common theory was that the Mound-Builders of New York and the Ohio River Valley were the remnants of the lost ten tribes of Israel who were carried away by Assyria in the seventh century AD. According to James Adair, an explorer and trader among the American Indians from 1735–1775, the Indians related that they were descended from a common ancestor who had twelve sons, echoing the notion of the Patriarch Jacob and his twelve sons. There were other similarities with the Hebrews as well that Adair found. For example, the Indians were monotheists, like the Hebrews, had a high priest, were divided into tribes, and appeared to have many feasts similar to those of the Hebrews, as well as the same time reckoning system.[28] Could this have been the fulfillment of Jacob's prophesy?

> Joseph is a fruitful bough, even a fruitful bough by a well; whose branches run over the wall.[29]

Did descendants of Joseph, through his sons Ephraim and Manasseh, truly journey over the wall of the ocean to North America? That would be consistent with the notion that the Mound-Builders and their descendants, which may include some American Indian tribes, are part of the lost ten tribes.

So are the Mound-Builders the ancient Nephite and Lamanite civilizations? In the book, *American Antiquities*, the characteristics of the Mound-Builders are summed up:

1. [They] were all of the same origin, branches of the same race, and possessed of similar customs and institutions.

2. They were populous, and occupied a great extent of territory.

3. They had arrived at a considerable degree of civilization, were associated in large communities, and lived in extensive cities.

4. They possessed the use of many of the metals such as lead, copper, gold, and silver, and probably the art of working in them.

5. They sculptured in stone, and sometimes used that material in the construction of their edifices.

6. They had the knowledge of the arch of receding steps; of the art

of pottery—producing utensils and urns forged with taste, and constructed upon the principles of chemical compositions and of the art of brick-making.

7. They worked the salt springs, and manufactured that substance.

8. They were an agricultural people living under the influence and protection of regular forms of government.

9. They possessed a decided system of religion, and a mythology connected with astronomy, which, with its sister science geometry, was in the hands of the priesthood.

10. They were skilled in the art of fortification.

11. The epoch of their original settlement, in the United States, is of great antiquity.[30]

These characteristics mirror those found in the Nephite civilization, which are described in the Book of Mormon.[31] But how would the Mound-Builders account for the two distinct nations, Nephites and Lamanites, and how is the genealogy of the American Indian linked to these Mound-Builders?

First, the Mound-Builders of the Woodland Epoch (1000 BC–AD 500) were separated into two distinct groups, the Hopewell and Adena nations. The Hopewell were a highly advanced race of Mound-Builders from New York, who migrated to the Ohio River Valley.[32] They have been referred to as the "New York Hopewell,"[33] and their lands included those encompassing the Hill Cumorah in upstate New York, the location where the Prophet Joseph Smith found the golden plates. The Hopewell were accomplished craftsmen and artisans.

On the other hand, the Adena appear to be less advanced, but more numerous, and lived south of the Hopewell. They are described as hunter-gatherers. The Hopewell vanish from history around AD 450. These are striking similarities to the Nephites (Hopewell) and the Lamanites (Adena).[34] Interestingly, as American settlers pushed west into Michigan, a large number of artifacts were discovered. They are referred to as the "Michigan Relics." A number of the relics are pictographs depicting two warring nations; one a nation of white skinned people with armor (their leader wearing a crown), and the other a nation of darker skinned people without armor (their leader wearing a feathered headdress). This is consistent with an old Indian legend of a great white race that pre-dated the Indian tribes, who were highly skilled artisans.[35]

As historian J. P. MacLean stated

> [This] country had been inhabited by a white people, who were familiar with arts of which the Indian knew nothing, and that after a series of battles with the Indians, they were exterminated.[36]

This understanding that the great white race of the Hopewells was destroyed in a war of extermination is well remembered in the legends of the American Indian. In discussing the area around the hill Cumorah, historian O. Turner professes that

> The evidence that this was one, at least, of their final battlefields, predominate. They are the fortifications, entrenchments and warlike instruments of an extinct race. That here was war of extermination, we may well conclude, from masses of human skeletons we find indiscriminately thrown together, indicating a common and simultaneous sepulcher from which age, infancy, sex, and no condition was exempt.[37]

Following the destruction of the Hopewells, a new mound building culture erupted in the heartland of the present day United States, known as the Mississippian Epoch. Eventually this civilization would spawn some of the Indian nations that the colonists found in the Americas and that Columbus met on the Isle of Hispaniola.[38]

THE PROPHESY OF EZEKIEL

The coming forth of the Book of Mormon, describing the ancient Nephite and Lamanite nations, was also prophesied anciently by the prophet Ezekiel.

> The word of the Lord came again unto me, saying: Moreover, thou son of man, take thee one stick and write upon it, For Judah, and for the children of Israel his companions: then take another stick, and write upon it, For Joseph, the stick of Ephraim, and for all the house of Israel his companions; And join them one to another into one stick; and they shall become one in thine hand.[39]

According to the prophesy, two sticks or scrolls (books) would be written; one for Judah and one for Joseph. The stick of Judah is obviously the Old Testament of the Bible, compiled by the Jews in the Septuagint[40] between 284 and 246 BC, as well as the New Testament, written by the Jewish disciples of Christ. It was not by mere happenstance that these books were called the Old and New Testaments; for they stand as witnesses that Jesus is the Christ, the only begotten son of the Father in the flesh. This second stick or book would also be a witness of Christ, a second witness, that would together with the first be one in the hand of the Lord. Where is this second book? To date, there is only one book that makes such a claim or fits such a description, and that is the Book of Mormon.[41]

The prophet Lehi was a descendant of Joseph through his eldest son, Manasseh. His family married into the family of Ishmael, who was also a descendant of Joseph, but through his younger son, Ephraim. These families migrated originally from the Northern Kingdom when that kingdom was conquered by the Assyrians. It was these families who wrote the Book of Mormon, a history of their descendants, the descendants of Joseph.[42] Their record is a second witness of the Lord Jesus Christ, that together with the Bible stand as witnesses of Christ, thus fulfilling the prophesy of Ezekiel.

NOTES

1. Petersen, *Where Have All the Prophets Gone?*, 19–21.
2. Ibid., 19.
3. Eusebius, *Ecclesiastical History* 1:26–28, quoted in Petersen, *Where Have All the Prophets Gone?*, 37–38.
4. B. H. Roberts, *A Comprehensive History of the Church of Jesus Christ of Latter-day Saints* ("History of the Church") (Provo, UT, Brigham Young University Press: 1965), 6:478–79.
5. Joseph Smith letter, dated September 6, 1842 (Nauvoo, IL).
6. *History of the Church*, 4:426.
7. Ibid., 4:208, 210–11. Emphasis added.
8. Acts 3:20–21. See also Matthew 17:11; Acts 1:6–7.
9. Ephesians 1:10. Emphasis added.
10. Revelation 14:6
11. Brown, *All Things Restored*, 19.
12. Daniel 2:38.
13. Daniel 5:28,31; Daniel 8:20.
14. Daniel 8:4–9, 21–22.
15. Daniel 7:7.

16. Daniel 7:23–25.

17. This most probably is the result of intermarriages with pre-existing populations in the Americas, many of whom may have come from Asian descent over the land bridge a thousand years earlier. This would also explain why the Lamanites had darker skin than the Nephites, who did not inter-marry.

18. The Book of Mormon speaks of the Lamanites being cursed with darker skin because of disobedience. Just as the Israelites of old had been forbidden to intermarry with the gentile nations surrounding Israel, so was this same prohibition given to the Lamanites. The curse was then the natural consequence of violating this prohibition.

19. See 2 Nephi 25:14–17 (where ancient Nephite prophets long foretold of hiding their records to come forth in a future dispensation)

20. The Church of Jesus Christ of Latter-day Saints has never taken an official position on Book of Mormon geography.

21. Phyllis Carol Olive, *The Lost Tribes of the Book of Mormon* (Springville, UT: Bonneville Books, 2001), 15, quoting John D. Balwin, *Ancient America in Notes on American Archaeology*, (New York: Harper and Brothers 1872), 17.

22. This is referred to as the "Woodland Period." However, those existing at the time of the Woodland Period were descendants of the Archaic Era of Mound-Builders (2500 BC–1000 BC). These Mound-Builders originated in southern Ontario and Northern New York. Were these the Jaredites in the Book of Mormon? No one knows.

23. Olive, *The Lost Tribes of the Book of Mormon*, 6, quoting Robert Silverburg, *Mound Builders*, (Athens: Ohio University Press, 1970), 10.

24. Olive, *The Lost Tribes of the Book of Mormon*, 36, 43–56. Phyllis Carol Olive, *The Lost Lands of the Book of Mormon*, (Springville, UT: Bonneville Books, 1998), 238–39.

25. Olive, *The Lost Tribes of the Book of Mormon*, 10–11.

26. Ibid., 15, quoting Silverburg, *Mound Builders*, 41.

27. Olive, *The Lost Tribes of the Book of Mormon*, 16.

28. Ibid., 22–23.

29. Genesis 49:22.

30. Olive, *Lost Tribes of the Book of Mormon*, citing Cecil E. McGavin and Willard Bean, T*he Geography of the Book of Mormon*, (Salt Lake City: Bookcraft, 1949), 68, quoting Bradford, *American Antiquities*, 60–70.

31. According to the Book of Mormon, another similar civilization existed prior to the Nephites and Lamanites, the Jaredites, who lived in the same region. According to the Book of Mormon, the Jaredites came to America after the confounding of the languages following the fall of the Tower of Babel and may have traveled extensively in Asia minor before making a voyage to America. This would explain the proximate beginning of the Mound-Builders more than 400 years before the arrival of Lehi and Ishmael, and their descendants. Some archeologists estimate that the Mound-Builder civilization may have begun as early as 2,000 to 3,000 BC, and stretched as far north as Quebec and Ontario in Canada.

32. Some archeologists believe that the Hopewell migrated as far west as Illinois.

33. Heironymous Rowe, "Hopewell Interaction Sphere" (February 6, 2010).

34. Olive, *The Lost Tribes of the Book of Mormon*, 119–42.

35. McGavin and Bean, *The Geography of the Book of Mormon*, 83.

36. Olive, *The Lost Lands of the Book of Mormon*, 284, quoting J.P. MacLean, *The Mound Builders*, 144.

37. Olive, *The Lost Lands of the Book of Mormon*, 284, quoting O. Turner, *Pioneer*

History of the Holland Purchase of Western New York, (Jewett, Thomas: Geo. H. Derby 1849), 19.

38. There are some Mormon historians who insist that 1 Nephi 13:12 requires that Columbus have visited North America for it to have been the promised land, but the promised land was said by Joseph Smith to be all of North and South America. However, these same historians who attempt to use this verse to downgrade the Mound-Builders theory in favor of a Guatemala geography have the same problem. Although Columbus visited central America, he specifically never visited the Maya in Guatamala.

39. Ezekiel 37:15–17.

40. The Septuagint is the Greek translation of the Old Testament, which purportedly was translated by seventy-two Jewish elders in seventy days. It was translated specifically for the Greek-speaking Jews living in Alexandria, Egypt. Bible Dictionary, The Church of Jesus Christ of Latter-day Saints (Salt Lake City, UT: 1989), 771.

41. Doctrine and Covenants 27:5; 2 Nephi 3:11–12; 1 Nephi 13:34–41.

42. Critics of the Book of Mormon suggest that DNA evidence does not support the ancestors of the American Indian (Lamanites) being of middle eastern descent. There are two problems with these analyses, (1) while there is some American Indian DNA that indicates Asian descent, there is also DNA found in 31 percent of self-identified American Indians, which indicates descent from Iranian and Iraqi Jews. See "Cohen Modal Haplotype," in David G. Stewart, Jr., "DNA and the Book of Mormon," *FARMS Review* 18/1 (2006): 109–138.

    Further, the Nephite and Lamanite settlements were a small percentage of the population then existing in the Americas. There is certainly evidence to suggest that the Lamanites intermarried with the pre-existing population as well, further diluting their DNA markers; (2) the Nephites and Lamanites were descended not from the Jews, but instead from the Tribes of Manasseh and Ephraim, two of the lost tribes carried away by the Assyrians. Consequently, without DNA from these two tribes, DNA testing of the American Indian is meaningless. See Generally, Erastus Snow, "Ephraim And Manasseh, etc.," (6 May 1882) *Journal of Discourses* 23:184. Molecular Anthropologist Michael H. Crawford wrote how the subjugation of the indigenous peoples by the European explorers may have effected the gene pool as well: "The conquest and its sequel squeezed the entire Amerindian population through a genetic bottleneck. The reduction of Amerindians gene pools from 1/3 to 1/25 of their previous size implies a considerable loss of genetic variability. . . . It is highly unlikely that survivorship was genetically random. . . . Thus, the present gene-frequency distributions of Amerindian populations may be distorted by a combination of effects stemming from genetic bottlenecks and natural selection. . . . This population reduction has forever altered the genetics of the surviving groups, thus complicating any attempts at reconstructing the pre-Columbian genetic structure of most New World groups." Ugo A. Perego, *The Book of Mormon and the Origin of Native Americans from a Maternally Inherited DNA Standpoint* (FAIR 2010), quoting Michael Crawford, *The Origins of Native Americans: Evidence from Anthropological Genetics* (Cambridge; Cambridge University Press, 1998). In other words, no DNA studies concerning the origins of the American Indian are conclusive.

CHAPTER 10

THE RESTORED CHURCH (THE MORMONS)

THE GREAT SECRET

In the spring of 1820 in upstate New York, the Great Awakening was continuing to occur. Revivalists from all Christian sects were preaching in open air auditoriums throughout Palmyra, New York. It was here that a family of pioneer stock was farming their claim. The grandfather, Assa Smith, had fought with General George Washington during the American Revolution. This was a typical New England family who was caught up in the excitement over religion. The father, Joseph Smith Sr., believed in God but did not believe that the true Church of Christ was upon the earth. Consequently, while his family traveled to each revival, he stayed at the homestead. It was during this time that one of his sons, a young fourteen-year-old farm boy, while seeking to know the truth about Christianity, was reading in the King James version of the Bible, James 1:5–6.

> If any of you lack wisdom, let him ask of God, that giveth to all men liberally, and upbraideth not; and it shall be given him.
>
> But let him ask in faith, nothing wavering. For he that wavereth is like a wave of the sea driven with the wind and tossed.

Young Joseph Smith Jr. decided that he should ask God which of all the Christian denominations he should join. He went to a grove of trees near his home and prayed. He recounted:

> After I had retired to the place where I had previously designed to go, having looked around me, and finding myself alone, I kneeled down and began to offer up the desires of my heart to God. I had scarcely done so, when immediately I was seized upon by some power which entirely overcame me, and had such an astonishing influence over me as to bind my tongue so that I could not speak. Thick darkness gathered around me, and it seemed to me for a time as if I were doomed to sudden destruction.
>
> But, exerting all my powers to call upon God to deliver me out of the power of this enemy which had seized upon me, and at the very moment when I was ready to sink into despair and abandon myself to destruction—not to an imaginary ruin, but to the power of some actual being from the unseen world, who had such marvelous power as I had never before felt in any being—just at this moment of great alarm, I saw a pillar of light exactly over my head, above the brightness of the sun, which descended gradually until it fell upon me.
>
> It no sooner appeared than I found myself delivered from the enemy which held me bound. When the light rested upon me I saw two Personages, whose brightness and glory defy all description, standing above me in the air. One of them spake unto me, calling me by name and said, pointing to the other—*This is My Beloved Son. Hear Him!*[1]

It was in this "First Vision" that Jesus Christ (Jehovah) told young Joseph that His gospel was to be restored to the earth, just as it had been done previously by the likes of Noah, Abraham, and Moses following periods of apostasy. From this time forth, the boy prophet of the Restoration began his sojourn to restore the gospel by restoring Hebrew Christianity, which was literally the tenets of the original Apostolic Church. The heresy that had been thought extinguished by the Hellenized Church was back some 1,500 years later. Not surprising, once the vision became known, the reformationists immediately began attacking young Joseph, even though he was only a teen. Said Joseph:

> I soon found, however, that my telling the story had excited a great deal of prejudice against me among professors of religion, and was

the cause of great persecution, which continued to increase; and though I was an obscure boy, only between fourteen and fifteen years of age, and my circumstances in life such as to make a boy of no consequence in the world, yet men of high standing would take notice sufficient to excite the public mind against me, and create a bitter persecution; and this was common among all the sects—all united to persecute me.[2]

A unique occurrence? From the perspective of Christian orthodoxy and the Hellenistic version thereof, it was not unique at all. The Cathar heresy had been allowed to fester. The lesson had been learned. Especially where the heresy in this case was Hebrew Christianity, the one heresy most feared by both the Roman Church and the Reformists. It needed to be extinguished early and not allowed to expand. Remember, Hebrew Christianity had been dominant; it was the original branch of Christianity for the first three hundred years after the death of Christ. It had been enormously popular. Much was at stake. Consequently, it was only logical that Joseph should be persecuted and dismissed publicly.

Consistent with past apostasies and dispensations, the opening up of the dispensation of the fulness of times, as prophesied by the Apostles Peter and Paul, began with the visitation of God the Father and Jesus Christ to a new spokesman, a new prophet. With that Joseph learned the first and most important restored truth—the very truth that had directly led to the destruction of the Hebrew Christians; namely, that God is a man.

Bible scholar W. D. Davies has proffered, "Mormonism is the Jewish-Christian tradition in an American key . . . What it did was to re-Judaize a Christianity that had been too much Hellenized."[3] Hence, in direct contradiction to the Nicene Creed, the true nature of the Godhead had been restored, for in the First Vision Joseph had seen the Father and the Son as two separate and distinct beings. He would go on to declare

> God to be a distinct personage, Jesus Christ a separate and distinct personage from God the Father, and that the Holy Ghost was a distinct personage and a Spirit: and these three constitute three distinct personages and three Gods.[4]

Three years later, Joseph was visited by an angel who said his name was Moroni, the last of his civilization, which had lived in the Americas. It was Moroni who instructed Joseph as to the location of a record of that civilization—the Nephite civilization—possibly the Hopewell Mound-Builders. As Joseph translated the ancient record, he learned about Christ's true and pure gospel, for the Nephite prophets of old had written extensively concerning it.

A Nephite prophet named Nephi (for whom the Nephite nation was named) discussed how the Godhead acts as one—in a unified voice. Modern Apostle James E. Talmage summarized Nephi's teachings:

> This unity is a type of completeness; the mind of any one member of the Trinity is the mind of the others; seeing as each of them does with the eye of perfection, they see and understand alike. Under any given conditions each would act in the same way, guided by the same principles of unerring justice and equity. The oneness of the Godhead, to which the scriptures so abundantly testify, implies no mystical union of substance, nor any unnatural and therefore impossible blending of personality. Father, Son, and Holy Ghost are as distinct in their persons and individualities as are any three personages in mortality. Yet their unity of purpose and operation is such as to make their edicts one, and their will the will of God.[5]

Subordinationism, as taught by Arius, was also back. Echoed the young prophet Joseph: "Any person that [has] seen the heavens opened knows that there are three personages in the heavens who hold the keys of power, and one [the Father] presides over all."[6] As previously stated, the Hebrew notion of the physicality of God was also restored. Said the Prophet Joseph Smith, "If you were to see [God] today, you would see him like a man in form," thus echoing again what was taught by the Apostles and the early Church Fathers; namely, that we are of the same creed and race as God.[7] The great secret of the ancient heresy had been revealed to Joseph.

> The God of Abraham, Isaac, and Jacob has often been distinguished from the god of the philosophers. The latter is allegedly only a human conception—a product of rational theologizing, with no explicit basis in biblical revelation. While the philosophers' God is variously conceived, it is usually said to be, among other things, absolutely unlimited in all

respects, wholly other, absolutely simple, immaterial, nonspatial, non-temporal, immutable, and impassible. By way of contrast, the biblical record describes the God of Abraham, Isaac, and Jacob as "the living God" who created man in his "own image and likeness" who spoke with Moses "face to face, as a man speaketh unto his friend." He is the loving God who is profoundly "touched with the feeling of our infirmities" and specifically involved in our individual and collective lives.[8]

Joseph Smith preached,

God himself was once as we are now, and is an exalted man, and sits enthroned in yonder heavens! *That is the great secret.* If the veil were rent today, and the great God who holds this world in its orbit, and who upholds all worlds and all things by His power, was to make Himself visible,—I say, if you were to see Him today, you would see Him like a man in form—like yourselves in all the person, image, and very form as a man; for Adam was created in the very fashion, image and likeness of God, and received instruction from, and walked, talked and conversed with Him, as one man talks and communes with another.[9]

Hellenized Christians called this doctrine an abomination, blasphemy. However, to the early Christians this was the essence of their relationship with God—a deeply personal relationship. They spoke of a familial tie. Mormons would then take the "great secret" to new heights, infusing within it an understanding of the universe not contemplated or understood by the earliest Christians.

THE CREATION AND PREMORTAL EXISTENCE OF MAN

The creation of this world was not by accident but was conceived of divine design by Elohim, a perfected and glorified man, for the benefit of His children.[10] Again, this familial tie.

Now, the word *create* came from the word *baurau* which does not mean to create out of nothing; it means to organize; the same as a man would organize materials and build a ship. Hence, we infer that God had materials to organize the world out of chaos—chaotic matter, which is element. . . . Element had an existence from the time he had. The pure principles of element are principles which can never be destroyed; they may be organized and re-organized, but not destroyed. They had no beginning, and can have no end.[11]

Obviously, if matter always existed and never was created, then the Hebrew belief in a premortal existence, as was written of in the Old Testament and preached by Christ and His Apostles during the meridian of time was only rational. Joseph Smith taught, "I am dwelling on the immortality of the spirit of man. Is it logical to say that the intelligence of spirits [are] immortal, and yet that it had a beginning? The intelligence of spirits had no beginning, neither will it have an end. That is good logic. That which has a beginning may have an end. There never was a time when there were not spirits; for they are [co-eternal] with our Father in Heaven."[12] From revelation, Joseph further learned of a council in heaven.

> The head God called together the Gods and sat in grand council to bring forth the world. The grand counselors sat at the head in yonder heavens, and contemplated the creation of the worlds which were created at that time. . . . In the beginning, the head of the Gods called a council of Gods; and they came together and concocted a plan to create the world and people it.[13]

It was there, in this premortal council, that Jehovah (Christ) and Lucifer (Satan), presented their plans of salvation for the welfare of mankind to the Father.[14] Satan, as noted by the Apostolic Fathers, was a son of God who fell from glory, as described by the Apostle John in the Book of Revelation.[15] His plan was rejected, and he rebelled against the Father.

DEIFICATION

With a restoration of the Hebrew beliefs in the nature of God came the inescapable conclusion of our own true natures; thus, the doctrine of deification was restored.[16] Joseph Smith revealed, "Here, then, is eternal life—to know the only wise and true God; and you have to learn to be Gods your[selves], and to be kings and priests to God, the same as all Gods have done before you, namely, by going from one small degree to another, and from a small capacity to a great one."[17] Men and women are of God's race, literal sons and daughters of God.[18] The familial tie then is not metaphorical but is instead a real one.

Critics, in attempting to dispel the new Mormon heresy, have scorned the Mormon faith in asserting that Joseph Smith's belief in deification is not backed up by the Bible, nor for that matter by the Book of Mormon. This, of course, is untrue. I previously discussed in this book the basis for deification from scripture within both the Old and New Testaments, as well as from the teachings of many of the Apostolic Fathers, like Origen. As for the Book of Mormon, it teaches that men and women can reap eternal life, which is the life God lives (such as, Godhood).[19] Joseph Smith taught, "The first principles of man are self-existent with God. God himself, finding he was in the midst of spirits and glory, because he was more intelligent, saw proper to institute laws whereby the rest could have a privilege to advance like himself. The relationship we have with God places us in a situation to advance in knowledge. He has power to institute laws to instruct the weaker intelligences, that they may be exalted with himself, so that they might have one glory upon another, and all that knowledge, power, glory, and intelligence, which is requisite in order to save them in the world of spirits."[20] These two main revealed doctrines, that of the true nature of God and of mankind's relationship to Him, have resulted in most of the other Christian denominations calling the Mormons non-Christians. It really isn't that Mormons are not Christians, it is that the restored doctrines of the Hebrews are different from those of orthodox Hellenized Christianity.[21]

THE GOSPEL

In the second century, Justin Martyr taught that the gospel had always been upon the earth in one form or another, thus explaining why the Old Testament was still of value to early Christianity and why Christ so often quoted from it. Joseph Smith likewise preached that the gospel was taught to Adam and Eve.[22] In his inspired translation of the Bible, the Prophet Joseph revealed that Moses received the fulness of the gospel originally on Mount Sinai.[23] Joseph Smith taught,

> We cannot believe that the ancients in all ages were so ignorant of the system of heaven as many suppose, since all that were eversaved, were saved through the power of this great plan of redemption, as much before the coming of Christ as since; if not, God has had

different plans in operation (if we may so express it), to bring men back to dwell with Himself. And this we cannot believe, since there has been no change in the constitution of man since he fell; and the ordinance or institution of offering blood in sacrifice was only designed to be performed till Christ was offered up and shed His blood—as said before—that man might look forward in faith to that time. . . . We may conclude, that though there were different dispensations, yet all things which God communicated to His people were calculated to draw their minds to the great object, and to teach them to rely upon God alone as the author of their salvation, as contained in His law.[24]

The gospel preached by Mormons is the same as was taught by the original Church;[25] namely, faith,[26] repentance,[27] baptism[28] by immersion,[29] and the receipt of the gift of the Holy Ghost.[30] This has been called the Doctrine of Christ.

Behold, verily, verily, I say unto you, I will declare unto you my doctrine.

And this is my doctrine, and it is the doctrine which the Father hath given unto me; and I bear record of the Father, and the Father beareth record of me, and the Holy Ghost beareth record of the Father and me; and I bear record that the Father commandeth all men, everywhere, to *repent* and *believe* in me.

And whoso believeth in me, and is *baptized*, the same shall be saved; and they are they who shall inherit the kingdom of God.

And whoso believeth not in me, and is not baptized, shall be damned.

Verily, verily, I say unto you, that this is my doctrine, and I bear record of it from the Father; and whose believeth in me believeth in the Father also; and unto him will the Father bear record of me, *for he will visit him with fire and with the Holy Ghost.*

And thus will the Father bear record of me, and the Holy Ghost will bear record unto him of the Father and me; for the Father, and I, and the Holy Ghost are one.

And again I say unto you, ye must repent, and become as a little child, and be baptized in my name, or ye can in nowise receive these things. And again I say unto you, ye must repent, and be baptized in my name, and become as a little child or ye can in nowise inherit the kingdom of God.

Verily, verily, I say unto you that *this is my doctrine*, and whoso buildeth upon this buildeth upon my rock, and the gates of hell shall not prevail against them.

And whoso shall declare more or less than this, and establish it for my doctrine, the same cometh of evil, and is not built upon my rock; but he buildeth upon a sandy foundation, and the gates of hell stand open to receive such when the floods come and the winds beat upon them.[31]

The Prophet Joseph Smith further taught, "Baptism is a sign to God, to angels, and to heaven that we do the will of God, and there is no other way beneath the heavens whereby God hath ordained for man to come to Him to be saved, and enter into the kingdom of God, except *faith in Jesus Christ, repentance, and baptism for the remission of sins, and any other course is in vain; then you have the promise of the gift of the Holy Ghost.*"[32] During the Apostasy, the Hellenized Church slowly de-emphasized the importance of baptism. Then during the Reformation, while some, such as the Baptists, returned to the baptismal ordinance as a foundational doctrine, many others, such as the Methodists, Calvinists, and Evangelicals, did not. Notwithstanding the move by orthodoxy away from water baptism, John 3:5, which answered the Pharisee Nicodemus's question on the necessity of baptism, is the only definitive statement from the Master. Commented the Prophet Joseph,

> this strong and positive answer of Jesus [referring to Nicodemus] as to water baptism, settles the question: If God is the same yesterday, today, and forever; it is no wonder he is so positive in the great declaration: 'He that believes and is baptized shall be saved, and he that believes not shall be damned!' There was no other name given under heaven, nor other ordinance admitted, whereby men could be saved: No wonder the Apostle said, being 'buried with him in baptism,' ye shall rise from the dead. No wonder Paul had to arise and be baptized and wash away his sins.[33]

Jesus, Himself, was baptized by immersion in the River Jordan by John the Baptist to show all mankind the way home to our Heavenly Father—in His words, "to fulfil all righteousness."[34] Apparently, the ordinance of baptism is more than simply the symbolic washing away of sin. It is the key to the door that opens eternal life. All must enter by that door. Yet to open it, all must possess the key. And the key cannot be a counterfeit; that is, one that is given out by an unauthorized servant of Jehovah. Just as John the Baptist was empowered to baptize, so too must those who perform the ordinance today possess the required authority.

Joseph Smith went on to emphasize the importance of also receiving the gift of the Holy Ghost:

> The gospel requires baptism by immersion for the remission of sins, which is the meaning of the word in the original language—namely, to bury or immerse. . . . I further believe in the gift of the Holy Ghost by the laying on of hands, by Peter's preaching on the day of Pentecost. You might as well baptize a bag of sand as a man, if not done in view of the remission of sins and getting of the Holy Ghost. Baptism by water is but half a baptism, and is good for nothing without the other half—that is, the baptism of the Holy Ghost. The Savior says, "Except a man be born of the water and of the Spirit, he cannot enter into the kingdom of God."[35]

Each week, Mormons renew their baptismal covenant through the taking of the sacrament, an ordinance similar to the Eucharist. However, the meaning of this ordinance to Mormons has special significance. The renewal is a reaffirmation of the covenant and comes with a promised remission of sins, so that each week Mormons start anew.

Mormons, however, reject the doctrine of infant baptism, as began to be practiced in the Hellenized Church.[36] Joseph Smith taught, "Baptism is for remission of sins. Children have no sins. Jesus blessed them and said, 'Do what you have seen me do.' Children are all made alive in Christ, and those of riper years through faith and repentance."[37] The age of accountability, eight years old, where children are capable of sinning, was later revealed to the Prophet Joseph.[38] The Prophet concluded, "The doctrine of baptizing children, or sprinkling them, or they must welter in hell, is a doctrine not true, not supported in Holy Writ, and is not consistent with the character of God. All children are redeemed by the blood of Jesus Christ, and the moment that children leave this world, they are taken to the bosom of Abraham."[39]

THE ATONEMENT AND THE RESURRECTION

Mormons believe that Jesus Christ is the Savior of the World.[40] He did this by suffering for all the sins and imperfections of mankind, which suffering and sacrifice is referred to as the Atonement.

> And he [meaning, Christ] shall go forth, suffering pains and afflictions

and temptations of every kind; and this that the word might be fulfilled which saith he will take upon him the pains and the sicknesses of his people.

And he will take upon him death, that he may loose the bands of death which bind his people; and he will take upon him their infirmities, that his bowels may be filled with mercy, according to the flesh, that he may know according to the flesh how to succor his people according to their infirmities.[41]

Further, what is not well understood in the greater Christian world of today is that the Atonement also encompasses the resurrection of the dead. It is of note that soon after conquering the Hebrews, the Hellenized Church changed the orthodox view of Christ's Resurrection from a physical resurrection to more of a spiritual one. With the restoration of Hebrew Christianity came the return to a belief in the physical resurrection of Christ.[42] "The fundamental principles of our religion are the testimony of the Apostles and Prophets, concerning Jesus Christ, that He died, was buried, and rose again the third day, and ascended into heaven; and all other things which pertain to our religion are only appendages to it," said Joseph Smith.[43] Just as Paul taught, the Mormons believe that "the Lamb of God hath brought to pass the resurrection, so that all shall rise from the dead."[44]

Mormons have a great reverence for the mortal body; for it not only houses the spirit but also shall become a permanent physical tabernacle, one that is glorified and perfected, immortal, all as a result of Christ.

> We came to this earth that we might have a body and present it pure before God in the celestial kingdom. The great principle of happiness consists in having a body. The devil has no body, and herein is his punishment. He is pleased when he can obtain the tabernacle of man, and when cast out by the Savior he asked to go into the herd of swine, showing that he would prefer a swine's body to having none. All beings who have bodies have power over those who have not.[45]

Mormons also believe, as did the Hebrews, in the concept of a Spirit World that exists between death and the resurrection. As explained by the Prophet Alma,

> Now, concerning the state of the soul between death and the resurrection—Behold, it has been made known unto me by an angel, that the spirits of all men, as soon as they are departed from this mortal body,

yea, the spirits of all men, whether they be good or evil, are taken home to that God who gave them life.

And then shall it come to pass, that the spirits of those who are righteous are received into a state of happiness, which is called paradise, a state of rest, a state of peace, where they shall rest from all their troubles and from all care, and sorrow.

And then shall it come to pass, that the spirits of the wicked, yea, who are evil—for behold, they have no part nor portion of the Spirit of the Lord; for behold they chose vile works rather than good; therefore the spirit of the devil did enter into them, and take possession of their house—and these shall be cast out into outer darkness; there shall be weeping and wailing, and gnashing of teeth, and this because of their own iniquity, being led captive by the will of the devil.

Now this is the state of the wicked, yea, in darkness and a state of awful, fearful looking for the fiery indignation of the wrath of God upon them; thus they remain in this state, as well as the righteous in paradise, until the time of their resurrection.[46]

THE PLAN OF SALVATION

The premortal existence can be compared to childhood. We lived there as spirits. We have no idea how long we were there—perhaps billions of years. Remember that time is relative and God has no fear of time; He is immortal. We graduated from that existence to this mortal sphere, our proverbial teenage years, where our spirits are given a mortal body. We must learn to control it, bend it to the will of our spirits. The mortal body, however, has passions and emotions that must be disciplined. This life is to grow and develop our character and attributes in the image of our Elder Brother Jesus Christ. He is our example. At death, we grow into immortal adults. Adults who happen to be of the same race and creed as God. In God's realm, all human beings are judged by the condition of their hearts.[47] According to John, it is Christ who will be our judge.[48] That is only fitting because only Christ, as our Savior, has the power to make us perfect through the washing away of our sins and imperfections.[49] That allows us to be placed upon a continuum of sorts, a continuum that is always progressing toward Godhood. Where you are placed along the continuum is up to you. It is your mortal agency to decide what kind of person you will become; one who has the characteristics of Christ: kindness, honesty, mercy, industry, and charity or one who is unlike Christ: angry, hard-hearted, self-centered, and lustful. It is up to the individual to decide. Many times, obstacles are placed in our way to see how we will deal with them. They are learning moments where our character is developed for good or ill.

Just as the Apostle Paul talked of degrees of glory in heaven, so Mormons believe. The continuum begins in outer darkness, progresses to a degree of glory that has been compared to the stars in the heaven (the telestial kingdom),[50] then on to a glory similar to the reflective light of the moon (the terrestrial kingdom),[51] and ultimately to the glory of the sun (the celestial kingdom).[52] All continue to progress along this spectrum for eternity. As Christ preached, "in my Father's house are many mansions: if it were not so, I would have told you. I go to prepare a place for you."[53] Hence within each of these kingdoms, there are many subkingdoms. We are always becoming better, perfecting ourselves in the image of Christ, moving forward along the continuum. This process has been referred to as the doctrine of "eternal progression." Eventually, if we persevere, endure to the end, we will become like our Father: a God, a Creator. To Hellenized Christianity, such is the world of fantasy. But to the prophets of the Old Testament and the Apostles of the New Testament, far from fairy tales, this was to be mankind's destiny.

Unlike the Hellenized reformers of the Middle Ages, Mormons do not consider themselves to be the only true Christians; rather Mormons believe that all who follow Christ are Christians and thus are not subject to damnation. Mormons believe that all of mankind is on a path toward perfection and Godhood. Some are further along than others, which denotes the separate kingdoms.

At this point, it is important to understand that Mormons believe salvation is ultimately obtained through a covenant relationship with Elohim, for only through this covenant relationship is man made perfect. That covenant is taken at baptism and is renewed through the taking of the sacrament of the Lord's Supper. Why is the covenant essential? Because it is through the covenant that men are afforded the guidance of the Holy Ghost.[54] The Holy Ghost is a purifier of the soul and this gift is often referred to as the baptism of fire. Through the companionship of the Holy Ghost, one's character is elevated and sanctified. Apparently, this companionship is mandatory to obtaining a celestial glory.

Consequently, Mormons may believe that they are farther along this continuum than those not of their religion because of the companionship of the Holy Ghost in their lives, but they are still on the same road as everyone else.

In Mormon theology only sons of perdition are truly damned and destined to hell.[55] Hell, however, is simply a place where Satan and his angels, a third of all the host of heaven, who were prevented from coming to this earth life and receiving a mortal body, live. It is referred to in the scriptures as "outer darkness." The fact that they are damned does not mean that they cannot progress, it simply means that for now their progression is stopped. Hence, they are not progressing along the continuum, but that lack of progress is of their own making. They rejected the Savior and His Atonement even while knowing that it was true. They are so hardened that they will never turn onto the road leading to eternal life.

So when other Christians talk about heaven, they are talking about the entire spectrum of kingdoms. When Mormons talk about the kingdom of God, they are only talking about the celestial kingdom. That is where Mormons part company with many Evangelical Christian sects.

Will we be happy in whatever kingdom we inherit in the afterlife? First, the prophet Joseph taught that any of the kingdoms is much better than mortality.[56] Second, we need to remember that Elohim is our Father. Christ makes this comparison in the Sermon on the Mount.

> Or what man is there of you, whom if his son ask bread, will he give him a stone?
>
> Or if he ask a fish, will he give him a serpent?
>
> If ye then, being evil, know how to give good gifts unto your children, how much more shall your Father which is in heaven give good things to them that ask him?[57]

Would you place your child in an unhappy place? Obviously not. Neither will our Heavenly Father. He will place each of us in the exact kingdom where we belong, are most comfortable, and happy. For example, although we may aspire to be placed in the celestial kingdom, if we only advance to have the character and attributes of a telestial glory, to be placed in the celestial kingdom would be very uncomfortable for us—we would not belong. Does this mean that we can never advance to the celestial kingdom? I don't know, but what I do know is that eternal progression never ends.

In sum, our spiritual existence is a progression from birth and childhood in the premortal existence, to adolescence on this mortal sphere, to adulthood in the hereafter. The Atonement allows us to progress toward eternal life, or Godhood, the life that Elohim, our Father, now has. The resurrection propels us forward along that continuum by providing us a glorified and perfected body, like the ones that our Father in Heaven and Jesus Christ possess, while the Atonement allows us the ability to correct our mistakes and become in character like our Savior.

THE PRIESTHOOD AND REVELATION

The priesthood is the authority of God the Father, which has been given to man to act in His name. It is the power that was used to create the universe, for it is literally the power of creation. Just like a wrench is the primary tool of the mechanic, so the priesthood is the primary tool of God. Mormons believe that this power is essential to the gospel. Without it, no ordinances can be performed. A marriage is not valid without a marriage certificate issued by the proper authority. To the state, without the proper marriage certificate, you are not married. Without the proper signature on a check, it cannot be cashed; it has no value. The authorization is necessary to make it effective, or make it acceptable to the bank. So it is with God. All of God's ordinances must be performed by those who have been sanctioned by God. Joseph Smith taught,

> The Priesthood was first given to Adam; he obtained the First Presidency, and held the keys of it from generation to generation. He obtained it in the Creation, before the world was formed. He had dominion given him over every living creature. He is Michael the Archangel, spoken of in the Scriptures.[58]

Hence, the priesthood has been held in every dispensation. However, the priesthood is not homogeneous. The scriptures point out two branches of the priesthood: the Melchizedek and the Aaronic or Levitical. "The Melchizedek Priesthood comprehends the Aaronic or Levitical Priesthood, and is the grand head, and holds the highest authority, which pertains to the priesthood and the keys of the kingdom of God in all ages of the world to the latest posterity on the earth, and is the channel through which all knowledge, doctrine, the plan of salvation, and every important matter is revealed from heaven."[59] The Prophet Joseph illuminated to the members of the Church that "no man can administer salvation through the gospel, to the souls of men, in the name of Jesus Christ, except he is authorized from God, by revelation, or by being ordained by someone whom God hath sent by revelation, as it is written by Paul."[60] Thus is the crux of the argument between Restorationist and Reformationist. One claims priesthood authority by ordination through revelation,[61] and the other does not. The position of the Restorationists is completely consistent with the Hebrew Christians.

With the restoration of the ancient Church also came a return to the ancient priesthood organization as practiced by the Hebrews; namely, the ordination of Apostles and prophets,[62] Seventies,[63] patriarchs,[64] high priests,[65] bishops,[66] priests,[67] teachers,[68] and deacons.[69] Questions Nibley,

> But must the church always have living prophets in its midst? Is it not enough that we have the words of the prophets of old preserved in holy writ? . . . The true church must and will always have living prophets. But that is unwelcome news to the world. It has always been poison. It is the one teaching that has made the restored gospel unacceptable to the wisdom of men. A dead prophet the world dearly desires and warmly cherishes; he is a priceless tradition, a spiritual heritage, a beautiful memory. But woe to a living prophet! He shall be greeted with stones and catcalls even by pious people. The men who put the Apostles to death thought they were doing God a favor, and the Lord tells us with what reverence and devotion men adorn the tombs of the prophets whom they would kill if they were alive.[70]

What is the fear of having a living prophet? It is not the fact that there is a living prophet, but rather what a living prophet means. It means that the heavens are not shut and revelation from God continues, including personal revelation.[71] What could be worse? The Hellenized Church has long remembered the disaster that was Montanus and his prophetesses, who contradicted the orthodox teachings by eluci- dating revelations to counter them. Nevertheless, revelation has been received from God throughout the ages; that is, until the aftermath of the Council of Nicaea, where the official position shut the heavens and limited all spiritual knowledge to the canon of scripture—the Bible.

Notwithstanding the official positions of the Catholic and Protestant Churches denying the existence of present-day revelation, the act of praying, which is still practiced within these churches, is an act of communication with God—in a word, revelation.

Said the Mormon prophet,

> Seeing that the Lord has never given the world to understand by any- thing heretofore revealed that he had ceased forever to speak to his crea- tures when sought unto in a proper manner, why should it be thought a thing incredible that he should be pleased to speak again in these last days for their salvation? Perhaps you may be surprised at this assertion, that I should say for the salvation of his creatures in these last days, since we have already in our possession a vast volume of his word which he has previously given. But you will admit that the word spoken to Noah was not sufficient for Abraham, or it was not required of Abraham to leave the land of his nativity and seek an inheritance in a strange country upon the word spoken to Noah, but for himself he obtained promises at the hand of the Lord and walked in that perfection that he was called the friend of God. Isaac, the promised seed, was not required to rest his hope upon the promises made to his father, Abraham, but was privileged with the assurance of his approbation in the sight of heaven by the direct voice of the Lord to him. If one man can live upon the revelations given to another, might not I with propriety ask, why the necessity, then, of the Lord speaking to Isaac as he did, as is recorded in the 26th chapter of Genesis? For the Lord there repeats, or rather promises again, to perform the oath which he had previously sworn unto Abraham.[72]

The Mormon belief in revelation, even personal revelation,[73] to guide one's own life was so important to the Church that it published it in its early periodicals and newspapers.

> We believe that we have a right to revelations, visions, and dreams from God, our Heavenly Father; and light and intelligence, through the gift

of the Holy Ghost, in the name of Jesus Christ, on all subjects pertaining to our spiritual welfare; if it so be that we keep his commandments, so as to render ourselves worthy in his sight.[74]

Another of the great powers of the priesthood is the power to seal on earth and in heaven,[75] as the Savior taught the Apostle Peter, "And I will give unto thee the keys of the kingdom of heaven: and whatsoever thou shalt bind on earth shall be bound in heaven: and whatsoever thou shalt loose on earth shall be loosed in heaven."[76]

This has been called in the Mormon faith the "Spirit of Elijah," after the prophet who called down fire from heaven to incinerate the offering of the priests of Baal and thereafter sealed the heavens for three and a half years. It was the Prophet Elijah who was taken up to heaven in a chariot of fire. In commenting on this sealing power, Joseph Smith remarked,

The spirit, power, and calling of Elijah is, that ye have power to hold the key of the revelation, ordinances, oracles, powers and endowments of the fulness of the Melchizedek Priesthood and of the kingdom of God on the earth; and to receive, obtain, and perform all the ordinances belonging to the kingdom of God, even unto the turning of the hearts of the fathers unto the children, and the hearts of the children unto the fathers, even those who are in heaven. Malachi says, "I will send you Elijah the prophet before the coming of the great and dreadful day of the Lord; and he shall turn the heart of the fathers to the children, and the heart of the children to their fathers, lest I come and smite the earth with a curse." Now, what I am after is the knowledge of God, and I take my own course to obtain it. What are we to understand by this in the last days? In the days of Noah, God destroyed the world by flood, and He has promised to destroy it by fire in the last days: but before it should take place, Elijah should first come and turn the hearts of the fathers to the children, etc. Now comes the point. What is this office and work of Elijah? It is one of the greatest and most important subjects that God has revealed. He should send Elijah to seal the children to the fathers, and the fathers to the children. Now was this merely confined to the living, to settle difficulties with families on earth? By no means. It was a far greater work. Elijah! what would you do if you were here? Would you confine your work to the living alone? No: I would refer you to the scriptures, where the subject is manifest: that is, without us, they could not be made perfect, nor we without them; the fathers without the children, nor the children without the fathers. I wish you to understand this subject, for it is important; and if you will receive it, this is the spirit of Elijah, that we redeem our dead, and connect ourselves with our fathers which are in heaven, and seal up our dead to come forth in the first resurrection; and here we want the power of Elijah to seal those who dwell on earth to those who dwell in heaven.[77]

In sum, the priesthood is viewed by Mormons as an essential power to administer the functions of the Church. Without it, the Church would cease to exist. With it, the Church progresses forward, having access to direct revelation from God and the power to bind and seal upon the earth and in the heavens.

ESOTERIC DOCTRINES

The esoteric doctrines (the mysteries) of Mormonism are performed in holy temples, where only worthy members of the Church can attend by presenting a temple recommend that bears the endorsements of the local ecclesiastical authorities.[78] These doctrines pertain to a belief in the salvation of both the living and the dead.[79] Within the temple, white clothing is required to be worn.[80] Temple ceremonies are divided into four areas: (1) vicarious baptism, confirmation, and ordination to the Melchizedek Priesthood; (2) washings and anointings, as was done during the time of Moses;[81] (3) the endowment, which consists of ordinances, instruction, covenants, and tests of knowledge,[82] and includes a prayer circle;[83] and (4) sealings, which consists of the highest ordinance in the Mormon faith, that of celestial marriage. This marriage is for time and all eternity, not simply until death.[84]

Therefore, if a man marry him a wife in the world, and he marry her not by me nor by my word, and he covenant with her so long as he is in the world and she with him, their covenant and marriage are not of force when they are dead, and when they are out of the world; therefore, they are not bound by any law when they are out of the world. . . .

And again, verily I say unto you, if a man marry a wife by my word, which is my law, and by the new and everlasting covenant, and it is sealed unto them by the Holy Spirit of promise, by him who is anointed, unto whom I have appointed this power and the keys of this priesthood; and it shall be said unto them—Ye shall come forth in the first resurrection; and if it be after the first resurrection, in the next resurrection; and shall inherit thrones, kingdoms, principalities, and powers, dominions, all heights and depths—then shall it be written in the Lamb's Book of Life, that he shall commit no murder whereby to shed innocent blood, and if ye abide in my covenant, and commit no murder whereby to shed innocent blood, it shall be done unto them in all things whatsoever my servant hath put upon them, in time and through all eternity; and shall be of full force when they are out of the world; and they shall pass by the angels, and the gods, which are set there, to their exaltation and glory in all things, as hath been sealed upon their heads, which glory shall be a fulness and a continuation of the seeds forever and ever. Then shall they be gods, because they have no end; therefore shall they be from everlasting to everlasting, because they continue; then shall they be above all, because all things are subject unto them. Then shall they be gods, because they have all power, and the angels are subject unto them.[85]

The Mormon doctrine of the eternal family is embedded in their temple worship, for Mormons believe that mankind will live beyond the grave in family units, just as we do here in this mortal sphere. Hence, the temple, as it was to the Hebrews, is paramount to Mormon theology.

> In the fourth decade of the nineteenth century the idea of the temple suddenly emerged full-blown in its perfection, not as a theory alone, but as a program of intense and absorbing activity which rewarded the faithful by showing them the full scope and meaning of the plan of salvation.[86]

Some have speculated that Joseph Smith simply reinvented the concept of a temple by putting together all of the fragments of the old world religions—Jewish, Orthodox, Masonic, Gnostic, Hindu, and Egyptian. However, according to Nibley, very few of the fragments of these temple ceremonies were available in Smith's day.[87] Throughout this book, there has been a discussion about surviving remnants of the temple concept and rites, which are found wherever there is organized religion in the world. "It is not surprising, therefore, that merely by looking about one may discover all sorts of parallels to Mormon . . . practices."[88] However, the full temple ceremonies in their entirety, which did not exist at the time of Joseph Smith, were restored to the earth.

Of temple worship,[89] Joseph Smith taught, "the Church is not fully organized, in its proper order, and cannot be, until the temple is completed, where places will be provided for the administration of the ordinances of the Priesthood."[90] Joseph continued,

What was the object of gathering the . . . people of God in any age of the world? . . . The main object was to build unto the Lord a house whereby He could reveal unto His people the ordinances of His house and the glories of His kingdom, and teach the people the way of salvation; for there are certain ordinances and principles that, when they are taught and practiced, must be done in a place or house built for that purpose. . . . It is for the same purpose that God gathers together His people in the last days, to build unto the Lord a house to prepare them for the ordinances and endowments, washings and anointings, etc. One of the ordinances of the house of the Lord is baptism for the dead. God decreed before the foundation of the world that that ordinance should be administered in a font prepared for that purpose in the house of the Lord. . . . Why gather the people together in this place? For the same purpose that Jesus wanted to gather the Jews—to receive the ordinances, the blessings, and the glories that God has in store for His Saints.[91]

It is perhaps this doctrine of baptism for the dead[92] that has drawn some of the most harsh criticism of the Mormon esoteric rites. In discussing this important doctrine, Joseph Smith preached,

The situation of the Christian nations after death, is a subject that has called forth all the wisdom and talent of the philosopher and the divine, and it is an opinion which is generally received, that the destiny of man is irretrievably fixed at his death, and that he is made either eternally happy, or eternally miserable; that if a man dies without a knowledge of God, he must be eternally damned, without any mitigation of his punishment, alleviation of his pain, or the most latent hope of a deliverance while endless ages shall roll along. However orthodox this principle may be, we shall find that it is at variance with the testimony of Holy Writ, for our Savior says, that all manner of sin and blasphemy shall be forgiven men wherewith they shall blaspheme; but the blasphemy against the Holy Ghost shall not be forgiven, neither in this world, nor in the world to come, evidently showing that there are sins which may be forgiven in the world to come, although the sin of blasphemy cannot be forgiven. Peter, also, in speaking concerning our Savior says, that "He went and preached unto the spirits in prison, which sometimes were disobedient, when once the long suffering of God waited in the days of Noah." Here then we have an account of our Savior preaching to the spirits in prison, to spirits that had been imprisoned from the days of Noah; and why did He preach to them? That they were to stay there? Certainly not! Let His own declaration testify: "He hath sent me to heal the broken hearted, to preach deliverance to the captives, and recovering of sight to the blind, to set at liberty them that are bruised." Isaiah has it—"To bring out the prisoners from the prison, and them that sit in darkness from the prison house." It is very evident from this that He not only went to preach to them, but to deliver, or bring them out of the prison house. . . . The great Jehovah contemplated the whole of the events connected with the earth, pertaining to the plan of salvation, before it rolled into existence, or ever "the morning stars sang together" for joy; the past, the present, and the future were and are, with Him, one eternal "now"; He knew of the fall of Adam, the iniquities of the antediluvians, of the depth of iniquity that would be connected with the human family, their weakness and strength, their power and glory, apostasies, their crimes, their righteousness and iniquity; He comprehended the fall of man, and his redemption; He knew the plan of salvation and pointed it out; He was acquainted with the situation of all nations and with their destiny; He ordered all things according to the counsel of His own will; He knows the situation of both the living and the dead, and has made ample provision for their redemption, according to their several circumstances, and the laws of the kingdom of God, whether in this world, or in the world to come.[93]

Thus, Mormons, just as their Hebrew Christian forefathers, believe that baptisms for the dead are essential to save our kindred dead who did not receive baptism in mortality. Far from being a morbid rite, to Mormons it is an outpouring of love and an indication of the manifest justice of God.

CELESTIAL MARRIAGE AND POLYGAMY

THE DOCTRINE OF PLURAL MARRIAGE

In Genesis 16 (around 2000 BC), and with the permission of Jehovah, Abram was given Hagar the Egyptian, Sarai's handmaid, to wife. Hagar bore Abram his first child, Ishmael. Four years later, Jehovah appeared to Abram, changing his name to Abraham and entering into a holy covenant with him (the Abrahamic covenant). This is the first instance of plural marriage documented in the Bible. Abraham went on to take another wife, Keturah, as well as many concubines, which also bore him children.[94] Abraham's grandson Jacob (who the Lord called Israel and who lived around 1800 BC) had four wives: Leah, Rachel, Bilah, and Zilpah.[95] From these four wives sprung the twelve tribes of Israel. On or about 1000 BC, king David took many wives and concubines, including Ahinoam, Abigail, Maacah, Haggith, Abital, Eglah, Michal, and Bathsheba. The last, Bathsheba, was without the sanction of Jehovah.[96] king David's son, Solomon, took seven hundred wives and three hundred concubines.[97]

Between 544 and 421 BC, the Book of Mormon recounts that the Prophet Jacob (the brother of Nephi) scolded the Nephites for following in the whoredoms of David (more specifically, his adultery with Bathsheba) and Solomon by having more than one wife. Preached Jacob, "Wherefore, my brethren, hear me, and hearken to the word of the Lord: For there shall not any man among you have save it be one wife; and concubines he shall have none."[98] When those in the congregation protested that Abraham and the other patriarchs practiced the doctrine of plural marriage, Jehovah, through his mouthpiece Jacob, retorted, "For if I will, saith the Lord of Hosts, raise up seed unto me, I will command my people; otherwise they shall hearken unto these things."[99] In sum, the doctrine of plural marriage is only practiced when Jehovah says it is to be practiced and not otherwise. In that instance, Jehovah had not authorized it.

THE MERIDIAN OF TIME, ESOTERIC DOCTRINES, CELESTIAL AND PLURAL MARRIAGE

At times, the Savior spoke only to the Apostles. The doctrines taught during these special events have been referred to by biblical scholars as "secret" teachings. A better term would be "sacred" teachings. As the Apostle Peter taught Clement, the bishop of Rome:

> Let such a one then hear this: The teaching of all doctrine has a certain order, and there are some things which must be delivered first, others in the second place, and others in the third, and so all in their order; and if these things be delivered in their order, they become plain; but if they be brought forward out of order, they will seem to be spoken against reason.[100]

Consequently, secrecy was a necessity because the overall Church was not yet ready to receive these sacred things—it would be imparted in the correct order and at the appropriate time when members of the

Church would be better prepared to receive them. It then bears to reason that the teachings that Christ gave to His Apostles following His Resurrection probably encompass the doctrines Christ had put off telling them because they were not yet ready. As Jesus had previously mentioned to His Apostles, "I have yet many things to say unto you, but ye cannot bear them now."[101] He further told them that "these things have I spoken unto you in proverbs: but the time cometh, when I shall no more speak unto you in proverbs, but I shall show you plainly of the Father."[102]

In the Clementine Homilies, Peter is reported to have stated, "Wherefore also He [meaning Jesus] explained to His disciples privately the mysteries of the kingdom of heaven."[103] Far from being abnormal, the practice of having secret or sacred doctrines was common in early Christianity.[104]

Marriage was instituted by God.[105] That it was encouraged is seen by Paul's direction to Timothy that bishops should be married.[106] Christ spoke of the joining of man and woman in one flesh sanctioned by God himself.[107] In fact, the leading Apostle, Peter, was married.[108]

Notwithstanding the open encouragement of marriage, it was regarded as an esoteric or secret ritual,[109] especially the idea that marriage continued beyond death. That this ritual was widely practiced is readily seen by the Apostolic Father Origen's complaint about those Christians who engaged in the practice of celestial, or eternal, marriage.

> Certain persons . . . are of the opinion that the fulfillment of the promises of the future are to be looked for in bodily pleasure and luxury. . . . And consequently they say, that after the resurrection there will be marriages, and the begetting of children . . . Such are the views of those who, while believing in Christ, understand the divine scriptures in a sort of Jewish sense, drawing from them nothing worthy of the divine promises.[110]

Clement, the bishop of Alexandria, disagreed with Origen's chastisement, instead stating that marriage "was good practice for life as a god," a reference to the continuation of marriage after the resurrection.[111]

Matthew 22:23–30 gives an interesting narrative concerning marriage and the resurrection. There, the Sadducees asked Christ about a situation where a woman outlived seven husbands, who were brothers, for each took her to wife in turn in order to raise up seed to the previously dead brother in order to satisfy the requirements of the law of Moses.[112] The Sadducees questioned the Savior as to whose wife she would be after the resurrection. Christ's response appears somewhat confusing. He states that "in the resurrection they neither marry, nor are given in marriage, but are as the angels of God in heaven." Some scholars have used Christ's answer as evidence that marriage does not continue beyond the grave, but that is not what Christ is saying at all. In the original Greek, the word used for "marry and given in marriage" refers not to the state of marriage, but to the actual marriage ceremony.[113] Hence, marriage exists in the resurrection, but marriage ceremonies are not performed in the resurrection. The marriages in this case, however, were ineffectual because the marriage ceremonies took place under the law of Moses rather than under the higher priesthood, which has the sealing power.[114] Hence, the marriages in this example were for this mortal life only.

Notwithstanding such, Christ's purpose was not to teach about marriage; rather it was to chastise the Sadducees for their rejection of the resurrection. Christ was saying that the Sadducees didn't understand the scriptures because if they did, they would understand that those who do not marry under the authority of the higher priesthood before the resurrection cannot obtain the blessings of a celestial marriage until after the resurrection, where marriages are once again performed. Until then, they are as the angels.

Biblical scholar Petersen has investigated the ancient practices in the Jewish temple of antiquity and has found it to be consistent with Christ's teachings to the Sadducees:

There were three buildings [within the temple] as places of offering in Jerusalem: the one which opens to the west was called "the holy"; another which opens to the south was called "the holy of holy"; the third which opens to the east was called the "holy of holies," where only the high priest might enter. Baptism is the "holy" house. The redemption is "holy of holy." "The holy of the holies" is the bridal chamber. . . . The woman is united to her husband in the bridal chamber. . . . Those who have united in the bridal chamber can no longer be separated. . . . If anyone becomes a son or daughter of the bridal chamber, he will receive the light. If anyone does not receive it while he is in the world, he will not receive it in the other place.[115]

Plural marriage appears to have been allowed in early Christianity under certain conditions.[116] Augustine noted that polygamy would have been openly allowed in early Christianity, as it was in the days of the Patriarchs, but for the laws and customs of Rome prohibiting it.[117] It is of note that Christ and the Apostles speak of plural wives existing in Abram's bosom (paradise).[118] Famed Christian Theologian Justin Martyr, in defending polygamy during the early second century, noted it was an esoteric doctrine of the early Christian church that was practiced in secret.[119]

Mormon scholar Stephen E. Robinson writes:

> In Western culture plural marriage is generally abhorred, but the roots of this abhorrence can hardly be described as biblical, for the Old Testament explicitly sanctions polygamy and the New Testament does not forbid it. The practice could not have been abhorrent to Jesus and the first-century Jewish Christians, for their culture was not Western, and plural marriage was sanctioned in the law of Moses, the holiness of which was endorsed by both Jesus and Paul. Indeed, it is possible that some Jewish Christians of the first century continued to practice plural marriage just as they continued Sabbath observance, circumcision, and other practices related to their cultural and religious background. The cultural milieu of Judaism and early Christianity simply cannot be the source of the Western horror of plural marriage, for plural marriages were common in the environment of the earliest Christian church.
>
> I do not deny that polygamy is now abhorred in Western culture generally and in modern Christianity particularly. What I deny is that the source of that abhorrence is biblical. It is derived not from the biblical heritage but the classical-the abhorrence of polygamy comes from Greece and Rome. As orthodox a figure as Saint Augustine knew that the prohibition of plural marriage in the church of his day was only a matter of Roman custom. . . . Though pagan culture could freely tolerate multiple sexual partners, it could tolerate only one wife. In that respect Greco-Roman culture was very similar to contemporary Western culture.
>
> Clearly, then, the antagonism to plural marriage was not biblical in origin, for the bosom of Abraham, where most Christians long to repose, is a polygamous bosom, and the house of Israel, into which most Christians seek admission, is a polygamous house.[120]

THE RESTORATION OF THE DOCTRINE OF PLURAL MARRIAGE

Of all the restored doctrines of the Hebrew Christians, the most polarizing was that of polygamy. In 1831, while studying the Bible, Joseph Smith reportedly came across this practice of the great Patriarchs. He inquired of the Lord and "learned that when the Lord commanded it, as He had with the Patriarchs anciently, a man could have more than one living wife at a time and not be condemned for adultery. He also understood that the Church would one day be required to live the law."[121] This created significant anxiety in Joseph. He knew such would be directly contrary to all nineteenth-century social norms. According to Lorenzo Snow, the Prophet revealed to him the "battle he waged in overcoming the repugnance of his feelings regarding plural marriage."[122] In fact, for a time, Joseph refused to engage in the practice. In response, the Lord sent an angel who stood over Joseph with a sword and an ultimatum: either restore the practice of plural marriage so as to restore all things as required by the dispensation of the fulness of times or forfeit his life so that another may be raised up in his stead.[123] Joseph was under no illusions, he knew that the introduction of plural marriage would result in increased criticism and persecution (notwithstanding the fact that at the time there were no criminal laws against plural marriage). Nevertheless, Joseph was committed to restore the ancient practice because the Lord had commanded it.

The Lord directed Joseph to keep the doctrine confidential, as it was an esoteric doctrine meant only for the most faithful and mature of believers. As a result, Joseph only told his closest friends about the revelation. The reaction of his friends was predicable. "After first learning of plural marriage, Brigham Young said he felt to envy the corpse in a funeral cortege and could hardly get over it for a long time."[124] Even the Prophet's own brother Hyrum Smith stubbornly resisted the practice for a time. Emma Smith, the Prophet's wife, vacillated back and forth, denouncing polygamy soon after Joseph's death, blaming it all on Brigham Young in October 1879.[125] In 1843, one year before his death, the Prophet Joseph committed to paper the revelation on plural marriage, known as section 132 in the Doctrine and Covenants. Soon thereafter, Emma reportedly tried to burn the original manuscript of the revelation.

Joseph Smith's biographer Richard Lloyd Dewey writes,

[Joseph] confided to John Taylor that the church could not continue until polygamy was established. Saints in retrospect believe it simply needed to be established for a time and not necessarily permanently. In Joseph's day, it would be a test for his followers, as many, if not most, would have difficulty accepting it. But the test would end for the church—at least for the mainstream church that would be head-quartered in Utah, 47 years later—when, as stated, polygamy was renounced in 1890 by the First Presidency.[126]

Contrary to conventional wisdom and popular belief, the practice of plural marriage was extremely unpopular within the Church membership. "Many members were descendants of the Puritans, a sexually conservative sect of Christianity. Consequently, early participants in plural marriage resisted and wrestled with the prospect, embracing the principle only after receiving personal revelation that they should sustain or participate in the practice. Yet, even with a confirmation from God, many struggled; others left the Church, unable to reconcile the doctrine with their cultural backgrounds."[127]

Brigham Young announced publicly from Salt Lake City on August 29, 1852, that the Church was practicing polygamy. Enemies of the Church immediately used polygamy as a powerful club to "attack and disparage the Church and Joseph Smith, and ultimately to delay Utah statehood until 1896. Anti-polygamy legislation, [which was upheld by the United States Supreme Court in *Reynolds v. United States*, 98 U.S. 145 (1878)], stripped Mormons of their rights as citizens, dis-incorporated the Church, and permitted the seizure of Church property before the manifesto of 1890 announced the discontinuation of the practice."[128]

PLURAL MARRIAGE IN UTAH

Plural marriage was a heavily regulated system of family life within the Church. Later in her life, Helen Mar Whitney, a plural wife of Joseph Smith, would write:

Plural marriage was the nineteenth-century LDS practice of a man marrying more than one wife. Popularly known as polygamy, it was actually polygyny. Although polygamy had been practiced for much of history in many parts of the world, to do so in "enlightened" America in the nineteenth century was viewed by most as incomprehensible and unacceptable, making it the Church's most controversial and least understood practice. Though the principle was lived for a relatively brief period, it had profound impact on LDS self-definition, helping to establish the Latter-day Saints as a "people apart." The practice also caused many nonmembers to distance themselves from the Church and see Latter-day Saints more negatively than would otherwise have been the case. Joseph stated that "the practice of this principle would be the hardest trial the Saints would ever have to test their faith."[129]

Contrary to popular nineteenth-century notions about polygamy, "the Mormon harem, dominated by lascivious males with hyperactive libidos, did not exist."[130] The image of sexual promiscuity and unabashed orgies were the sad creation of non-Mormon travelers to Salt Lake City.[131]

B. H. Roberts provides a concise and basic understanding on what was involved and expected in the Utah practice of plural marriage:

> The Saints did not accept into their faith and practice the plural-wife system with the idea that it increased the comfort, or added to the ease of anyone. From the first it was known to involve sacrifice, to make a large demand upon the faith, patience, hope and charity of all who should attempt to carry out its requirements. Its introduction was not a call to ease or pleasure, but to religious duty; it was not an invitation to self-indulgence, but to self-conquest; its purpose was not earth-happiness, but earth-life discipline, undertaken in the interest of special advantages for succeeding generations of men. . . . It was indeed a principle of religion to them, a holy sacrament, and not at all designed to become a general practice under merely human laws. It is unfortunate that the world outside of the Church was not impressed with this phase of the subject; for then it would have been apparent that the things the world argued against and fought against—a general plural marriage system free for all to adopt, considered to be destructive of the monogamous system and the menace to the home itself—was not the thing upheld and contended for by the Latter-day Saints, who believed that the privilege of plural marriage is to be limited to persons of high character, approved lives, and living under the most sacred obligations to chastity, and granted this privilege of the marriage system only under the most carefully guarded permission amounting to divine sanction.[132]

No one knows for sure the percentage of Church members who

participated in plural marriages. However, some studies have put a maximum at between 20 and 25 percent of Mormon adults. Leaders of the Church were expected to set an example and hence it was the norm for those men to have more than one wife. "Public opposition to polygamy led to the first law against the practice in 1862, and, by the 1880s, laws were increasingly punitive." Ultimately, this led "to a harsh and effective federal anti-polygamy campaign known by the Mormons as "the Raid." Wives and husbands went underground and hundreds were arrested and sentenced to jail terms in Utah and several federal prisons. This campaign severely affected the families involved, and the related attack on the Church organization and properties greatly inhibited its ability to function."[133] "Following a vision showing him that continuing plural marriage endangered the temples and the mission of the Church, not just statehood, President Wilford Woodruff issued the Manifesto in October 1890, announcing an official end to new plural marriages."[134]

Polygamous families, who were formed before the 1890 Manifesto, continued to exist well into the twentieth century. The Church did not require these families to divorce. However, new plural marriages were allowed only in Mormon settlements outside the United States in Canada and northern Mexico. The issue came up again at the "House hearings on Representative-elect B. H. Roberts and Senate hearings on Senator-elect Reed Smoot.[135] "President Joseph F. Smith thereafter issued a "Second Manifesto" in 1904. Since that time, it has been official Church policy to excommunicate any member practicing or advocating the practice of polygamy."[136]

MIRACLES AND GIFTS OF THE SPIRIT

Mormon's have a steadfast belief in the use of the priesthood power to perform miracles and serve others.[137] The early history of the Church records many instances of miraculous events. For example, on November 27, 1839, in Buffalo, New York, then Apostle Brigham Young calmed a storm. The Prophet Joseph Smith was documented to have raised William D. Huntington from the dead at Nauvoo, Illinois. Yet another example occurred on January 9, 1935 when Hyrum Grant was raised from the dead by elders of the church. Also documented was Mary Ellen Jensen being raised from the dead on March 3, 1891 by then Apostle Lorenzo Snow at Brigham City, Utah.[138]

One of the most common of miracles, if a miracle can be said to be common, is the healing of the sick. Christ set the example of healing those who came to him with a desire and faith to be healed. The Hebrew Christians practiced healings as well, thus demonstrating the importance of the doctrine.[139] Joseph Smith taught that to invoke the power of God to heal the sick necessitates that one use the "laying on of hands [as] the sign or way marked out by James, and the custom of the ancient Saints as ordered by the Lord." He further explained, "we cannot obtain the blessing [of healing] by pursuing any other course except the way marked out by the Lord."[140]

The Day of Pentecost was repeated in the latter days at the dedication of the Kirtland Temple in Ohio. During the dedicatory prayer, the Prophet Joseph Smith asked, "Let it be fulfilled upon them as in the days of Pentecost. . . . Let the gift of tongues be poured out upon thy people, even cloven tongues as of fire, and the interpretation thereof. And let thy house be filled, as with a rushing mighty wind, with thy glory."[141] As was recorded at the time, after the dedicatory services, "a noise was heard like the sound of a rushing mighty wind, which filled the temple, and all the congregation simultaneously arose, being moved upon by an invisible power; many began to speak in tongues and prophesy; others saw glorious visions; and I beheld the temple was filled with angels, which fact I declared to the congregation."[142]

The gift of tongues was manifested in various documented instances in the early days of the Church besides the above instance at Kirtland, Ohio.[143] Joseph Smith records, "I read the 13th Chapter of First Corinthians, also a part of the 14th Chapter, and remarked that the gift of tongues was necessary in the Church . . . the gift of tongues by the power of the Holy Ghost in the Church, is for the benefit of the servants of God to preach to unbelievers, as on the day of Pentecost."[144] Where there is present the gift of tongues, there must also be the Interpretation of Tongues manifested.[145]

Another gift of the spirit is that of seership. Prophets of the Old Testament used seer stones to read ancient texts and assist in the receiving of revelation. These seer stones were called "Urim and Thummim," and are interpreted to mean "Lights and Perfections."[146]

> And thou shalt put on the breastplate of judgment the Urim and the Thummim; and they shall be upon Aaron's heart, when he goeth in

before the Lord: and Aaron shall bear the judgment of the children of Israel upon his heart before the Lord continually.[147]

Seer stones were used by Nephite prophets, just as they had been used by Israelite prophets.[148]

A set of seers stones was found by Joseph Smith with the golden plates. It was through these seer stones that Joseph was able to translate the ancient record by the gift and power of God.[149]

Other miraculous events in the Mormon Church parallel those of the Hebrew Christians, including receiving prophesy,[150] visions,[151] dreams,[152] ministering of Angels,[153] and the casting out of evil spirits.[154]

Miscellaneous Doctrines

MISSIONARY WORK

One of the most recognized tenants of the Mormon Church is missionary work.[155]

> Send forth the elders of my church unto the nations which are afar off; unto the islands of the sea; send forth unto foreign lands; call upon all nations, first upon the Gentiles, and then upon the Jews.[156]

Missionaries went out two by two, in a similar manner as the early Apostles.[157] This emphasis on converting new members comes from a desire to share the gospel with others and provide an opportunity for them to receive essential ordinances. The concept of eternal families has had an enormous appeal, as shown by the enormous growth in Church membership over the past thirty years. The Mormon Church continues to be one of the fastest growing religious sects in the World.

LAW OF TITHING AND OF THE FAST

Just as Abraham gave his tithes to Melchizedek, the king of Salem,[158] so too the Prophet Malachi preached,

> Will a man rob God? Yet ye have robbed me, But ye say, Wherein have we robbed thee? In tithes and offerings. Ye are cursed with a curse; for ye have robbed me, even this whole nation. Bring ye all the tithes into the storehouse, that there may be meat in mine house, and prove me now herewith, saith the Lord of hosts, if I will not open you the

windows of heaven, and pour you out a blessing, that there shall not be room enough to receive it.[159]

Mormons adhere to this same ancient doctrine.[160] Through it, members of the Church claim the blessings promised by Malachi.

"And this shall be the beginning of the tithing of my people. And after that, those who have thus been tithed shall pay one tenth of all their interest annually; and this shall be a standing law unto them forever, for my holy priesthood, saith the Lord."[161]

Mormons generally combine the payment of tithes and offerings with fasting. "Organize yourselves; prepare every needful thing; and establish a house, even a house of prayer, a house of fasting, a house of faith, a house of learning, a house of glory, a house of order, a house of God."[162] Mormons are encouraged to take the money equivalent to the price of two meals, which would have been spent on food, and contribute it to the poor as a fast offering. It is from these funds that the local congregations assist their members who may have fallen on hard times. From Church Headquarters comes assistance worldwide. Deseret Industries, a company operated by the Church, provides a franchise of thrift stores throughout the western United States to assist the needy. Welfare farms and ranches, together with canning facilities, bishops' storehouses, and employment centers are some of the other facilities meant to assist members and others within the community who may be in need of assistance. Mormons have a strong work ethic and believe strongly in being self-reliant. Church leaders encourage members to store a year's supply of food and fuel, to help sustain them in emergencies. Emergency fairs are quite common at local Mormon meetinghouses. When members receive welfare help from the Church, they are expected to work for it by volunteering to work at Deseret Industries, bishops' storehouses, farms, ranches, granaries, and the like. The late President Ronald Reagan toured the Church's welfare facilities in the 1980s, commenting that the Church's welfare program was a model for others.

HEALTH CODE

Brigham Young University is the perennial top "Stone Cold Sober" college in the country according to *U.S. News and World Report*. Scientific studies have long showed that Mormons tend to be healthier and live longer than other people. Donny and Marie Osmond were famous for drinking milk instead of imbibing alcohol. The Mormon health code has many elements that are similar to those practiced by early Christians and Jews. Mormon's call this code, "the Word of Wisdom," after Section 89 of the Doctrine and Covenants. In this revelation received by the Prophet Joseph Smith on February 27, 1833, in Kirtland, Ohio, members were encouraged to avoid tobacco, alcohol, and coffee, as well as other foods. Members were promised that if they adhered to this code, they

> shall run and not be weary, and shall walk and not faint. And I, the Lord give unto them a promise, that the destroying angel shall pass by them, as the children of Israel, and not slay them.[163]

SACRAMENT AND THE SABBATH DAY

Just as Christ instituted the sacrament of the Lord's supper the night before His crucifixion in the upper room of a house to His Apostles, so too do the Mormons.

> Listen to the voice of Jesus Christ, your Lord, your God, and your Redeemer, whose word is quick and powerful. For, behold, I say unto you, that it mattereth not what ye shall eat or what ye shall drink when ye partake of the sacrament, if it so be that ye do it with an eye single to my glory—remembering unto the Father my body which was laid down for you, and my blood which was shed for the remission of your sins.[164]

The sacrament is generally held in conjunction with the Sabbath day observance. To Mormons, the Sabbath (Sunday after the order of the Apostles) is a day set aside to Elohim and Jesus Christ.

> And that thou mayest more fully keep thyself unspotted from the world, thou shalt go to the house of prayer and offer up thy sacraments upon my holy day. For verily this is a day appointed unto you to rest from your labors, and to pay their devotions unto the Most High; Nevertheless thy vows shall be offered up in righteousness on all days and at all times; But remember that on this, the Lord's day, thou shalt offer thine oblations and thy sacraments unto the Most High, confessing their sins unto thy brethren, and before the Lord. And on this day thou shalt do none other thing, only let thy food be prepared with singleness of heart that thy fasting may be perfect, or, in other words, that thy joy may be full.[165]

THE GATHERING OF ISRAEL

Before the Great and Dreadful Day of the Lord, as spoken of by the ancient prophets, the House of Israel is to be gathered from the four corners of the earth. For this reason, Mormons believe in the restoration of the Jews to Jerusalem. In speaking of the Jews, an ancient Nephite Prophet foretold,

> And it shall come to pass that they shall be gathered in from their long dispersion, from the isles of the sea, and from the four parts of the earth; and the nations of the Gentiles shall be great in the eyes of me, saith God, in carrying them forth to the lands of their inheritance. Yea, the kings of the Gentiles shall be nursing fathers unto them, and their queens shall become nursing mothers; wherefore, the promises of the Lord are great unto the Gentiles, for he hath spoken it, and who can dispute?[166]

Together with the return of the Jews, is the return of the lost ten tribes of Israel.[167] These are the descendants of the Northern Kingdom of Israel, who were carried off to the north countries by the Assyrians and became lost to history. These tribes shall return.

> And they who are in the north countries [the lost ten tribes] shall come in remembrance before the Lord; and their prophets shall hear his voice, and shall no longer stay themselves; and they shall smite the rocks, and the ice shall flow down at their presence. And an highway shall be cast up in the midst of the great deep. Their enemies shall become a prey unto them. And in the barren deserts there shall come forth pools of living water; and the parched ground shall no longer be a thirsty land. And they shall bring forth their rich treasures unto the children of Ephraim, my servants.[168]

AGENCY

Mormons believe in the "agency" of man. To most, it is referred to by another name: freedom. The ability to choose and take responsibility for our actions, and thereby grow in character, is an underlying foundation to Mormon theology. Mormons believe that the premortal battle referred to in Revelation 12, fought between Michael the Arc Angel and the devil, was about the "agency" of man. Moses tells of a council in heaven before the world was.

And I, the Lord God, spake unto Moses saying: That Satan, whom thou hast commanded in the name of my Only Begotten, is the same which was from the beginning, and he came before me, saying—Behold, here am I, send me, I will be thy son; and I will redeem all mankind, that one soul shall not be lost, and surely I will do it; wherefore give me thine honor. But, behold, my Beloved Son, which was my Beloved and Chosen from the beginning, said unto me—Father, thy will be done, and the glory be thine forever. Wherefore, because that Satan rebelled against me, and sought to destroy the *agency of man*, which I, the Lord God had given him, and also, that I should give unto him mine own power; by the power of mine Only Begotten, I caused that he should be cast down; and he became Satan, yea, even the devil, the father of all lies, to deceive and to blind men, and to lead them captive at his will, even as many as would not hearken unto my voice.[169]

Joseph Smith preached, "All persons are entitled to their agency, for God has so ordained it. He has constituted mankind moral agents, and given them power to choose good or evil; to seek after that which is good, by pursuing the pathway of holiness in this life, which brings peace of mind, and joy in the Holy Ghost here, and a fulness of joy and happiness at His right hand hereafter; or to pursue an evil course, going on in sin and rebellion against God, thereby bringing condemnation to their souls in this world, and an eternal loss in the world to come."[170] As a result of this strongly held belief in the "agency of man," Mormons soundly reject any notion of pre-destination as taught by Hellenized Christianity, especially among the protestant faiths. Instead, Mormons believe in the concept of foreordination. Under this concept, due to God's foreknowledge of the character of our spirits, He can predict how we will react under any circumstance pertaining to His plan. Thus, Elohim foreordained spirits in the premortal life to fulfill missions here in this mortal sphere. These missions are for the fulfilling of God's wishes and plans. Notwithstanding the foreknowledge of God, we are still free to choose whether or not we will do as the Father has foretold; thus retaining our free agency. Many times, we are given missions in which our Father in Heaven knows that we will fail. Yet it is important for His children to experience the failure for themselves. One such case concerned the king of Tyrus during the days of Ezekiel the Prophet. Apparently the king had been one of the cherubim that guarded the way to the tree of life in the Garden of Eden. However, he lost his position in heaven due to his iniquity and wickedness, which he wrought as the king of Tyrus.[171] Notwithstanding his lofty position in the premortal life, the king was allowed to choose his own path and ultimately fail. The Lord knew what would transpire but allowed it to happen and did not intervene because He respected the agency of man and its importance to His plan of salvation for His children. King David is yet another example where one so close to the Lord was allowed to make his own choices, leading to tragedy and heartache. Mormons believe that the Lord will not protect us from ourselves or our own unrighteous decisions. Rather, learning from those decisions and changing course is where true character is developed.

THE AFTERLIFE

Joseph Smith taught, "'But,' says one, 'I believe in one universal heaven and hell, where all go, and are all alike, and equally miserable or equally happy.' What! We're all are huddled together—the honorable, virtuous, and murderers, and whoremongers, when it is written that they shall be judged according to the deeds done in the body? But St. Paul informs us of three glories and three heavens. He knew a man that was caught up to the third heaven. . . . Jesus said unto His disciples, 'In my Father's house are many mansions; if it were not so, I would have told you. I go to prepare a place for you, and I will come and receive you to myself, that where I am ye may be also.'"[172] Hence, Mormons adhere to the theology that "heaven" is not simply one place. Rather it consists of many kingdoms, among which are designated by the Apostle Paul, a celestial kingdom (sun), a terrestrial kingdom (moon), and a telestial kingdom (stars).[173]

This belief plays into the Mormon concept of eternal progression and godhood that have been previously discussed. For the Mormon God is not only a just God, but also a merciful one. He rewards each of His children according to their desires and character. Each of us go to dwell in a kingdom or mansion where we are with others who are like us and with whom we will be comfortable. Our Heavenly Father, just as our earthly father, wants us to be happy. Accordingly, we advance to a location where we will be most happy. Those progressing in character farthest, who become like our Father in Heaven and Jesus Christ, will dwell as Gods under their direction, and live in family units with their loved ones. Thus beginning the cycle of life again, for as husband and wife, we begin to create worlds and populate them with our spirit children. As God has declared,

> For behold, this is my work and my glory—to bring to pass the immortality and eternal life of man.[174]

According to Mormons, that will be our goal as well if we advance to Godhood. We will work to bring to pass the eternal lives of our children. Once the restoration was complete and thus, the mission that had been entrusted to the Mormon Prophet Joseph Smith fulfilled, he followed in the footsteps and tradition of the early Apostles, sealing his testimony of the restoration with his own blood, becoming a martyr for the gospel of Jesus Christ and triggering the final dispensation of this world.

NOTES

1. Joseph Smith—History 1:15–17.
2. Ibid., 1:22.
3. Bickmore, *Restoring the Ancient Church*, chapter 2, quoting W. D. Davies, *Israel, the Mormons, and the Land, Reflections on Mormonism: Judeao-Christian Parallels* (Provo, UT: Religious Studies Center, Brigham Young University, 1978), 91.
4. *History of the Church*, 6:474; Joseph Smith, *Teachings of the Prophet Joseph Smith* (TPJS), ed. by Joseph Fielding Smith (Salt Lake City: Deseret Book, 1976), 370–71.
5. James E. Talmage, *A Study of the Articles of Faith* (SLC: Deseret Book, 1988), 37.
6. TPJS, 312.
7. TPJS, 345–46. See Doctrine and Covenants 130:22.
8. David L. Paulsen, "The God of Abraham, Isaac and Joseph Smith: Defending the Faith," FAIR Conference (2004).
9. *History of the Church*, 6:303–5.
10. "What does it mean on a grand scale to assert that the universe is the product of an intelligent designer? In a scientific age that exalts rationalism and chance, what empirical evidence could possibly support such a claim? As humans contemplating the immense complexity of the cosmos, might certain features of the universe suggest that our 'home' has in fact been carefully crafted for our benefit? Can our own human experiences of creativity and design illuminate the concept of a cosmic designer?" Dr. Walter L. Bradley, "Is There Scientific Evidence for the Existence of God? How the Recent Discoveries Support a Designed Universe," *Leadership U.*, 1–2 (10 June 2004). The scientific theory is called "Intelligent Design." Atheists would contend that such is simply a hoax—a new form of Creationism. That is an easy way to avoid discussing the subject or testing its principles; for who could argue with its premise?
    We can drop sugar, flour, baking powder, and an egg on the floor, but they won't turn into a cake by themselves. We have to mix and bake them according to a recipe.

Throwing steel, rubber, glass and plastic together doesn't make a car. It takes skillful engineering. How much more, then, would intelligence be needed to design life? If brilliant scientists have failed to create it, how could blind stupid chance? James Perloff, *Tornado in a Junkyard* (Arlington, MA: Refuge Books, 1999), 70.

"Intelligent Design," however, is not a new theory from Creationists. In fact, it pre-dated Darwin's Theory of Evolution and was first brought to the forefront by an eighteenth-century philosopher, William Paley. Paley, *Natural Theology* (London: Wilks and Taylor, 1802). "Anyone who can contemplate the eye of a housefly, the mechanics of human finger movement, the camouflage of a moth, or the building of every kind of matter from variations in arrangement of proton and electron, and then maintain that all this design happened without a designer, happened by sheer, blind accident—such a person believes in miracles far more astounding than any in the Bible." Perloff, 62 quoting David Raphael Klein, "Is There a Substitute for God?" *Reader's Digest* (March 1970), 55.

There is also the misconception that "Intelligent Design" does not follow the scientific model. In reality, it does. First, Intelligent Design looks at the laundry list of requirements necessary, from the scientific perspective, to create a world such as ours and inhabit it with biological life-forms. Second, Intelligent Design looks at the scientific probabilities that such requirements could be met. Third, Intelligent Design tests the significance of those probabilities.

According to British mathematician Roger Penrose, the statistical probability of the occurrence of a universe in which life can form is one in ten to the 10,123rd power with the probability of one in ten to the 50th power being equivalent to a probability of zero. Roger Penrose, *The Emperor's New Mind*, (Oxford University Press, 1989); Michael Denton, *Nature's Destiny* (New York: The Free Press, 1998), 9; Harun Yahya, *The Maths of Probability* (2003), 1–2. One noted biologist, Edward Conklin, put it this way: "The probability of life originating from accident (or chance) is comparable to the probability of an unabridged dictionary resulting from an explosion in a print shop." Ralph Epperson, "How Did the Universe Begin?" *Does God Exist?* 32, no. 1: Jan/Feb 2005), 4.

Consequently, using the scientific theory, there is considerable evidence of a creator—God. As Geneticist Robert Griffith jokingly remarked, "If we need an atheist for a debate, I go to the philosophy department. The physics department isn't much use." Harun Yahya, The Maths of Probability (2003), 3 quoting Hugh Ross, *The Creator and the Cosmos*, (Nav Press Publishing Group, 2001), 123.

11. TPJS, at 350–52; Journal of Discourses of the General Authorities of the Church of Jesus Christ of Latter-day Saints, *Journal of Discourses*, 26 vols (2006), 6:6.
12. TPJS, 353–54. See Abraham 3:22–26.
13. *Journal of Discourses*, 6:5.
14. Moses 4:1–2; *Journal of Discourses,* 6:8; Abraham 3:27–28.
15. Moses 5:13; Doctrine and Covenants 76:25.
16. Doctrine and Covenants 84:38; Doctrine and Covenants 132:20.
17. TPJS, 346–47; *Journal of Discourses,* 6:4.
18. Moses 6:36, 51.
19. 2 Nephi 31:18; Jacob 6:11; Enos 1:3; Mosiah 26:20; 3 Nephi 15:9; Moroni 7:41.
20. *History of the Church*, 6:310–12.
21. Another example of this is the doctrine of Original Sin taught by the Catholic Church. The Mormons, as did their Hebrew ancestors, rejected such a doctrine, finding instead that little children are "alive in Christ," Moroni 8:22; See Articles of Faith 1:2.

22. Moses 6:52–60.
23. JST Exodus 34:1–2.
24. *History of the Church*, 2: 15–16.
25. Pearl of Great Price, Article of Faith 4.
26. 2 Nephi 25:23; Doctrine and Covenants 49:11–14.
27. 2 Nephi 9:23–24; 3 Nephi 27:16–20; 2 Nephi 31:17–21; Doctrine and Covenants 49:11–14. Repentance: "The Greek word of which this is the translation denotes a change of mind, i.e., a fresh view about God, about oneself, and about the world. Since we are born into conditions of mortality, repentance comes to mean a turning of the heart and will to God, and a renunciation of sin to which we are naturally inclined." Bible Dictionary, 760. An example of this "change of heart" can be seen in Luke, chapter 7, wherein Jesus is invited to the house of a Pharisee to eat. The Pharisee intentionally had an adulterous woman serve Christ. The purpose was to test the Savior to see if He would recognize the woman as a sinner and refrain from having her touch Him. Instead, Jesus allowed this woman to wash His feet with her tears and anoint His feet with ointment. He then used this as an object lesson for the Pharisee by recounting the kindnesses received from the woman, while contrasting that with the fact that he had received none of the normal courtesies from the Pharisee host. Apparently, this woman was experiencing this "change of heart." Christ provides the following insight:

    Wherefore I say unto thee, Her sins, which are many, are forgiven; for she loved much: but to whom little is forgiven, the same loveth little. And he said unto her, Thy sins are forgiven. And they that sat at meat with him began to say within themselves, Who is this that forgiveth sins also? And he said to the woman, Thy faith hath saved thee; go in peace. (Luke 7:47–50.)

    See Mosiah 4:2–3; 5:7 (People of king Benjamin receive remission of sins due to their faith in Christ and change of heart); Alma 5:14, 26 ("have ye experienced this mighty change in your hearts?"); Alma 36:16–20 (Alma the Younger received forgiveness of his sins when he cried for mercy to Christ, thus exercising faith in Him and having a change of heart); Alma 19:33 (king Lamoni and his household experienced a "change of heart"); Helaman 15:7 ("faith and repentance bringeth a change of heart . . ."); Doctrine and Covenants 21:9 (Christ died "for the remission of sins unto [those with a] contrite heart"). Since God is not a "respecter of persons," all of God's children may receive a "remission of sins" by experiencing this "change of heart." (Acts 10:34.)
28. Doctrine and Covenants 84:74; Moroni 6:1–4; Doctrine and Covenants 20:37; Doctrine and Covenants 68:8–12; Doctrine and Covenants 39:19–24; Moses 6:59–62; 2 Nephi 9:23–24; 3 Nephi 27:16–20; 2 Nephi 31:5–21; 3 Nephi 11:23–24; Doctrine and Covenants 49:11–14.
29. Doctrine and Covenants 13:1; 20:73–74; 76:51.
30. "Baptism by water is but half a baptism, and is good for nothing without the other half—that is, the baptism of the Holy Ghost." (TPJS, 314.) The reception of the Holy Ghost is also referred to as a baptism by fire. See 2 Nephi 31:13–14; 3 Nephi 9:20; Mormon 7:10; Doctrine and Covenants 19:31; 20:41. The gift of the Holy Ghost is given by the laying on of hands. Doctrine and Covenants 49:11–14.
31. 3 Nephi 11:31–40 (emphasis added).
32. *History of the Church*, 4:554–55 (emphasis added). "God has set many signs on the earth, as well as in the heavens; for instance, the oak of the forest, the fruit of the tree, the herb of the field—all bear a sign that seed hath been planted there; for it is a decree of the Lord that every tree, plant, and herb bearing seed should bring forth

of its kind, and cannot come forth after any other law or principle. Upon the same principle do I contend that baptism is a sign ordained of God, for the believer in Christ to take upon himself in order to enter into the kingdom of God, 'for except ye are born of water and of the Spirit ye cannot enter into the kingdom of God,' said the Savior. It is a sign and a commandment which God has set for man to enter into His kingdom. Those who seek to enter in any other way will seek in vain; for God will not receive them, neither will the angels acknowledge their words as accepted, for they have not obeyed the ordinances, nor attended to the signs which God ordained for the salvation of man, to prepare him for, and give him a title to, a celestial glory." *History of the Church*, 4:554–55.

33. Joseph Smith, "Baptism" *Times and Seasons* (September 1, 1842).
34. Matthew 3:13–17.
35. *History of the Church*, 5:499.
36. Moroni 8:12–22; Doctrine and Covenants 74:7
37. *History of the Church*, 5:499.
38. Doctrine and Covenants 68:27.
39. *History of the Church*, 4:554.
40. Mosiah 4:6–8; Alma 22:13–14; Doctrine and Covenants 20:26–32; Moses 6:53–54; Mosiah 3:11; Doctrine and Covenants 29:1–5, 41–45; 76:1, 41–42, 69–70; 107:18–19; 19:2–5, 16; 21:9; 35:2; 1 Nephi 11:32–33; Doctrine and Covenants 34:3; 3 Nephi 11:11; 45:4–5; 88:6; 122:8; Alma 42:9–15; 2 Nephi 9:6–12.
41. Alma 7:11–12.
42. Alma 11:43.
43. *History of the Church*, 3:30.
44. Ibid., 6:366.
45. L. John Nuttall, "Extracts from William Clayton's Private Book," Journal of L. John Nuttall, 7–8 (1857–1904).
46. Alma 40:11–14. See Doctrine and Covenants 138.
47. "Above all else, God wants our hearts. Imperfect performance can be corrected, sins can be remitted, mistakes can be erased—but God can do nothing with an unwilling and rebellious heart until it repents. Weakness can be saved; rebellion cannot. 'Behold, the Lord requireth the heart and a willing mind.' (Doctrine and Covenants 64:34)." Stephen E. Robinson, *Believing Christ* (Salt Lake City: Deseret Book, 1992), 54. See also 1 Samuel 16:7; Proverbs 23:7; Matthew 5:8; 3 Nephi 12:8; Luke 16:15; 3 Nephi 9:20; Ether 4:15; Moroni 4:3; 6:2; Doctrine and Covenants 6:16; 137:9; 21:9; 20:77.
48. John 5:22.
49. Moroni 10:32.
50. Doctrine and Covenants 76:81–90, 98–112.
51. Doctrine and Covenants 76:71–80, 91, 97.
52. Doctrine and Covenants 76:50–70, 92–96.
53. John 14:2.
54. Note the sacramental prayers wherein the covenant is renewed. Our part of the covenant is to "be willing" to be called Christians, remember Christ in our lives, and keep the commandments, while God promises in return the companionship of the Holy Ghost. See Moroni 4:3; 5:2.
55. A son of perdition is one who has a perfect knowledge through the Holy Ghost that Elohim is our Father and Jesus Christ is our Savior, but then goes about preaching against them. These are they who crucify the Savior anew.

56. Doctrine and Covenants 76:89.

57. Matthew 7:9–11.

58. *History of the Church*, 3:385–88.

59. Ibid., 4:207.

60. *Times and Seasons*, (February 1840), 54.

61. Doctrine and Covenants 107:1–6, 8, 13–14.

62. Doctrine and Covenants 84:63; 88:127.

63. Doctrine and Covenants 107:25.

64. Doctrine and Covenants 107:39–52; 124:91.

65. Doctrine and Covenants 107:10.

66. Doctrine and Covenants 84:29.

67. Doctrine and Covenants 84:111.

68. Doctrine and Covenants 84:30.

69. Doctrine and Covenants 84:30.

70. Nibley, *The World and the Prophets*, 5.

71. Article of Faith 9; Brown, *All Things Restored*, at 142–43; Jacob 4:8–10; Doctrine and Covenants 8:2–3; Doctrine and Covenants 43:2–7; Doctrine and Covenants 82:2–4; 2 Nephi 28:29–30; 2 Nephi 29:3–14.

72. Lucy Mack Smith, *The History of Lucy Smith, Mother of the Prophet*, (Signature Books, 2001), 229–32.

73. 1 Nephi 15:7–11; Enos 1:1–19; Mosiah 4:11–12; 24:8–25; Alma 10:22–23; 37:36–37; 3 Nephi 18:15–25; Moroni 10:4–5; Doctrine and Covenants 112:10.

74. *Times and Seasons*, (February 1840), 54.

75. Doctrine and Covenants 128:8–10 (Elijah appears to Joseph Smith and restores the sealing powers).

76. Matthew 16:19.

77. *History of the Church* 6:251–53.

78. Alma 12:9–11.

79. Doctrine and Covenants 110:13–16; 128.

80. Boyd K. Packer, *The Holy Temple*, (Bookcraft, 1980), 71–79, 155; Brown, *All Things Restored*, 95.

81. Doctrine and Covenants 124:37; 124:39; Brown, *All Things Restored*, 94.

82. John A. Widtsoe, "Temple Worship," *The Utah Genealogical and Historical Magazine* 12 (1921), 58; James E. Talmage, *The House of the Lord* (Bookcraft, 1962), 99–100.

83. *Encyclopedia of Mormonism*, 4 vols. (Macmillian, 1992), 4:1444, 3:1430. Joseph Smith instituted the prayer circle for Mormons. It is a solemn ordinance, "guarded by [a] secret and a 'mystery' for initiates only." The circle consists of "ordinary men and women of the church, with a high priest presiding." Nibley, *Mormonism and Early Christianity*, 82–83.

84. Doctrine and Covenants 132:15–17.

85. Doctrine and Covenants 132:15, 19–20.

86. Nibley, *Mormonism and Early Christianity*, 370.

87. Ibid., 383.

88. Ibid., 369.

89. Doctrine and Covenants 124:39.

90. *History of the Church*, 4: 603.

91. Ibid., 5:423–25, 427.

92. Doctrine and Covenants 124:29–34; 128:12–13.

93. *History of the Church*, 4: 596–97.

94. Genesis 25:1; 6.
95. Genesis 29–30.
96. 2 Samuel 3; 11.
97. 1 Kings 11:3.
98. Jacob 2:27.
99. Jacob 2:30.
100. Clementine Recognitions 3:34, ANF 8:123.
101. John 16:12.
102. John 16:25.
103. Clementine Homilies 19:20, ANF 8:336.
104. Ignatius, Epistle to the Trallians 5 in ANF 1:68; Hippolytus, Apostolic Tradition, 23:14, in Hanson, *Tradition in the Early Church*, 32.
105. Genesis 1:26–28; Genesis 2:18, 21–24; Ecclesiastes 3:14; Matthew 19:3–8; 1 Corinthians 11:11–12; Hebrews 13:4; 1 Timothy 5:14; 4:1–5.
106. 1 Timothy 3:1–12.
107. Matthew 19:4–9.
108. Luke 4:38.
109. Robert M. Grant, *After the New Testament* (Fortress Press, 1967), 184; 1 Corinthians 1:11; Ephesians 5:22–33.
110. Origen, De Principiis 2:11:2, ANF 4:297.
111. Walter Wagner, *After the Apostles* (Augsburg Fortress Publishers, 1994), 180.
112. Deuteronomy 25:5.
113. Marc A. Schindler, "Doesn't Matthew 22:23–30 Contradict the LDS Doctrine of Eternal Marriage?" FAIR (2002).
114. Doctrine and Covenants 132:15–17.
115. Petersen, *Where Have All the Prophets Gone?*, 105, quoting from the Gospel of Philip, in Schneemelcher, New Testament Apocrypha, 1, vv. 76–77, 79, 122a, 127, 197–98, 204, 206.
116. Tertullian, Exhortation to Chastity 6, ANF 4:53.
117. Augustine, Reply to Faustus 22:47, NPNF 1:4:288.
118. Luke 16:19–31.
119. Martyr, Dialogue with Trypho, 141.
120. Stephen E. Robinson, *Are Mormons Christians?* (Salt Lake City: Bookcraft, 1991), 92–93.
121. Ludlow, *Encyclopedia of Mormonism*, "Polygamy" (authors: Daniel Bachman & Ronald K. Esplin).
122. *The Biography and Family Record of Lorenzo Snow*, 60–70 (Salt Lake City, 1884), cited in Ludlow, *Encyclopedia of Mormonism*.
123. Hyrum L. Andrus, *Doctrines of the Kingdom* (Bookcraft, 1974), 471–472. One of several statements from Andrus' notes reads: "Hyrum Smith told Benjamin F. Johnson: 'I know that Joseph was commanded to take more wives, and he waited until an angel with drawn sword stood before him and declared that if he longer delayed fulfilling that command that he would slay him.'"
124. Brigham Young, "Plurality of Wives, Etc.," *Journal of Discourses*, reported by G. D. Watt 14 July 1855, vol. 3 (London: Latter-day Saint's Book Depot, 1856), 266 and Andrus, *Doctrines of the Kingdom*, 472, both cited in Ludlow, *Encyclopedia of Mormonism*. Brigham Young states: "It is not through lust that men and women are to practice this doctrine, but it is to be observed upon righteous principles; and, if men and women would pay attention to those instructions, I would promise, in

the name of the Lord, that you would never find them lustful in their dispositions, and you might watch them as closely as you pleased. . . . Some of these my brethren know what my feelings were at the time Joseph revealed the doctrine; I was not desirous of shrinking from any duty, nor of failing in the least to do as I was commanded, but it was the first time in my life that I had desired the grave, and I could hardly get over it for a long time. And when I saw a funeral, I felt to envy the corpse its situation, and to regret that I was not in the coffin, knowing the toil and labor that my body would have to undergo; and I have had to examine myself, from that day to this, and watch my faith, and carefully meditate, lest I should be found desiring the grave more than I ought to do."

125. Orson Pratt, *Journal of Discourses*, 13:194.
126. Dewey, *Joseph Smith* (Arlington, VA: Stratford Books 2005), 520.
127. Ludlow, *Encyclopedia of Mormonism*.
128. Ibid.
129. Helen Mar Whitney, "Scenes and Incidents in Nauvoo," *Woman's Exponent*, X (November 1, 1881), 83, as cited in Andrus, *Doctrines of the Kingdom*, 471–472.
130. Ludlow, *Encyclopedia of Mormonism*.
131. Richard S. Van Wagoner, *Mormon Polygamy: A History* (Salt Lake City: Signature Books, 1989), 89.
132. B. H. Roberts, *The Truth, The Way, The Life: An Elementary Treatise on Theology* (Provo, UT: BYU Studies, 1991), 557.
133. *History of the Church*: c 1878–1898, Late Pioneer Utah Period cited in Ludlow, *Encyclopedia of Mormonism*.
134. Ludlow, *Encyclopedia of Mormonism*.
135. Smoot Hearings, United States Congressional Record cited in Ludlow, Encyclopedia of Mormonism.
136. Ludlow, *Encyclopedia of Mormonism*.
137. Mormon 9:7–25.
138. Brown, *All Things Restored*, 150–53
139. Brown, *All Things Restored*, 138–141; Doctrine and Covenants 42:43–44; 3 Nephi 17:7–10.
140. *History of the Church*, 4:555.
141. Doctrine and Covenants 109:35–37.
142. *History of the Church*, vol. 2, 428.
143. Brown, *All Things Restored*, at 134–36.
144. *History of the Church*, 4:485.
145. Brown, *All Things Restored*, at 136–38.
146. Leviticus 8:8; Numbers 27:21; Deuteronomy 33:8; 1 Samuel 28:6; Ezra 2:63; Nehemiah 7:65.
147. Exodus 28:30.
148. Mosiah 8:13–18; Mosiah 28:13–16; Ether 3:22–24.
149. Joseph Smith used the Urim and Thummim to translate the Book of Mormon. Pearl of Great Price, Smith 2:35, 59.
150. Brown, *All Things Restored*, 144–45.
151. Ibid., 145–46.
152. Ibid., 146–48.
153. Ibid., 148–150.
154. Ibid., 153–55.
155. Doctrine and Covenants 58:64.

156. Doctrine and Covenants 133:8.
157. Doctrine and Covenants 52:10; 61:33–35.
158. Genesis 14:20.
159. Malachi 3:8–10.
160. Doctrine and Covenants 64:23.
161. Doctrine and Covenants 119:3–4.
162. Doctrine and Covenants 88:119.
163. Doctrine and Covenants 89:20–21.
164. Doctrine and Covenants 27:1–2. See also 3 Nephi 18:1–2; Moroni 4–5; Doctrine and Covenants 20:75–79.
165. Doctrine and Covenants 59:9–13.
166. 2 Nephi 10:3–9. See 3 Nephi 20:29–46.
167. Doctrine and Covenants 110:11.
168. Doctrine and Covenants 133:26–30.
169. Moses 4:1–4 (emphasis added).
170. *History of the Church*, 4:45.
171. Ezekiel 28:11–19.
172. *History of the Church*, 5:425–26.
173. Doctrine and Covenants 76.
174. Moses 1:39.

CHAPTER 11

CONCLUSION: MORMONS ARE THE HEBREW CHRISTIANS

Twenty-first Century Mormons and Hebrew Christians at the meridian of time are one and the same. Although separated by two thousand years of existence, their identities cannot be clearer. Their doctrines are nearly identical, as are their organizational structures and content. The affinity between Mormons and Christian Jews of today is indicative of a shared historicity. But perhaps more significant are their parallel histories and the way in which the western world views them both; namely, as antithetical to Christendom! Just as with the Hebrew Christians before them, there is something about the Mormons that strikes fear into the hearts of mainstream Christianity; otherwise, the greater Christian world would not care one way or another as to whether or not Mormons are Christians. The animosity with which other Christian sects have attacked the Mormons cannot be otherwise explained away; the Mormons didn't migrate to the Salt Lake Valley willingly. They were driven there by angry mobs, fleeing for their lives across the Mississippi River in the midst of winter, leaving behind nearly all of their possessions. The Mormons fled the jurisdictional boundaries of the United States to escape the kind of persecution that drove the Puritans to immigrate to America. How ironic that a country founded upon religious liberties would turn its back on one of its own—the famous statement of US President Martin Van Buren pretty much sums things up; upon learning of the injustices inflicted on the Mormons and the demand for action by the Prophet Joseph Smith, he retorted "Gentlemen, your cause is just, but I can do nothing for you."[1]

What could cause such vengeance and hostility by the Christian majority? In short, theology; for the theology of the Mormons and their Hebrew predecessors threatens the very foundations of the orthodox Christian world.

Hebrew Christianity was very popular until its demise at the Council of Nicaea in AD 325. A resurgence of Hebrew Christianity could make lasting in-roads into the current Christian community; and hence, the fear of the Hellenized world. A recent message board erected at a Baptist Church best describes the fear. It reads, "Don't read the Book of Mormon and pray about it; that's how the Mormons deceive you." Knowledge is power and the best way to keep power is to censor the amount of information available.

Nevertheless, human beings yearn to know what the Mormons are teaching: Where did I come from before my life on earth? Why am I here—what is my purpose for existence? Where am I going after this mortal life is over? The answers to those three questions haunt most people and a religion that can adequately answer them, is a powerful religion indeed. Philosophers have made it their life's work to solve such theological questions. Here is how the Hebrew Christians, and thereafter, the Mormons answer them.

THE CREATOR—GOD

Is it so improbable that there exists a race of creators; gods; glorified and perfected beings who designed, created, and maintain the Universe; a divine creator? The Bible refers to one of these beings as Elohim, the Father God. That is what the Hebrew Christians believed at the meridian of time. It is what the Mormons believe today.

In the Book of Abraham, it records that mankind existed as "intelligences" before the world and this universe were even in existence.[2] I do not purport to know what an "Intelligence" is or even its substance, if any. Perhaps we simply existed as disembodied consciences.

Whatever the case, Elohim, who is literally in the creation business, and his wife (yes, God is married to a Goddess), through their combined procreative powers produced spirit bodies for each of these Intelligences. Thus, we, collectively mankind, became the literal offspring of God. We are part of His race, as we discussed earlier. We lived with Elohim and His wife in a premortal sphere. Just where that was is the subject of speculation. However, we do know that Abraham was told that one day in Elohim's time is equivalent to one thousand earth years.[3]

Therefore, using basic astronomy we can make some educated guesses about our premortal abode. Within our Milky way galaxy, planets in a solar system revolve around a sun with the planets closest to the sun having shorter days and those farther away having longer days. Solar systems revolve around the nucleus of the galaxy using the same principle. At the nucleus or center of the galaxy, theoretically time virtually stops. So is the throne of Elohim in the galactic nucleus? That is a discussion for another day.

PREMORTAL LIFE

While residing in this premortal existence, we grew and developed as spirit children. If the creation of our spirit bodies was our birth, then this premortal existence would be equivalent to our infancy and childhood. Where was Jehovah ("Jesus Christ") during this premortal life? He was living alongside us, for He was the first spirit child born. That is the reason He is called the Firstborn of the Father for He was the first spirit body created by Elohim. It was during this premortal experience, as discussed in the Book of Revelation, that a War in heaven occurred.[4] Satan and his followers, who apparently numbered a third of the hosts of heaven, fought against Jehovah and His followers, who were captained by Michael the Arc Angel, the same who would become Adam, the first mortal man upon the earth. In the Book of Moses, it tells of a Great Council in heaven. During this Council, Elohim was presented with two plans, one from Jehovah and the other from Satan, whom Isaiah identifies as Lucifer, the Son of the Morning.[5] Elohim was to consider how this mortal existence on earth was to play out in the further development of His children.

His spirit children were to receive mortal bodies of flesh and bones. Apparently the combining of spirit and mortal flesh is an essential part of the progression of our race. However, it is also the most delicate of times. The corporeal body is not an easy thing to tame. It comes with passions and emotions, which are unfamiliar to a spirit. The mastering of the physical body is a daunting task, but one that must be accomplished to progress further. One who fails to master the mortal body will never become a creator like Elohim.

Consequently, two plans were presented. The first plan, Jehovah's plan, was the same plan that Elohim's race had always adhered to. Spirit children would come to earth in mortal tabernacles, a set of guidelines would be established and presented as to how mortal bodies could be mastered, these spirit children would then be given their "agency" to choose whether to follow these guidelines or disregard them, giving into the passions and emotions of their physical bodies.

The second plan, that of Satan, eliminated "agency" and instead of a Savior, an appointed representative of Elohim would force all spirits to obey the guidelines. There would be no choice.

Under Jehovah's plan, many of the spirit children would fail. But under Satan's plan, all would succeed and return to the presence of Elohim. Elohim chose the first plan and designated Jehovah to be the Savior (the "Christ"). Why the first plan and not the second? Because it is through trials and tribulations that we learn and develop. That is how a spirit masters the physical body. There really is no other way. The second plan was an attempt at a shortcut. It would be the easy way out. It is no surprise that there was a war over this—a third of heaven wanted that easy way and Satan was willing to lead them. The kicker to the second plan was that after all of the spirit children returned to Elohim, Satan would use those who were now loyal to him to dethrone the Father. He wanted the glory of it all to be his. Jehovah, on the other hand, gave deference and all glory to His Father.[6]

So which side did we pick? If you are reading this, you picked Jehovah's side. What happened to Satan and his followers? As the Apostle John states, they lost the war in heaven and were thrust out.[7] They became the devil and his angels, and they are on this earth with one and only one goal, to thwart the plan of Jehovah. They believe that if they can succeed, then they will have a second opportunity to dethrone the Father.

Mortal Life

So we are born into this Earth life with mortal bodies enveloping our spirits. Our task is to master the physical body and its passions and appetites, and thus become as our Father in Heaven. It is to become a perfect man or woman. As noted previously, because perfection is not possible in this mortal life—as we all sin, and the laws by which our race lives demands such perfection, a Savior was provided for us. That is someone who could meet out the justice that perfection demands, but at the same time provide us with the mercy imperfection requires.

The guidelines for mastering physical bodies is the gospel of Jesus Christ. It was brought into this world at the time of Adam's Fall. It was preached by all of the Patriarchs—Enoch, Noah, Abraham, Isaac, Jacob, and Moses. However, like rebellious teenagers, mankind periodically rejected the gospel—falling into apostasy. Jehovah would then re-introduce the gospel in a successive dispensation.

During the dispensation known as the "meridian of time," Jehovah was made flesh and became Jesus of Nazareth.[8] He established His Church with a specific organization and re-introduced His gospel. Through His Church, the gospel was taught to His spirit brothers and sisters. The purpose: to assist the Father's children to live up to their divine potential, to become creators like their Father.

The Hebrew Christians— the Mormons of today

When other Christians say that Mormons are not Christians because they believe in a different God, a different Christ, ask them to describe their God. Ninety-nine percent of the time, they will describe a benevolent grandfatherly figure and a corporeal Christ who answers their prayers. This, however, is not the Hellenistic God, without body, parts or passions, as set forth in the Nicene Creed. The Hellenized God does not answer prayers, the cannon of scripture is closed, there is no revelation. Remarkably, most Christians are instead describing the Hebrew God—the Mormon God.

In truth, it is not so surprising. The Hebrew Christians were the majority sect of Christianity in the first three centuries after the crucifixion. Those beliefs ran deep and have never completely faded, even as Hellenized Christianity became dominant following the Council of Nicaea. Is it any wonder why this Hebrew legacy is feared by mainline Christian sects today?

The Hellenized Church—namely, the Catholic Church—has had many offshoots. Protestantism arose because of the suppression of Hebrew Christian doctrines that made biblical sense to the likes of Martin Luther and John Calvin. However, the entirety of Hebrew Christian thought was not restored and the Protestant Churches became simply an adaptation of the mother Hellenized Church. They adhered to many of the same ecumenical councils and the theology there espoused. Hence, for them as well as the Catholic Church, true Hebrew Christian theology was tantamount to an assault on all Christendom. It was the "great heresy" come back from the dead. The Church of the nineteenth century thought it had been eradicated 1,500 years ago, yet it was back—resurrected from the grave. In the fourth century, this heresy had battled the Greek version of the gospel for supremacy and almost won.

As the once dominant sect, Hebrew Christianity had enjoyed the praise and adulation of the masses. Now it had returned. Although its name had changed, the doctrine was the same. The Hebrew Christians were now Mormons—members of the restored (not reformed) Church of Jesus Christ.

The reaction to the restoration was swift. Reported Joseph Smith:

> Some few days after I had this vision, I happened to be in company with one of the Methodist preachers, who was very active in the before mentioned religious excitement; and, conversing with him on the subject of religion, I took occasion to give him an account of the vision which I had had. I was greatly surprised at his behavior; he treated my communication not only lightly, but with great contempt, saying it was all of the devil, that there were no such things as visions or revelations in these days; that all such things had ceased with the apostles, and that there would never be any more of them. I soon found, however, that my telling the story had excited a great deal of prejudice against me among professors of religion, and was the cause of great persecution, which continued to increase; and though I was an obscure boy, only between fourteen and fifteen years of age, and my circumstances in life such as to make a boy of no consequence in the world, yet men of high

standing would take notice sufficient to excite the public mind against me, and create a bitter persecution; and this was common among all the sects—all united to persecute me. It caused me serious reflection then, and often has since, how very strange it was that an obscure boy, of a little over fourteen years of age, and one, too, who was doomed to the necessity of obtaining a scanty maintenance by his daily labor, should be thought a character of sufficient importance to attract the attention of the great ones of the most popular sects of the day, and in a manner to create in them a spirit of the most bitter persecution, and reviling. But strange or not, so it was, and it was often the cause of great sorrow to myself.[9]

Strange indeed. That is unless these men of great religious influence saw in young Joseph the restoration of Hebrew Christianity and the danger its doctrines presented to their Hellenized sects. In a land of religious freedom, as the United States was in the nineteenth century, it is indeed an odd phenomena that while the Puritans came to escape religious persecution, the Mormons fled for the very same reasons, only the country of religious freedom for the Mormons was—Mexico—not the United States.

A startling fact not often repeated in the history of the United States was that starting in the 1840s, the State of Missouri legalized the killing of Mormons. What could have caused such governmental acts so foreign to the purposes and intent of the Declaration of Independence and the United States Constitution? It would appear that the very nature of our nation had been subverted. The Revolution and War of 1812 had been fought based upon principles of liberty from taxation without representation and freedom of thought and religion. Of those colonists who died to make this nation free, the treatment of the Mormons became a mockery to their cause and service. When the Mormons appealed to the congress and president for aid, none came. They were persecuted and driven from the United States in much the same manner as Nero had persecuted the Hebrew Christians of old. And that is the catch, the Mormons were simply walking in the footsteps of those Hebrew Christians that had gone before them. They had returned and the Hellenized Church would and did do anything it could to thwart the restoration of a long dead, but popular sect of Christianity.

The Hellenized Church, however, failed. The Mormon Church has thrived, becoming one of the fastest growing religions of the twentieth and twenty-first centuries. The Hebrew Christians and their legacy have returned, and with that return has come the Mormon mystique, which is really nothing more than that of an eternal perspective— a perspective that gives a rational explanation to our existence. It answers the questions that have troubled mankind and gives purpose to our lives. We are a godly race. It is our race that created the universe and all living creatures therein and it is our legacy to continue that creation story.

NOTES

1. *History of the Church*, 4:80.
2. Abraham 3.
3. Abraham 3:4.
4. Revelation 12:7–9.
5. Isaiah 14:12–15.
6. Moses 4:1–4.
7. Revelation 12.
8. John 1:14.
9. Joseph Smith—History 1:21–23.

INDEX

A

Abraham 14, 18, 20–24, 26, 29, 37, 41, 58, 79, 138, 187, 189, 202, 204, 210, 217, 222, 226, 232, 248, 251

Adam 10–21, 23, 30, 32, 68, 81, 101, 116, 121, 187–88, 205, 207, 215, 222, 249, 251

Apostasy 5, 11, 18–20, 23, 28–29, 49, 59, 65, 71–73, 81, 173–77, 187, 192, 202, 209, 251

Arianism 130, 142, 144–46, 148, 158

B

Bogomils 101, 162–276, 170

C

Cathars 164–68, 170–71

Constantine the Great 143–44

Council of Nicaea 2, 94, 123, 130, 145, 149, 151, 217, 248, 252

E

Ebionites 76–78, 91, 93, 126

Enoch 15, 18–19, 23–24, 187, 189, 251

G

Gnostic Christianity
    Creation 95–96, 162
    Deification 98
    Esoteric doctrines 98
    Nature of Christ 96–97
    Resurrection 96–98, 128

P

R

ABOUT THE AUTHOR

D avid L. Thomas is a practicing attorney and student of early Christian history. This work is the result of a decade of research and study. Dave graduated from Brigham Young University with a BS in finance and received his juris doctorate from the College of William & Mary. He served in the US Army as a Judge Advocate before settling in Utah to work as a county attorney. He is active in the community, having served in the Utah legislature, on the State Board of Education, and on his local city council. He lives in South Weber, Utah, with his wife, Lynn, and their four children.

NOTES

N O T E S